How To Conquer
Health Problems
Between Ages
50 And 120

Books by Vernon Coleman

The Medicine Men (1975)
Paper Doctors (1976)
Everything You Want To Know About Ageing (1976)
Stress Control (1978)
The Home Pharmacy (1980)
Aspirin or Ambulance (1980)
Face Values (1981)
Guilt (1982)
The Good Medicine Guide (1982)
Stress And Your Stomach (1983)
Bodypower (1983)
An A to Z Of Women's Problems (1984)
Bodysense (1984)
Taking Care Of Your Skin (1984)
A Guide to Child Health (1984)
Life Without Tranquillisers (1985)
Diabetes (1985)
Arthritis (1985)
Eczema and Dermatitis (1985)
The Story Of Medicine (1985, 1998)
Natural Pain Control (1986)
Mindpower (1986)
Addicts and Addictions (1986)
Dr Vernon Coleman's Guide To Alternative Medicine (1988)
Stress Management Techniques (1988)
Overcoming Stress (1988)
Know Yourself (1988)
The Health Scandal (1988)
The 20 Minute Health Check (1989)
Sex For Everyone (1989)
Mind Over Body (1989)
Eat Green Lose Weight (1990)
Why Animal Experiments Must Stop (1991)
The Drugs Myth (1992)
How To Overcome Toxic Stress (1990)
Why Doctors Do More Harm Than Good (1993)
Stress and Relaxation (1993)
Complete Guide To Sex (1993)
How to Conquer Backache (1993)

How to Conquer Arthritis (1993)
Betrayal of Trust (1994)
Know Your Drugs (1994, 1997)
Food for Thought (1994, revised edition 2000)
The Traditional Home Doctor (1994)
I Hope Your Penis Shrivels Up (1994)
People Watching (1995)
Relief from IBS (1995)
The Parent's Handbook (1995)
Oral Sex: Bad Taste And Hard To Swallow? (1995)
Why Is Pubic Hair Curly? (1995)
Men in Dresses (1996)
Power over Cancer (1996)
Crossdressing (1996)
How to Conquer Arthritis (1996)
High Blood Pressure (1996)
How To Stop Your Doctor Killing You (1996, revised edition 2003)
Fighting For Animals (1996)
Alice and Other Friends (1996)
Spiritpower (1997)
Other People's Problems (1998)
How To Publish Your Own Book (1999)
How To Relax and Overcome Stress (1999)
Animal Rights – Human Wrongs (1999)
Superbody (1999)
The 101 Sexiest, Craziest, Most Outrageous Agony Column
    Questions (and Answers) of All Time (1999)
Strange But True (2000)
Daily Inspirations (2000)
Stomach Problems: Relief At Last (2001)
How To Overcome Guilt (2001)
How To Live Longer (2001)
Sex (2001)
How To Make Money While Watching TV (2001)
We Love Cats (2002)
England Our England (2002)
Rogue Nation (2003)
People Push Bottles Up Peaceniks (2003)

novels
The Village Cricket Tour (1990)
The Bilbury Chronicles (1992)
Bilbury Grange (1993)
Mrs Caldicot's Cabbage War (1993)
Bilbury Revels (1994)
Deadline (1994)
The Man Who Inherited a Golf Course (1995)
Bilbury Country (1996)
Second Innings (1999)
Around the Wicket (2000)
It's Never Too Late (2001)
Paris In My Springtime (2002)
Mrs Caldicot's Knickerbocker Glory (2003)

short stories
Bilbury Pie (1995)

on cricket
Thomas Winsden's Cricketing Almanack (1983)
Diary Of A Cricket Lover (1984)

as Edward Vernon
Practice Makes Perfect (1977)
Practise What You Preach (1978)
Getting Into Practice (1979)
Aphrodisiacs – An Owner's Manual (1983)
The Complete Guide To Life (1984)

as Marc Charbonnier
Tunnel (novel 1980)

with Alice
Alice's Diary (1989)
Alice's Adventures (1992)

with Dr Alan C Turin
No More Headaches (1981)

with Donna Antoinette Coleman
How To Conquer Health Problems Between Ages 50 And 120 (2003)

How To Conquer Health Problems Between Ages 50 And 120

The Beginner's Guide To An Active And Joyful Later Life

Vernon Coleman &
Donna Antoinette Coleman

European Medical Journal

Published by the European Medical Journal, Publishing House,
Trinity Place, Barnstaple, Devon EX32 9HJ, England.

Reprinted 2004

ISBN: 1 898947 15 5

A catalogue record for this book is available from the British Library.

Printed by J.W. Arrowsmith Ltd., Bristol

NOTE

This book is not intended to be, and cannot be, an alternative to personal, professional medical advice. Readers should immediately consult a trained and properly qualified health professional, whom they trust and respect, for advice about any symptom or health problem which requires diagnosis, treatment or any kind of medical attention.

While the advice and information in this book are believed to be accurate at the time of going to press, neither the author nor the publisher can accept any legal responsibility or liability for errors or omissions which may be made.

Readers should always consult a qualified doctor before changing or stopping medication, before changing their diet or before beginning any exercise programme.

Dedication
To our families, with love and gratitude

Contents

Introduction: Age is a state of mind

Some people are old at 30; they look physically tired and appear to be worn out mentally. They look and behave much older than they really are. Other individuals are still young and full of vitality even though they are well into their 80s.

Why? What is the difference between the world weary 30-year-old and the vivacious 80-year-old?

There are three factors which have a crucial effect on how old you look – three factors which decide whether you are tired at 30 or sizzling at 80.

First, there is no doubt that most individuals' attitudes and expectations are likely to be coloured by the attitudes and expectations of those around them. Expectations can be subdivided into two categories – the general expectations of society and the specific expectations of family and friends.

Society expects us to be frisky and slightly irresponsible at 16 but sedate and sensible at 70. There is no sound reason for this – it's just the way things are. In fact, it is perfectly possible to argue that it makes far more sense to be irresponsible at 70 (when you have less to lose) than at 16 when you have your whole life ahead of you.

The expectations of family and friends are likely to be similarly restricted and narrowly based. 'Act your age!' is a common admonition. 'You're too old for that!' is another. Both these phrases should be banned from the English language (and, indeed, any other language in which they appear).

There is absolutely no reason why a 70 or 80-year-old shouldn't start a new business, get married or take up motor cycling if he or she wants to and feels able to. The average 70-year-old has 97 per cent of the brain power he or she had at 25 (plus all the extra wisdom accumulated over the years).

The second important constraint is, of course, likely to be a physical one. If your body is in poor condition then you are undoubtedly going to find it easier and more comfortable to sit and watch television than to travel around the world, or force yourself to find and tackle new challenges. As we get older our bodies do tend to creak a bit. Parts that used to work well and without strain slowly begin to show signs of wear and tear. But much physical incapacity can be overcome – if you've a mind to do it.

And it is, of course, the third possible constraint – the mental one – which is by far the most important. Attitude of mind is vital in every aspect of life – not least in the art of staying young and active. If you *think* you are old, past it and incapable of accepting and taking on new challenges then you will probably *become* old, past it and incapable of accepting and taking on new challenges.

If, whatever your age, you have passions, hopes and ambitions and you are determined to ignore the artificial constraints of society, and the warnings of your nervous friends and relatives, and see those passions and hopes and ambitions through to fruition then the chances are that you will be able to overcome any physical obstacles in your way and succeed.

Hopefully, the advice and information in this book will help you (at best) avoid or (at worst) deal with many of the health problems which are commonly accepted as being a part of old age.

Finally, a word of advice.

If anyone – doctor, nurse, social worker, relative or friend – ever says to you: 'It's your age – what do you expect?' boot them out of the house and tell them not to come back.

Age and health are only loosely related. The machinery does tend to get a little worn as time goes by but that doesn't mean it will inevitably stop functioning efficiently or effectively. You need to isolate, define and tackle your existing health problems one by one. And you need to look hard at your lifestyle to identify all the ways in which you can best preserve your health for the future.

The information in this book is designed not just to help those suffering from these problems to live longer, healthier lives (and to minimise the discomfort and danger to which their diseases expose them) but also to help those who are not suffering from these problems understand how best they can avoid them.

It is a sad fact that as medical knowledge increases so the quality of medical care (and caring) seems to deteriorate. As it becomes increasingly difficult for doctors to keep up with new advances in medicine (even in their own speciality) so it becomes increasingly difficult for patients to find the truth about the diseases from which they are suffering (or which they fear).

On the whole doctors have never been particularly good at sharing medical information with their patients. And there is no doubt that the increasing complexity of much information has made this aspect of their job more difficult. But the major reason why patients find it so difficult to discover the truth about significant illnesses which may threaten their lives, and the lives of the ones they love, is that everyone (doctors and patients) is these days bombarded with vast quantities of misinformation. Lobbyists and public relations specialists feed doctors with the half-truths they want disseminated, and keep from them inconvenient and unprofitable truths. How else can one explain the fact that the vast majority of doctors (and, therefore, their patients) do not know that the best way to treat heart disease does not involve drugs or surgery? How else can one explain the fact that the vast majority of doctors (and, therefore, their patients) do not know that 80 per cent of all cancers can be avoided?

Information is the most valuable resource on earth – far more valuable than gold or platinum. Information gives you power over many things but most important of all it gives you power over your own health – and increases your chances of survival in an increasingly dangerous and dishonest world.

But how can you possibly keep up when there are so many lobbyists and PR organisations busy laying traps and false information in order to sell specific products and particular points of view?

Much of the material you read in newspapers and magazines has been 'planted' by public relations experts – wanting to sell or protect a particular product. The same is true of TV and radio programmes. There are just as many spin-doctors in the world of health care as there are in politics.

In order to navigate these traps – and to differentiate between the truth and the fallacies – you need help.

Why should you trust us to provide you with that help?

Well, we have nothing to sell you but the truth. We don't have a practice to run or to protect. We don't accept sponsorship or advertising from anyone.

And we have a track record which is, we believe, second to no one in the world of medicine. A full list of accurate predictions and warnings which were first made in Vernon Coleman's books, in his newsletter, in his newspaper columns or on his website would take up several pages in this book.

This book has been written to help you to look after yourself; to enable you to take charge of, and responsibility for, your own medical care.

Vernon Coleman and Donna Antoinette Coleman

Alzheimer's disease

At any age, few things are more frightening than the idea of losing your mind. But, for an increasing number of people over 50, this nightmare is becoming a reality.

Alzheimer's disease was virtually unheard of just a few decades ago. Today, Alzheimer's disease, the commonest genuine cause of dementia, affects one in ten people.

Scientists have claimed that Alzheimer's disease is commoner now because people are living longer. This is nonsense. Visit any cemetery and the chances are high that you will find plenty of graves for people who died in their 80s or 90s around 100 years ago. (You will also find plenty of graves for young children – showing just how high the incidence of infant and child mortality used to be and why the *average* life expectancy was so short.)

The incidence of Alzheimer's disease has risen because the population has increased. And the incidence of Alzheimer's will continue to rise steadily as the population increases.

* * *

Alzheimer's is a terrible disease: gradually robbing the sufferer of his or her memory, judgement, reasoning skills, speech and dignity. The disease also has an effect on the emotions as well as on behaviour. Here are three basic facts:

1. Alzheimer's, a physical, progressive condition for which there is no known cure, causes degeneration of the nerve cells in the cerebral cortex of the brain as well as loss of brain mass.
2. Alzheimer's affects both men and women; no sex or nationality is immune to the disease.
3. The incidence of Alzheimer's steadily increases with age: it occurs in up to 30 per cent of people over the age of 85. However,

although this is uncommon, Alzheimer's disease can affect people as young as 35. When it occurs at an early age Alzheimer's is known as early-onset familial Alzheimer's disease and it tends to progress much more rapidly than late-onset Alzheimer's. For many years, early-onset Alzheimer's was known as pre-senile dementia (dementia that is not associated with advanced age). Early-onset Alzheimer's disease can be an inherited disease.

* * *

Alzheimer's disease was first described in the early 1900s by a leading German neurologist called, Alois Alzheimer. While doing an autopsy on the brain of a 51-year-old patient who had died with symptoms similar to that of 'senile dementia', Dr Alzheimer was astonished to discover a new type of dementia. This new type of dementia involved three pathological changes to the brain – plaques over the brain's surface, tangled cells (called, neurofibrillary tangles) and a loss of brain cells. All these changes are the cause of the symptoms associated with Alzheimer's.

* * *

Alzheimer's disease is one of the commonest – and probably the best known – cause of dementia in people over the age of 65.

Dementia (which is a Latin word meaning 'loss of mind') is a gradual deterioration in mental function: affecting memory, thinking, judgement, concentration, learning, speech and behaviour.

Some people believe that dementia is a normal part of the ageing process (hence the term 'senile dementia'), but it is not. There are many people in their 80s and 90s who still have all their mental faculties intact; thousands have gone on to achieve great things in their advanced years. Dementia is neither a natural nor an inevitable consequence of ageing.

Dementia is not itself a disease but is a general word for the symptoms displayed as a result of a number of different diseases. (In much the same way that 'cancer' and 'infection' aren't specific diseases.)

When someone displays symptoms of dementia, it's the doctor's job to identify the underlying cause.

Besides Alzheimer's, other disorders that can cause dementia include: Parkinson's disease, advanced syphilis, vitamin B12 deficiency, Huntington's disease, Creutzfeldt-Jacob disease (aka Mad Cow disease), Down's Syndrome, Pick's disease, strokes, Lewy Body disease, late-multiple sclerosis, brain tumours, hormone deficiencies, chronic alcoholism, drug abuse (of both illegal and prescription drugs) and head injuries. Some of these disorders are treatable.

Drugs, depression and illness can all mimic the symptoms of Alzheimer's disease. (How many people diagnosed as having Alzheimer's disease really have Mad Cow disease? Your guess is as good as your doctor's.)

Indeed, it is possible that prescription drugs – not Alzheimer's – are the commonest cause of dementia. It is likely that half of all cases of alleged dementia could be cured simply by stopping unnecessary prescription drug use. Sedatives, hypnotics, anxiolytics and anti-depressants are the commonest cause of problems, with benzodiazepine tranquillisers and sleeping tablets such as Valium, Mogadon and Ativan probably being some of the commonest culprits.

Symptoms of Alzheimer's disease

Because the disease begins very gradually, the symptoms of Alzheimer's may go unnoticed for a while.

Mild forgetfulness, which is so common in the early stages of the disease, may simply be put down to 'getting older' (though there is no specific reason why memory should deteriorate with age).

However, as the disease progresses, the symptoms become more noticeable, especially the memory loss. It is usually the loss of memory that motivates sufferers or their relatives to seek medical attention.

Not every sufferer of Alzheimer's will follow the course of the disease exactly. The disease, which usually develops gradually, progresses faster in some people than it does in others.

It is also important to be aware that even though the commonest symptoms of the disease are shared by the majority of sufferers, no two people will experience identical symptoms.

The symptoms which appear on the list below are not inevitable. But knowing a little about the possible progression of Alzheimer's can help you plan for the future. Forewarned is forearmed.

1. The following symptoms usually occur in the early stages of Alzheimer's disease:

1. Forgetfulness, especially of recent events. Sufferers may remember events that took place a year ago, but lose all recollection of what occurred an hour ago. In the very early stages of Alzheimer's, it is only short-term memory loss which is affected; memory loss deteriorates as the disease progresses. It is not uncommon for sufferers to become highly defensive when questioned about their failing memory, this is because they usually feel embarrassed or frightened by it. Some sufferers even go to great lengths to hide their memory loss from friends and relatives.
2. Difficulty in making decisions.
3. An inability to do tasks which require some intellectual ability, such as simple mathematical calculations, managing the household finances, etc.
4. Repetitious questioning – the same question may be asked over and over again because the sufferer has lost all memory of having asked that question previously. Stories may also be repeated for the same reason.
5. Misplacing objects – the sugar may be put in the fridge for example, because the sufferer is not able to remember where it is normally stored.
6. Constantly losing things.
7. Difficulty in finding the right word when talking (Anomia).
8. Frequently losing train of thought during conversations.
9. Apathy.
10. Forgetting the names of objects and calling them by a different name, for example, a chair may be called a bench or a cupboard might be called a wardrobe.
11. Loss of concentration.
12. Forgetting familiar names.
13. Listlessness.
14. Inability to learn new information – this is due to loss of short-term memory which is essential when it comes to learning anything new.
15. Depression and anxiety.
16. Getting lost in familiar places – the sufferer may forget their

usual route back home from their local supermarket or from a friend's house.

17. Sleep disturbances.
18. Disorientation in time – a sufferer may be confused as to what day, month or year it is.
19. Poor judgement – the Alzheimer sufferer may put on a thick woolly jumper even though it's the middle of summer and the temperature is ninety degrees in the shade.
20. Increasing difficulty with speech. The sufferer may withdraw from intellectual conversations as a result.
21. Personality changes – a previously trusting person may suddenly become suspicious of everyone they encounter, even their loved ones. Other personality changes may include: hostility, jealousy, outbursts of anger and sometimes violence.

* * *

2. Symptoms usually occurring in the later stages of Alzheimer's disease:

1. Carelessness – frequently leaving the cooker on or, if they smoke, leaving burning cigarettes lying around. This type of carelessness can be life-threatening both to the sufferer as well as to the people around them.
2. Mood swings – sobbing uncontrollably one minute and laughing hysterically the next for no apparent reason.
3. Simple everyday tasks becoming increasingly difficult.
4. Lack of personal hygiene.
5. Personality changes becoming more apparent.
6. Increasing problems with speech.
7. Wandering – roaming from room to room as if looking for something.
8. Repetition of simple but usually purposeful activities. For instance, repeatedly smoothing down a fold in the tablecloth.
9. Behaviour may become increasingly bizarre.
10. Severe deterioration of comprehension.
11. Loss of sexual inhibitions.
12. Strong denial that anything is wrong.
13. Extreme lack of motivation.
14. Severe sleep disturbances.

3. Symptoms usually occurring in the advanced stages of Alzheimer's disease:

1. A failure to recognize familiar faces. The patient may not be able to identify their spouse and may confuse him/her with another family member. It is also quite common for sufferers not even to recognize themselves when they look in the mirror and because of this, they may complain of a stranger being in the room.
2. The sufferer can no longer find his or her way around their own home.
3. Loss of the ability to read and write.
4. Personality changes becoming more severe and problematical.
5. The sufferer may experience hallucinations.
6. A complete failure to recognize ordinary, everyday objects.
7. Speech becomes unintelligible.
8. A total dependency on others for help with: toileting, bathing, eating, dressing, etc.
9. Bowel and bladder incontinence.
10. An inability to walk or even sit up.
11. Severe confusion and disorientation.
12. Paranoid delusions.
13. An inability to swallow.
14. Finally, a complete loss of memory and speech as well as muscle function.

Death usually occurs in about five to ten years after diagnosis though in some cases, the sufferer can have the disease for as long as 20 years.

Sufferers do not usually die from the primary brain damage caused by Alzheimer's, but invariably from a complication of the disease. This is a consequence of the increasing debility that the disease causes to the sufferer. Once sufferers become immobile, they are far more susceptible to infection.

Finally, it is important to point out that individuals who experience some or all of the symptoms associated with Alzheimer's should not panic. Most of us experience lapses of memory from time to time: we might lose our keys, forget an important date in the calendar or lose our train of thought during conversation. These lapses of memory are quite normal and are simply due to absent-mindedness.

However, if forgetfulness comes on suddenly or gets noticeably worse, it is time to seek help. Remember that the symptoms of Alzheimer's can be caused by a wide variety of illnesses, some of which can be treated.

* * *

Alzheimer's disease can be very difficult to diagnose because some of the symptoms are very similar to that of other illnesses. To find the underlying cause of your symptoms, your doctor may refer you to a neurologist at the hospital, or he or she may make a diagnosis based on your symptoms and medical history alone.

To be 100 per cent certain that someone is suffering from Alzheimer's disease an autopsy on the brain needs to be performed, but the next best option is for a specialist to carry out some tests to try to make an accurate diagnosis. The tests, which are performed to help diagnose Alzheimer's disease, are usually about 90 per cent accurate. However, with the aid of state-of-the-art equipment, researchers are becoming increasingly adept at spotting the disease.

Tests for Alzheimer's disease

When doctors suspect that a patient might have Alzheimer's disease they are likely to perform the following tests:

1. Psychiatric examination – this is to rule out depression or any other mental illness that can mimic the symptoms of Alzheimer's disease.
2. Blood tests – to detect illnesses that can cause dementia-type symptoms.
3. Mental test – to assess brain function such as: memory, the ability to do simple addition or subtraction, comprehension, etc.
4. EMG (Electromyography) – to test the large muscles in the body. (In some diseases of the brain, this activity can malfunction.)
5. Neurological examination – the nervous system is examined to look for other illnesses which might be causing similar symptoms, such as Parkinson's disease, previous strokes, brain tumours, etc.
6. CAT scan (Computerised Axial Tomography) – takes pictures of the brain to check for any anomalies.
7. Physical examination – like the neurological and the blood tests,

this examination is also used to rule out any other underlying disorders.

8. EEG (Electroencephalogram) – to assess abnormalities in brain wave activity.

9. Medical history assessment – this may involve interviews with the patient and his or her partner or with one or two members of his/her family. This is to find out how he/she is functioning with day-to-day living and to learn about any previous or any familial illnesses.

10. MRI scan (Magnetic Resonance Imaging) – is very much like the CAT scan. An MRI scan may be used if nothing shows up from the CAT scan.

11. SPECT scan (Single Photon Emission Computerised Tomography) – unlike the MRI and the CAT scanners which look at the structure of the brain, the SPECT scan looks for a change in the function of brain tissue. The person being scanned is given an injection of glucose together with a mild radioactive material. This substance, called radionuclide, circulates in the brain. The SPECT scan then measures the amount of radionuclide in various parts of brain tissue. (The brain's main source of energy is glucose; in people suffering with Alzheimer's, certain areas of the brain do not absorb as much glucose as would be normal.)

Diagnosis

A diagnosis will be issued once an evaluation of the test results have been made.

It is important to get a diagnosis as early on in the disease as possible because this enables everyone concerned to plan for the future.

It is, incidentally, important to remember that most doctors still dramatically under-estimate the importance of iatrogenesis – or doctor-induced disease. It is perfectly possible for a team of doctors to perform all these tests and yet forget to find out if a patient is taking a tranquilliser or sedative which could be causing all the symptoms. (And even when the doctors know that a patient is taking prescription drugs they are likely to ignore, forget or downplay the possible side effects.)

Treatment

Unfortunately, there is no known cure (yet) for Alzheimer's, but there are drugs available which may help to slow down the progression of the disease. (Although, some of the drugs commonly used in the 'treatment' of patients with Alzheimer's disease may exacerbate existing symptoms and produce new ones.)

It is claimed that anticholinesterase drugs may prevent the symptoms from getting any worse, but sadly, these drugs seem to work only for a short period of time. In addition, drugs of this type tend to be more effective in the very early stages of the disease; this is another reason why it is important to see your doctor as early as possible if you suspect that you (or a family member) could have Alzheimer's. These drugs are not suitable for every Alzheimer's disease sufferer.

Research has suggested that vitamin E and ginkgo biloba might help ease some of the symptoms and even slow down the progression of Alzheimer's disease a little. You must always consult your doctor before taking (or giving) any alternative form of treatment.

Most of the time, the orthodox medical treatment for Alzheimer's involves controlling the other symptoms that can accompany the disease, such as behavioural problems, depression and sleeplessness. By treating these symptoms, life for the sufferer as well as for the carer is made slightly more comfortable.

But there is good news.

It is possible to reverse some of the symptoms of Alzheimer's disease by exercising the brain. Actively using the mind helps develop surplus brain tissue which can compensate for the tissue which has been damaged by Alzheimer's disease.

Vernon Coleman's book *How To Live Longer* contains an extensive chapter explaining how to exercise the brain and improve mental skills and agility, as well as memory and general brain power.

Caring

Anyone caring for a patient with Alzheimer's disease should remember the following advice:

1. Keep tasks simple.
2. Keep your voice calm and try not to argue with the sufferer if he

or she becomes difficult, argumentative or aggressive. This will only make them worse. If you find yourself losing patience, then leave the room if you can to cool down. If the person you're caring for develops hurtful and aggressive behaviour, try to understand that it's the disease that is causing them to behave like this.

3. Try to stick to a routine; the slightest change is likely to cause irritability and confusion.

4. Make the house as safe as possible. Lack of judgement and poor memory can cause many dangers in the home. Gas cookers and open fires can be especially dangerous. Keep the house clutter-free and remove any potential dangers, such as loose carpets or unsafe stair rails.

5. Alzheimer's disease sufferers are prone to wander. Make sure that the person you're caring for has some form of identification on them just in case they wander away from home.

6. Don't be afraid to ask for help when you need it. Asking for help doesn't mean that you have failed as a carer; looking after someone with Alzheimer's disease can be extremely stressful as well as very distressing. Alzheimer's is a progressive, degenerative disease and because of this, your job is likely to become more and more demanding as the person you're caring for becomes increasingly less capable. Remember, you are not superhuman. Ask for and take whatever help you can get.

7. Patients with advanced stages of Alzheimer's may need inpatient care.

Causes and prevention of Alzheimer's disease

Although many theories have been proposed, no-one really knows what causes Alzheimer's, though scientists are learning more about the disease all the time. Nevertheless, for the time being, all we can do is try to avoid the possible risks until more is known about them.

1. Scientists have discovered abnormal levels of aluminium in the brains of Alzheimer's disease sufferers. However, no-one really knows whether aluminium causes Alzheimer's or whether the diseased brain has a tendency to absorb higher levels of this element. But until some hard evidence is found, the sensible thing

to do is to avoid aluminium as much as you can. Avoid cooking in pots and pans that are made of aluminium.

2. Some researchers believe that Alzheimer's disease may be caused by a viral infection. Again, until more evidence is found, it's best to avoid factors that are likely to increase your chances of developing the disease. To reduce your risk of getting viral infections you must avoid things that are likely to weaken your immune system such as: smoking, drinking, lack of exercise, poor diet and stress and do whatever you can to boost your immune system. (Vernon Coleman's book *Superbody* is packed with advice on how to keep your immune system strong.)

3. The brain needs regular exercise in order to keep it healthy. Research has shown that exercising the brain may decrease your chances of getting Alzheimer's or even slow down the progression of the disease. Doing crosswords, mental arithmetic, learning a new language or learning to play an instrument can all help to exercise the brain.

4. Some scientists have led people to believe that smoking prevents Alzheimer's – this is ludicrous. There are fewer smokers with Alzheimer's disease because smokers tend not to live long enough to get Alzheimer's disease. (Remember too that smokers are much more likely to develop strokes – another major cause of dementia.)

When to see the doctor

Many people with symptoms of dementia do not bother seeking medical help because they believe that nothing can be done for them – this is not true. Much can be done to improve the quality of life for both the sufferer and the carer. An investigation to identify the cause(s) of your symptoms is extremely important because some illnesses that cause dementia are treatable. Remember: dementia is not an inevitable part of ageing.

Arthritis (osteoarthritis)

Osteoarthritis usually affects people in their 50s or 60s. It seems to affect women slightly more often than men and in addition to the joints of the spine usually also affects the knees, hips, hands and feet. To start with there is usually only one joint affected but, as time goes by, osteoarthritis can spread to many parts of the body. Unlike rheumatoid arthritis (to which it bears remarkably few similarities other than that both are joint diseases) osteoarthritis does not involve damage to other parts of the body. Osteoarthritis is a much simpler disease to understand than rheumatoid arthritis. The main symptoms are stiffness and aching which develop as the cartilage between the bones gradually gets thinner and thinner. Eventually the bones end up rubbing on one another. Although osteoarthritis is often caused by excess wear and tear, it can be inherited and may affect younger adults.

What are the causes of osteoarthritis?

We reach our physical peak in our late teens and early 20s and from then on it is all downhill. Our vision becomes less acute and our hearing more indistinct. Our bones become weaker and more likely to fracture, our muscles lose some of their strength and our joints stiffen up and start to creak a little. Most of these changes are gradual and painless and go unnoticed until we suddenly try to do something that we used to be able to do with ease, and find that our bodies let us down.

It is the changes inside our joints which so often lead to the development of osteoarthritis. A normal healthy joint is perfectly designed for the job it has to do. Those joints which have a synovium and which are filled with synovial fluid are particularly impressive from an engineering point of view: they are strong and they have a magnificently sophisticated self-lubricating system. Each one of the synovial joints in a normal, healthy body is as slippery and as efficient as any man-made joint could ever hope to be.

Synovial joints have three special attributes:

1. The synovial fluid inside the joint is made of a special substance which loses water and becomes thicker when the pressure on the joint is greater. This means that the lubricant automatically becomes more efficient and more protective when the need for lubrication is at its greatest.
2. The two cartilaginous surfaces of a synovial joint are

extraordinarily slippery and would move smoothly together even without a lubricant.

3. Although the cartilaginous surfaces look smooth they are full of tiny indentations – rather like a golf ball. The result is that synovial fluid is trapped between the two surfaces – thereby reducing the amount of friction still further.

To get an idea of the amount of work each of your joints has to do just stop and think for a moment of the number of times that you move your arms and legs in a fairly ordinary sort of day. Getting up, sitting down and walking about all put pressure on your joints. Obviously, all this action means that our joints must eventually begin to wear out. And that is often what happens as we get older. Our cartilages wear down and the production of lubricating fluid becomes a little sluggish.

But, although osteoarthritis may be partly a consequence of ageing, that is not by any means the whole story. For a start most of us are so accustomed to the fact that our joints are strong, resilient and hard-wearing that we do very little to look after them or to help protect them from unnecessary wear and tear. The worst thing that most of us do to damage our joints is to allow ourselves to become overweight. If you are 14 pounds overweight then your joints will be constantly carrying an unnecessary load. (Try picking up 14 pounds of sugar or flour and walking around with it for five minutes or so. That is what your joints have to put up with for every minute of your waking day.) The heavier you are – and the more excess weight you are carrying – the greater the strain on your joints will be. If you are overweight then the chances are high that it will be the joints in your hips, knees and ankles – your weight-bearing joints – which suffer from osteoarthritis first.

We make things even worse by taking exercise that puts a tremendous strain on our bodies, by battering our bones and our cartilages and by putting totally unreasonable demands on the resilience of our joints. When we are young our bones are resilient and capable of absorbing an enormous amount of stress. But as we age our bones become less elastic and less capable of taking any sort of punishment. The result is that your joints have to take increasing amounts of the shock when you walk, run, jump, dance or leap about.

Your joints are at their best when you are about 20 years old. Every year after that means a year's additional decay. By the time you are 30 your joints may be noticeably stiffer and more vulnerable. After the age of 40 weight bearing joints in particular are likely to start creaking and causing trouble. Jogging, running, tennis, squash, football and aerobics all put a tremendous strain on your joints (particularly if you are not wearing shock-absorbing footwear). And, of course, if you are overweight then the strain will be increased even more.

Although osteoarthritis is usually a consequence of old age or overuse it is not always a result of natural wear and tear. Sometimes osteoarthritis may develop in younger people who are not overweight and who have done relatively little exercise. When this happens it may be because salts have been deposited in the cartilages, because inflammation or infection has damaged the joint or because the two parts of the joint do not fit together properly as a result of some congenital abnormality (the hip joint is the one most commonly affected by congenital problems).

Who gets osteoarthritis?

Anyone can get osteoarthritis – at any age – but it doesn't usually start before the age of 30 or 40 years old and it is commonest after the age of 50. It affects women more than men and it does seem to affect some families more than others. People who are overweight are prone to osteoarthritis and if you have ever had an injury in a joint then you will be more likely to get osteoarthritis in that joint.

How common is osteoarthritis?

It is difficult to say how many people get osteoarthritis because most sufferers manage without seeking medical help, but millions are disabled by osteoarthritis and it is probably the commonest cause of disability in the Western world.

How quickly does osteoarthritis develop?

It is rare for osteoarthritis to develop quickly. It usually starts slowly and builds up gradually over a period of years. Often, osteoarthritis develops so slowly that the sufferer may become quite seriously crippled without ever really noticing or complaining of any severe pain or disablement. It is, however, possible for an injury (even a relatively minor one) to exacerbate or accelerate osteoarthritis in a joint.

Which joints does osteoarthritis affect?

Osteoarthritis normally only affects joints below the waist. The hips, knees, ankles, hands and feet are the joints most commonly affected. Sometimes some of the joints in the back may be affected. Occasionally, only one joint will be affected by osteoarthritis but it is more common for two or three joints to be involved.

1. The hips

The hip is a ball and socket joint which has a wide range of movement (only the shoulder joint has a wider range) but because it is an important weight bearing joint it is the most common joint in the body to be affected by osteoarthritis. People who are overweight are particularly likely to be affected. When osteoarthritis develops in the hip it causes increasing stiffness and even the slightest movement may be painful. Walking can be very difficult and even movements in bed can cause excruciating pain. When a hip is affected by osteoarthritis it gradually changes in shape and the end result can be that the leg on that side may effectively become noticeably shorter than the other leg – making walking particularly difficult and putting an additional strain on the rest of the body. Because people who have damaged hips may be unable to move about enough to look after themselves properly, osteoarthritis of the hip is by far the commonest single cause of disablement today.

2. The knees

Osteoarthritis in the knees can cause a wide range of deformities. It can make the knees look knobbly. It can produce a 'bow-legged' look or a 'knock-kneed' look. Patients with osteoarthritis of the knees often have difficulty in walking up and down stairs. The noises which osteoarthritis of the knees make are awful and it is possible to hear creaking and grating noises whenever osteoarthritic knee joints are moved.

3. The ankles

Although they have to carry the weight of the whole body the ankles are less likely than the hips or knees to develop osteoarthritis – possibly because the normal range of movement in the ankle joint is less than the range of movement in the hips or knees and the amount of wear and tear is, therefore, considerably less. The ankle joint is only responsible for up and down movements of the foot – other movements (such as rotating and tilting) are produced by joints within the foot.

4. The feet

The commonest joint in the foot to be affected by osteoarthritis is the joint at the base of the big toe. Problems in this joint are usually caused by long-term pressure produced by shoes that don't fit properly. Women – who are more likely to wear tight shoes, high-heeled shoes and shoes that are designed to look fashionable rather than to provide the feet with any protection or support – are far more likely to suffer from this particular type of osteoarthritis than men are.

5. The shoulders

Only rarely affected by osteoarthritis – and usually only after injury.

6. The elbows

Like the shoulders the elbows are only rarely affected by osteoarthritis – and, again, usually only after injury. The rarity of osteoarthritis in the shoulders and the elbows shows quite clearly just how important excess weight can be in the development of osteoarthritis of the knees and hips.

7. The hands

When osteoarthritis affects the hands it most commonly affects the joint at the base of the thumb and the joints at the ends of the fingers. Small, hard nodules often form at the backs of affected joints in the hand and although these are usually painless they can add to the stiffness of the joints.

Symptoms

Pain is by far the most important symptom of osteoarthritis and can vary from a dull and persistent but often bearable ache to a sharp, gnawing pain. Usually worse after joints have been used a lot (that invariably means at the end of the day) the pain of osteoarthritis is produced when pain receptors around the bones and ligaments are stimulated. The dull, deep and generalised ache in and around the affected joints is caused by changes in the pressure within the bones – which is itself a result of the failure of the joint to function properly. The sharper, more acute pain of osteoarthritis is usually produced when a ligament catches on or is stretched by a piece of irregular bone in the joint. In addition to these 'internal' pains there may sometimes be a feeling of tenderness over an affected joint.

The second significant symptom of osteoarthritis is stiffness which is usually worst in the mornings or after any period of rest or inactivity. Most sufferers of osteoarthritis find that their joints are worse if they spend a long time in the same position.

Since it is the knees and hips which are most commonly affected sufferers often have difficulty in walking, stooping, bending and stretching. They may also have difficulty in getting into and out of soft, 'comfortable' chairs. Regular, gentle movements of a joint help to keep stiffness at bay although when a joint is affected by osteoarthritis its range of movement is usually less than the range of movement in a perfectly healthy joint.

Finally, there may be some swelling of osteoarthritic joints. In particular, nodules may appear around the finger joints, and the knee joints may swell as fluid accumulates. Osteoarthritis does not usually come and go and nor does it have 'active' and 'inactive' phases in the way that rheumatoid arthritis does. Usually, once a joint develops osteoarthritis it remains osteoarthritic for life.

Tests

The X-ray is the most important investigation. X-ray pictures of suspected joints will show how much damage has been done, what changes there have been to the bones and whether there is any narrowing of the joint space between the bones. Blood tests are of limited value but doctors sometimes take a sample of fluid from a joint to check for any signs of inflammation and to look to see if there are any crystals present in the joint.

Treatment

Osteoarthritis cannot be 'cured' by any miracle pills (although surgeons can replace a damaged joint with a 'new' one) but there are many ways in which the symptoms can be controlled and the development of the disease can be minimised.

What doctors can do

1. Drugs

Drugs will not cure osteoarthritis, nor will they affect the progress of the disease or prevent further damage, but they can help relieve pain and by relieving pain they can help keep joints mobile and thereby stop further stiffening developing. Painkilling drugs such as aspirin and paracetamol are the drugs most commonly used to give relief to sufferers from osteoarthritis and by relieving pain and combating inflammation they help reduce the amount of stiffness patients have to deal with. Many doctors also prescribe other drugs in the non-steroidal anti-inflammatory group but steroids are unlikely to be useful in the treatment of osteoarthritis since the symptoms are usually caused by physical wear and tear within the joint rather than by inflammation.

2. Injections

If there is any inflammation in the joint, a steroid injection may be useful. However, since osteoarthritis is usually caused by wear and tear rather than inflammation steroid injections are unlikely to be as effective as they can be in the treatment of rheumatoid arthritis.

3. Surgery

Since the 1960s, surgeons around the world have been replacing osteoarthritic hip joints with artificial joints and today hip replacement operations are commonplace and immensely successful. Indeed, hip replacement surgery has been so successful that many surgeons are now replacing other joints – particularly knees and joints in the hands.

The operation to remove and replace an osteoarthritic hip joint is relatively safe and straightforward to perform (it has been done on patients in their 90s). The osteoarthritic hip joint is simply removed and a metal and plastic replacement is glued into the patient's own bones. The success rate is high with most patients standing on their own feet a day or two after the operation and walking within two or three weeks. Advances are constantly being made in the design of joint replacements and, in particular, in the type of materials used to provide an effective long-life replacement. It is, as you can imagine, difficult to mimic the efficiency of the human joint but artificial joints are being made which can last for 15 years of fairly active movement.

Joint replacement is not the only type of surgery offered to patients with osteoarthritis. Sometimes it is possible to cut through the bone near to an osteoarthritic joint and to take pressure off the joint by realigning the bone. This sort of operation is called an osteotomy and in addition to removing pain and pressure from the area it can also stimulate the body to heal itself.

4. Physiotherapy
A physiotherapist can help to reduce pain and stiffness and to keep joints mobile.

5. Alternative therapies
Because osteoarthritis is a disease which is usually caused by wear and tear within a joint (or joints) there is little that alternative or complementary therapists can do to provide permanent relief of symptoms. However, alternative and complementary therapists are often able to help relieve pain. Many patients have found that acupuncture is an extremely effective way of combating pain.

Self-help

If you have arthritis of any kind you should try to lose any excess weight. Osteoarthritis, which commonly affects large, weight bearing joints such as the hips and the knees is particularly likely to be made worse if you are overweight.

If you are going to lose weight permanently then you really have to make sure that you change your eating habits permanently. Vernon

Coleman's book *Food for Thought* contains an extensive chapter explaining how to lose weight and how to stay slim for ever.

Arthritis (rheumatoid arthritis)

There is little doubt that rheumatoid arthritis is one of the commonest of all crippling, long-term diseases. Although it usually affects the smaller joints – particularly those of the hands and wrists and feet – it can also affect the joints of the spine. However, when this happens the spine is usually the last part of the body to be affected and by then other joints will probably be affected. The neck is usually the first part of the spine to be involved.

The initial symptoms of rheumatoid arthritis are usually pain, tenderness, swelling and stiffness of the affected joints. These symptoms, which can arrive quite suddenly or which may develop slowly over a lengthy period of time, are nearly always worst first thing in the morning. Many joints can be affected and sufferers who have rheumatoid arthritis badly may complain that their whole bodies are affected. The pain and aching is often also accompanied by a general feeling of tiredness, listlessness and of being run down. The symptoms of rheumatoid arthritis are unusual in that they may sometimes disappear almost completely without any warning – though, sadly, they usually come back again.

Rheumatoid arthritis is much commoner in women than in men. For every two men who get the disease there are usually four or five female sufferers. This difference may be due to some genetic factor carried on the female sex chromosomes. Rheumatoid arthritis also runs in families and if your parents, grandparents or brothers or sisters have or had rheumatoid arthritis then your chances of suffering from the disease are increased. Although the disease can start at any age it usually affects people between the ages of 30 and 60, most commonly starting in early adulthood or early middle age. Rheumatoid arthritis has been found in countries all over the world and it affects members of all races but it is more common – and tends to be more severe – among the inhabitants of Northern Europe. No one really knows whether this is due to the climate, to genetic factors or to a localised infection.

It is difficult to say how common the disease is because not all sufferers seek medical help. Obviously, some patients have far more severe symptoms than others and they will nearly all visit their doctor for advice. However, patients with mild symptoms are likely to struggle on without visiting the doctor. Some will manage without any treatment at all while others will treat themselves or visit alternative medical practitioners.

The causes

There is no known single cause of rheumatoid arthritis. Instead it seems likely that a number of different factors are responsible for the development of rheumatoid arthritis.

1. Infection

It is possible that the development of the disease may be triggered by a virus.

2. Inherited factors

Some genes transmitted from generation to generation seem to determine susceptibility to rheumatoid arthritis (i.e. whether or not you get it) while others determine the extent to which the disease develops (i.e. how badly you get it).

3. Food

It seems possible that certain types of food may make rheumatoid arthritis more likely. Meat – and meat products – may be a cause of rheumatoid arthritis.

4. Auto-immune reaction

Normally, your immune system helps to protect you against attack from infectious diseases. But, because the changes which take place inside the joints when rheumatoid arthritis develops are similar to the changes which take part in other parts of the body when antibodies produced by the human body are fighting an infection, many experts now believe that under some circumstances your body's immune system may be triggered to attack your joints – and in particular the lining of the joints – producing an inflammation of the synovial membrane which causes the well-known symptoms of the disease. One of the blood tests commonly done to confirm the presence of rheumatoid arthritis in joints checks for a special protein in the blood stream. This special protein is an antibody – similar to the antibodies which your body produces when it overcomes an infection such as influenza. No one really understands yet exactly how or why your body's immune defence system should attack the linings of your joints (it seems such a silly and pointless thing to do). But it may be nothing more complicated than a simple case of mistaken identity.

Cells called macrophages wander around your body looking for foreign looking cells. If they find any they produce a chemical signal which calls for help. Within a short space of time the foreign looking cells will be surrounded by cells called 'killer lymphocytes' which grab foreign cells and either poison them to death or eat them alive. This is, in principle, how your body's immune defence system works.

Neither the macrophages nor the 'killer lymphocytes' are usually triggered into action by your body's own cells. However, if any of your body's own cells have become damaged and have lost their identifying marks then your 'killer lymphocytes' will deal with them just as effectively and as unsympathetically as they will deal with foreign viruses, bacteria or fungi.

In rheumatoid arthritis your macrophages and 'killer lymphocytes' may be triggered into action by the fact that certain cells in your body – notably the cells of the synovial membranes in your joints – have changed in some way. It is thought that this is where the virus may come into play, for it is possible that a virus that you have picked up may change your synovial membrane in some slight way so that it looks 'foreign' to your macrophages and 'killer lymphocytes'.

What happens to the joints in rheumatoid arthritis?

The normal job of the synovium – the membrane which covers the joint – is to produce a constant supply of synovial fluid, the oily substance which lubricates, moistens and feeds the cartilage on the ends of the two opposing bones. It is the cartilages which take all the pressure when a joint is in action and it is the synovial fluid which ensures that the cartilages stay in good condition. When rheumatoid arthritis develops and the synovial membrane becomes inflamed the membrane swells up as the blood vessels supplying it open up to bring more 'killer' blood cells into the area.

If you have a boil, the blood vessels supplying that area will open up in an attempt to take more white blood cells to the area to help tackle the infection. Your body's internal defence systems rely on your blood supply to get to trouble spots and when and wherever there is a problem the localised blood vessels open up to ensure that the local blood supply is increased to the absolute maximum. This is exactly what happens to the synovium in an inflamed joint that has rheumatoid arthritis. Your body assumes that there must be some external agent present (a bacteria, virus or some other foreign organism) causing the inflammation and so it sends teams of specialist 'killer' blood cells to the area to try to clear up the problem.

In addition to becoming swollen the synovium also starts to go red and to feel hot as the blood flow increases. Because the synovium gets its nourishment from its blood supply the increased flow means that it starts to over-produce synovial fluid and within a relatively short time the whole joint will become swollen with fluid and painful to touch or to move. Instead of making movement easier the extra synovial fluid makes movement more difficult than ever. Occasionally, particularly in the knee joint, the excess fluid inside the joint can build up to such a high pressure that it bursts the joint capsule and escapes into the muscles of the calf.

The joint will by now be showing all the typical symptoms of rheumatoid arthritis: it will be swollen, it will feel hot to the touch, it will look red and it will be stiff and painful to move. Meanwhile, because the inflammation is still there, your body assumes that the underlying infection which it wrongly believes has caused the inflammation is simply proving too powerful and too resistant to the 'killer' cells in your blood supply. So your body responds by increasing the flow of blood still further – pumping ever increasing amounts of blood into the tissues and making things worse rather than better. All this means that the synovium just gets bigger and bigger and grows more and more, gradually spreading over more and more of the inside of the joint.

Eventually, the expanding synovium will start to damage the cartilage – the essential load-bearing surface on the ends of the opposing bones of the joint. Instead of being nice and slippery and allowing the joint to move easily and smoothly, the cartilage will become rough and pitted and will make movement difficult and uncomfortable. In advanced rheumatoid arthritis the joints which are affected will become deformed as well as swollen and stiff. If the tendons and bursae which lie over the joint are also affected by the inflammation then they will be damaged in much the same sort of way and the area around the joint will become tender to the touch and difficult to move.

One of the tragedies of rheumatoid arthritis is undoubtedly the fact that the problems which develop are caused by the body's own defence mechanisms mistakenly diagnosing a case of mild inflammation as being caused by an underlying infection; overreacting and then pumping unwanted blood cells into the area in such huge quantities that the joint becomes permanently damaged. It is rather like the fire brigade turning out to a small fire and causing far more damage with their high pressure water hoses than has been caused by the flames.

Normally, inflammation is a useful trigger. It encourages your body's own defence mechanisms to act quickly and decisively, limiting the amount of damage, getting rid of the cause of the inflammation and encouraging the healing process. As soon as it is clear that the underlying cause of the inflammation has been dealt with your body will stop sending in 'killer' blood cells. But in rheumatoid arthritis the inflammation doesn't go away and it is your body's reaction rather than the inflammation itself that does most of the damage. The consequences can be long-lasting and, if untreated, permanently disabling.

Rheumatoid arthritis does not just affect your joints

Rheumatoid arthritis is primarily a disease of the joints. It causes stiffness, swelling, tenderness and pain in and around the joints.

But if you are a sufferer it will not only be your joints which will be affected. Because the inflammation inside your joint (or joints) triggers an auto-immune reaction, and inspires your body to send an increased blood supply into the joints which are involved, the disease will affect your health in many other ways. Patients who suffer from rheumatoid arthritis often complain that they feel tired, easily exhausted, irritable and edgy. Most victims claim that they also have vague aches and pains in many different parts of their bodies. It is quite common for rheumatoid arthritis sufferers to complain that they constantly feel as though they have the 'flu. Many have night sweats and quite a few find that they lose weight (though this can be an advantage, for losing excess weight can help reduce the severity of the symptoms associated with arthritis).

Many people with rheumatoid arthritis show a slight rise in body temperature (partly because of the increased blood flow and partly because your body knows that one of the best ways to combat an infection – which it thinks you have is by increasing your general body temperature). And because the blood system is concentrating on producing and disseminating 'killer' blood cells there may be a shortage of red cells – the sort which normally carry oxygen to the tissues. This shortage of red blood cells can lead to anaemia and to breathlessness and tiredness.

Finally, although it is usually the joints – and particularly the synovial membranes – which are affected by the inflammation associated with rheumatoid arthritis that same inflammation can sometimes affect other parts of the body. The skin, kidneys, eyes, nerves, heart, lungs and tendons can all be affected by inflammation occasionally, and when this happens all sorts of other symptoms can develop. Bones may become thin and easily broken, lungs may be scarred and the skin may be ulcerated.

How quickly does rheumatoid arthritis develop?

Very occasionally rheumatoid arthritis will start suddenly. It is possible for someone to go to bed feeling fit and perfectly healthy and to wake up the next morning with all the symptoms of rheumatoid arthritis in one or more joints. But it is much more common for the disease to develop slowly over a period of weeks or even months. The disease usually starts in the joints of either the hands or the feet. In a typical patient the joints of the fingers will become stiff and swollen and painful to move. Because it hurts to move the joints the patient will probably want to rest them as much as possible. And so the muscles will become weak and will start to shrink. The stiffness in the joints which are affected by rheumatoid arthritis is usually worst first thing in the morning. Gradually, as the pain and stiffness in the small joints gets worse and worse, so the generalised symptoms of tiredness and weakness will also develop.

Which joints does rheumatoid arthritis affect?

Any joint in the body that contains a synovial membrane can develop rheumatoid arthritis. The small joints of the hands and feet are the ones most commonly affected to begin with. The joints in the middle of the fingers and at the bases of the fingers are probably the ones which are affected most frequently. Next, usually come the wrists and the knees. The ankles, elbows, shoulders and hips are affected less frequently.

Rheumatoid arthritis can last a long time – but usually comes and goes

The 'bad news' is that once rheumatoid arthritis has started to develop it will usually last for many years before burning itself out and ceasing to cause any more damage. The 'good news' is that the disease comes and goes and most sufferers notice that their symptoms quieten down after a year or two – although they may flare up occasionally. During an 'active' phase of the disease patients usually feel terrible in themselves and invariably wake up feeling stiff. Joints which are affected have to be loosened slowly and painfully and they often begin to get stiff and painful again in the late afternoon or early evening. Most sufferers who have 'active' rheumatoid arthritis have to do things slowly. Some patients have noticed that 'active' phases of their rheumatoid arthritis can be triggered by certain types of food or by doing too much. But others find it quite impossible to spot any factor as being responsible for a painful attack. During an 'active' phase the inflamed synovium usually does damage to the inside of the joint and so afterwards the amount of movement in the joint will probably be slightly reduced. The hands, which have small and apparently vulnerable joints, seem to suffer most and to show the most dramatic long-term changes.

After a few years rheumatoid arthritis usually begins to settle down and the 'active' phases become less and less common. In some patients this 'settling down' occurs after just a year or two. In others it can take 20 or 30 years. Even if your arthritis has been 'active' for many, many years you should never give up hope that it will one day become 'inactive'. If your arthritis has been 'active' for many years your joints may have been permanently damaged and disfigured by the time it settles down.

The joints of the hands – which often look worst affected and which may be so badly damaged that fine movements are difficult or even impossible – are usually least painful in the chronic or non-active stages of the disease. In contrast, the joints of the hips and knees – which have to carry a lot of weight – may not show a great deal of deformity but may be constantly painful.

Tendons can also be affected

Although rheumatoid arthritis is primarily a joint disease it can sometimes affect the tendons by which muscles are attached to the bones which make up a joint. Tendons are thin and rather cord-like and when a muscle contracts the tendon is used to pull the bone into place. Inevitably, the pressure on and in the tendon can be very high.

Tendons can be affected in two ways.

First, tendons themselves may develop patches of inflammation. When this happens a lump or nodule may develop inside or on top of the tendon. Normally, tendons slide in and out of place quite smoothly and easily – often travelling through fairly close fitting tunnels so that they do not interfere with (or get troubled by) other tissues. But when a nodule develops on a tendon the tendon may have difficulty in sliding in and out of its tunnel. To begin with the tendon may move in and out of position with an audible 'click' but if the lump gets big enough the tendon will eventually start to stick in one position. For a while it may be possible to force the lumpy tendon through its tunnel but if the lump becomes too big the tendon will stick permanently in one position.

Second, because the narrow tissue tunnels through which many tendons pass are lined with exactly the same sort of synovial membrane as that which lines and lubricates the inside of the joint, the inflammation of rheumatoid arthritis may cause the inside of the tunnel to become swollen. The result will be that the tunnel becomes narrower and stickier – and so, not surprisingly, the tendon will tend to stick in one position. If the tendon remains stuck in one position for long enough there is a real danger that the inflamed synovial membrane will start to 'eat' it in just the same way that the inflamed synovial membrane inside a joint will eat into the cartilage surfaces on the tops of the bones. Eventually, there is a danger that the tendon will become weak and may tear apart with the result that the muscle is no longer connected to the bone that it is supposed to move. Inevitably, the result is then a paralysis. Putting a joint in a splint can sometimes help encourage the torn tendon to heal itself and if that fails it is often possible to repair a tendon surgically – simply sewing together the two separated halves.

Joint damage may result in disablement

Patients with rheumatoid arthritis sometimes become disabled because of the damage done inside the joints that are affected. If the hands are badly affected by damaged joints or displaced or torn tendons, the fingers may bend to one side or individual fingers may bend in a variety of different directions, making it difficult to use the hands. If the toes are badly affected then walking may be made difficult. Patients who have bad arthritis in their feet complain that walking – even in comfortable shoes – is like walking on a stony beach in bare feet. If the toes become displaced in the same way that fingers often are, then the foot probably won't fit into a normal shoe. If the elbows are badly affected then the sufferer may have difficulty in bending or straightening his arm. This can make all sorts of things – from washing to eating to tooth cleaning – extremely difficult. If the knees or hips are badly deformed then walking can be difficult.

If you have painful arthritis in your knees that keeps you awake at night you may want to relieve your pain by putting a pillow under your knees. Don't do this. If your knees stiffen in a bent position (as they may) you will be permanently stuck with bent knees – and you will find walking extremely difficult.

Not surprisingly the constant pain and disablement caused by rheumatoid arthritis often cause depression. It would be a surprise if such a far-reaching and devastating disease did not make many sufferers miserable. Patients with rheumatoid arthritis often find it difficult to get out and about. They find sports difficult to play and often it is easier to stay at home slumped in an easy chair than to go out. But staying slumped in a chair or in bed can produce problems itself. First, there are the physical hazards. Staying immobile for long periods can result in muscles becoming weaker than ever, and in bones becoming thinner and more likely to break. Areas of skin which support the body can develop pressure sores. Sitting or lying down for long periods means that the body's need for food goes down – and since most people who spend long periods sitting or lying eat too much that means a dangerous and destructive weight gain. Infections are far more likely in people who don't move about and remain active and, of course, the joints are more likely to get so stiff that movement becomes quite impossible. Finally, people who spend a lot of time keeping still tend to become less tolerant of pain when it occurs. And thus a vicious circle develops. Second, there are the mental hazards. If you allow your rheumatoid arthritis to run your whole life you will quickly become demoralised and miserable. Boredom and anxiety and fear quickly lead to an increased susceptibility to stress and a far greater liability to depression.

Tests

Because rheumatoid arthritis is common and because the symptoms are pretty obvious it isn't usually too difficult to make the diagnosis clinically – without any hospital or laboratory tests. But the diagnosis isn't always easy to make – particularly in the early stages of the disease.

1. Blood tests may show the existence of a substance called 'the rheumatoid factor' and may show that there is inflammation in the body. Blood tests can usually provide useful results early on in the history of the disease.
2. X-rays may show that the edges of the bones are damaged. But X-rays do not usually show up any noticeable abnormalities until the rheumatoid arthritis has been present for many months or even years.
3. Testing the synovial fluid – taken out of the joint – may show the presence of the disease

Repeating tests may enable doctors to tell how fast the disease is progressing.

Can rheumatoid arthritis be treated?

Rheumatoid arthritis *cannot* be cured but it *can* be treated and it is much easier to prevent complications developing than it is to treat them once they have developed. Never forget that although rheumatoid arthritis can disable you it is extremely unlikely to kill you.

If you approach your arthritis gloomily – anxious about possible disablement and depressed by the fact that there is no 'magic' cure available – then the disease will do you far more damage than if you approach the problem in a positive, even aggressive, frame of mind. The more you know about the disease the greater your chance of combating it successfully. There are many things that your doctor can do to help you – and you must always talk to your doctor before starting or changing any treatment. But there are also many things that you can do to help yourself – and approaching your disease in a positive frame of mind is one of the most important.

What doctors can do

1. Drugs (to be taken by mouth)

There are scores of drugs available for the treatment of arthritis – in all its forms – and the number of drugs available is growing every month. Many patients with rheumatoid arthritis need to keep taking drugs for months or even years and that means that there are huge potential profits to be made by companies which can market safe and effective drugs. It is hardly surprising, therefore, that many drug companies produce at least one drug designed for the relief of the joint symptoms such as pain and stiffness which are commonly caused by rheumatoid arthritis.

The 'non-steroidal anti-inflammatory drugs' are the ones most commonly prescribed, and drugs in this category work in three different ways:

1. They reduce inflammation
2. They help conquer pain
3. They reduce any fever that may be present

Selecting the right drug for the right patient is always something of a problem. Some patients will respond to one drug while others will respond best to another substance. It is often a question of trial and error before the right drug is found. Surprisingly, perhaps, the drug that is still most widely prescribed – and which still seems to offer the greatest number of patients the greatest amount of relief – is aspirin; the first 'non-steroidal anti-inflammatory drug'. Aspirin has an unfortunate reputation for causing stomach bleeding but when used properly and carefully and prescribed in the soluble form it is as safe as most of the competing products. During the last decade or so an enormous number of 'safe' alternatives have been produced and time and time again it has been shown that many of the 'newest' and 'latest' drugs may also produce side effects if used in decent quantities or for fairly long periods. The main disadvantage with aspirin is that it needs to be taken fairly regularly and patients using it invariably have to take tablets every four hours or so. Some patients do develop allergies to aspirin, and tinnitus (noises in the ears) and deafness can also be a problem occasionally.

Because aspirin is made by numerous different companies and sold at very competitive prices most drug companies prefer to manufacture and promote their own alternatives – which can be sold at a much higher price and which can, therefore, be far more profitable. There are, therefore, scores of alternatives available which have roughly similar properties. It is impossible to recommend any one of these drugs as being better than any other, and new drugs are launched virtually every month. Although there are many chemical differences between the drugs which are available, most work by relieving both pain and inflammation. Most doctors have their own favourite drugs with which they become familiar, though some doctors do tend to prescribe the latest (and probably the most expensive) product that the drug salesmen tell them about. The only advantage of the huge variety of 'non-steroidal anti-inflammatory drugs' (known as NSAIDS) is that if you fail to get relief from one drug there will almost always be another drug for you to try.

Corticosteroids suppress inflammation so effectively that when they were first introduced they were hailed as 'miracle' drugs. They mimic the actions of corticosteroid hormones produced within the body as an internal anti-inflammatory. Unfortunately, although (or perhaps that should be 'because') they are very powerful, corticosteroids can cause very serious side effects. They can produce stomach troubles, blood pressure problems, bone disorders, skin diseases and a characteristic swelling of the face and body. There is also a danger that if you take a corticosteroid for too long your body's own production of steroids will shut down and you will become dependent on the tablets you are taking.

Sadly, many doctors do not really understand exactly how drugs work and what they can and cannot do. However, if you are going to benefit properly from the drugs you are prescribed it is vitally important that you understand just how drugs work and what you can expect from them.

One survey showed that a majority of patients – and this includes patients who are at home and patients receiving inpatient hospital attention – receive only one quarter of the dose of painkiller they need in order to provide them with proper relief. This is not, of course, because doctors or nurses are mean-spirited or uncaring. There are several reasons for the medical profession's failure to give patients enough painkillers.

First, it is very easy for both doctors and nurses to underestimate the amount of pain a patient is suffering. Lots of patients try to be brave and try not to show just how much pain they are in. Inevitably, therefore, when doctors prescribe pills they don't prescribe in large enough doses or quantities.

Second, both doctors and nurses worry a lot about their patients getting hooked on the drugs they are taking. They worry about this because some painkillers – and in particular the morphine derivatives – are addictive. In fact this fear is to a very large extent unfounded. It is very rare for patients to get hooked on painkillers – even if they need to take quite large doses for long periods of time. Indeed, the risk of addiction seems to be greater if a patient does not receive his drug often enough or in adequate quantities to control the pain. When a patient has to suffer pain and wait for his drug he is more likely to get hooked on that drug than when the dosage and the timing are designed to enable the patient to avoid pain or to control the pain properly.

One of the most important things you should remember is that you will suffer far less if you take your painkillers regularly according to the clock rather than waiting for the pain to return before taking them. If you only take your painkiller when your pain is terrible your body will be weakened and you will be learning to link your drug with relief from pain: that is what is likely to lead to drug dependence. Anyone taking a drug of any kind should talk to his or her doctor about the medication. Find out what the drug is prescribed for; find out whether the drug is likely to be needed as a long-term measure or a short-term measure and ask your doctor to explain to you how the drug does its job. If your doctor doesn't know the answers to these questions then maybe your questions will help to make sure that he does a little homework so that he can answer your questions and learn a little more himself.

You should know the answers to the following questions about any drugs you are prescribed:

1. How many times a day should they be taken?
If a drug has to be taken once a day it doesn't usually matter at what time of day it is taken as long as it is taken at the same time of day. A drug that needs to be taken twice a day should usually be taken at intervals of 12 hours. And a drug that needs to be taken three times a day should usually be taken at eight hour intervals if you are going to get the best out of it.

2. Does it matter whether the drug is taken before, during or after meals?
Some drugs are not absorbed properly if taken with food – other drugs may cause stomach problems and need to be taken with meals.

3. For how long must a drug be taken?
Some drugs need to be taken as a complete course – others can be stopped when symptoms cease. It is essential that you know which of the drugs you take fall into which of these categories.

4. What side effects can you expect?
You should ask your doctor if there are any particular side effects that you should watch out for. And if you notice any side effects while taking a drug you should get in touch with your doctor straight away, report what you have noticed and ask him whether you should keep on with the pills or whether you should stop them. Common side effects with pain relievers include: indigestion, constipation, dizziness and nausea and vomiting. But it is important to remember that all drugs can cause side effects and that the range of possible side effects is virtually infinite.

2. Suppositories

When you swallow a tablet or a pill the active constituent in that pill gets into your bloodstream and therefore the rest of your body by being digested as it travels along the intestinal tract. As far as the drugs used to control arthritic symptoms are concerned the main danger with this method is that the walls of the stomach may be irritated by the drug. Indigestion is, indeed, the commonest side effect associated with many of the drugs which are widely used in the treatment of rheumatoid arthritis. However, drugs do not have to be given by mouth in order to be absorbed through the digestive system and into the blood stream. In some countries the other end of the intestinal tract – the rectum – is considered a far more sensible place from which to start the absorption process. A drug taken as a suppository will be absorbed into the body just as quickly as a drug taken in tablet form but there will be a much reduced chance of any intestinal irritation. Although there may be obvious difficulties for patients with severe rheumatoid arthritis (putting a suppository into your rectum may be tricky if you have deformed, arthritic hands) the advantages are considerable and many drugs are available in this form.

3. Injections

Drugs taken by mouth or in suppository form have to travel throughout the whole body in order to have an effect on painful and inflamed joints. It is often more efficient and more effective to put the drug directly into the joint concerned. This does not only mean that the joint gets the full benefit of the drug but it also means that the patient concerned may be spared whatever side effects which may be associated with the drug when it is used generally. When joints are being injected (these are known as intra-articular injections) it is obviously important that the person handling the needle knows exactly what he is doing. Improperly administered injections can do far more harm than good. Some general practitioners do inject straight into joints but the majority of patients will usually be dealt with by some sort of specialist – usually either an orthopaedic surgeon or a rheumatologist. The shoulders, wrists, elbows and knees are the joints most commonly tackled in this way, although other joints (fingers, toes and hips, for example) can be dealt with by injection.

The drug used for the injection is usually a corticosteroid. The risks associated with drugs in this group are much smaller when the drugs are injected directly into a joint than when they are taken by mouth and allowed to spread throughout the whole body.

Before giving an injection into a joint the doctor will usually clean the area with an antiseptic and then give a local anaesthetic to numb the skin and the tissues just under the skin. The doctor usually confirms that he has the needle in the right place – right inside the joint – by withdrawing some of the fluid through the needle before giving the injection. Improvement usually follows about three days after an injection and will last for several months. A steroid injection can be repeated two or three times a year if necessary. Since infection can develop after an intra-articular injection it is important to tell your doctor straight away if you develop any unusual symptoms (such as increased pain, swelling, redness or heat) after the injection.

If a joint is swollen with an accumulation of fluid it may be possible to reduce the amount of pain, swelling and stiffness by withdrawing some of the excess fluid from the joint before giving an injection.

4. Surgery

Although surgery is used fairly frequently in the treatment of osteoarthritis its use is relatively rare in the treatment of rheumatoid arthritis. Here, however, are some of the operations that are sometimes performed in the treatment of this disease:

1. Synovectomy

If the joint lining or synovium is badly inflamed it may be possible to prevent damage to the joint by removing the inflamed synovium completely. This operation needs to be performed at an early stage in the progress of the disease – before too much damage has been done. Similarly, if the tunnels through which the tendons pass are affected by an inflamed synovium an operation to remove the damaged tunnel may prevent problems in the future. These operations are usually performed at an early stage to prevent severe disabling or crippling developing.

2. Joint replacement

Joint replacement operations were originally devised for use on patients with osteoarthritis where large joints such as the hip are commonly affected. Large joint operations have been so successful (nine out of ten operations on patients who need hip replacement surgery are successful) that surgeons are now replacing knee, elbow, shoulder, ankle and finger joints.

3. Nerve relief

If a nerve is trapped by inflamed or swollen tissues the numbness, continuous pain and 'pins and needles' that is produced can be excruciating. An operation to free the nerve and remove the pressure can produce spectacularly successful results.

5. *Physiotherapy*

A good physiotherapist will probably want to see you walk and sit and move before he or she even begins to examine you. By watching the way that you move the physiotherapist will be able to tell a great deal about your arthritis, the state of your joints and the extent of your pain. Then, when he or she has studied your movements, he or she will want to examine you. Physiotherapists don't just use their hands to heal their patients – they also use them to find out what is wrong. By moving your joints and by feeling your muscles a physiotherapist will be able to measure the extent of the damage done by your arthritis and will be able to work out how best he or she can help you.

In addition to watching their patients move, and examining them with their hands, many physiotherapists also like to look at any X-rays that may have been taken – or, at the very least, to look at the X-ray reports written by the radiologist. They will also want to look at any blood tests which may have been done.

Once they have thoroughly researched the patient's condition physiotherapists can start with their treatment. Unlike drugs, which are often designed to offer nothing more than short-term relief, physiotherapy is usually designed to provide some form of long-term improvement. The type of treatments physiotherapists use varies a great deal of course but their repertoire of therapies include massage, manipulation and exercise.

The sort of manipulation techniques used by physiotherapists are rather similar to the ones which are used by chiropractors and osteopaths. It is vitally important that joints and bones which are damaged are never manipulated (and it is especially important that a damaged spine is never manipulated in any way since if it were there would be a risk of causing permanent damage to the spinal cord). It is also unwise to allow anyone to manipulate an inflamed joint or a bone which is weakened (this means that many patients with arthritis will probably not be suitable candidates for manipulation). When the joints and bones are suitable for manipulation the operator will often be able to unlock joints that have become fixed simply by using his or her hands. When properly used, manipulation can help to relieve joint stiffness and muscle spasm.

A professional masseur (or masseuse) will stroke, knead and stretch your skin and muscles in order to relax them and to help take the stress and strain out of your joints. A good massage will help to break up toughened tissues and may even be able to help improve a poor blood supply. You can, of course, have a massage from a friend but a professional masseur is likely to be able to help relieve pains and stiffness far more effectively. As with manipulation you should not allow anyone to massage you unless your doctor has given his or her approval.

6. Ultrasound

Because it shows up soft tissues which cannot be shown very well on X-ray pictures, doctors use ultrasound to help them make a diagnosis. Physiotherapists on the other hand use ultrasound, which consists of high frequency sound waves, as a treatment aid to help them to mend injured ligaments, joints and muscles. Ultrasound is believed to help in several ways: it speeds up the ordinary, natural healing process; it increases the blood flow in the area and it also reduces the amount of inflammation.

7. Short wave diathermy

Like ultrasound a full course of short wave diathermy is likely to involve two or three sessions a week for several weeks. And like ultrasound those who use this technique, which uses high frequency electromagnetic waves to create heat within the tissues, claim that there are few, if any, significant side effects and that it is painless.

Physiotherapists use short wave diathermy because they claim that it can help to increase the flow of the blood, speed up the healing processes which normally and naturally help to repair the body and reduce any swelling which exists. The precise type of treatment they use will depend upon the tissues involved for different types of treatment affect tissues at different layers.

8. Interferential therapy

Unlike short wave diathermy and ultrasound, some experts claim that interferential therapy, another form of electrical treatment, does little to help speed up long-term recovery and is more likely to provide a short-term solution to pain. Like short wave diathermy and ultrasound this type of therapy is usually given two or three times a week for several weeks.

9. TENS

TENS devices are very safe and can be extremely effective.

Self-help

1. Lose unnecessary weight. Every pound of excess weight will put an additional strain on your joints, making existing rheumatoid arthritis worse and threatening otherwise healthy joints.
2. Give up meat. A vegetarian diet is more healthy and may help relieve symptoms if you are a sufferer from rheumatoid arthritis.
3. Learn to deal with stress. Stress can exacerbate the symptoms of rheumatoid arthritis.

Backache (see also slipped disc)

Backache is one of the commonest long-term health problems in the Western world. It is also one of the most poorly understood and one of the most badly treated disorders. If you have back trouble you should always visit your doctor so that he can make sure that you don't have a broken bone – or some other specific, treatable condition. Sadly, however, the two words which most accurately sum up the way most doctors treat backache are 'criminally' and 'incompetent'.

Visit your doctor with a back problem and the chances are that his first move will be to give you a prescription for the latest 'wonder' painkiller. Your doctor is unlikely to try to find out why your back problem developed. And he or she is unlikely to offer you much in the way of a long-term solution. He will simply do what he was told to do by the last drug company representative to wander into his consulting room. Modern medical practice has many lows but the treatment of backache is down there at the bottom alongside the treatment of cancer, heart disease, arthritis, asthma, depression and infectious diseases.

If your back problem persists – despite the prescription of wonder drugs – then your doctor will probably send you for an X-ray. This will give you a feeling that something is happening but the chances are high that it will be a complete waste of time and money. The chances of the X-ray providing useful information are probably worryingly close to your chances of winning the lottery. Indeed, unless he is a complete raving idiot (sadly, not as impossible as you might suspect) your doctor may not have even expected the X-ray to identify a treatable problem.

Your doctor will probably not have expected the X-rays he has ordered to find any abnormality because he knows that the vast majority of back problems are caused not by broken or damaged bones but by muscle or joint disorders. And, surprise, surprise, muscle disorders do not show up on X-rays.

The muscle and joint problems which lead to most back problems are usually caused not by accidents or falls but by stress, poor posture, high fashion shoes or some other lifestyle trigger.

When the X-ray report comes back with 'no abnormality found' written (or printed) across it the chances are that your doctor will reach for his prescription pad again – and give you a bottle of some other new wonder drug.

Drugs can provide short-term relief but they won't cure the problem. After many years of research, and countless millions spent on advertising, the best painkiller and anti-inflammatory is almost certainly a drug whose existence may not exactly be a surprise to you. It's name is aspirin. We recommend the soluble variety.

Soluble aspirin, taken in the dose recommended by the manufacturer, is probably safer and more effective than anything else around. This says a great deal about the effectiveness of the pharmaceutical industry. It also says a good deal about the intelligence of doctors who can usually be conned into prescribing the latest and most expensive pharmaceutical sewage instead of recommending aspirin. (Some doctors, poor things, probably feel embarrassed about recommending something that can be bought over the pharmacy counter for pennies).

If the drug your doctor prescribes doesn't work then the next move will probably be a referral to a surgeon.

What doctors can do

Back surgery can be a real shot in the dark. It probably helps occasionally. But often it doesn't. Far more surgeons than patients have benefited from back surgery. How many cars, boats and holiday homes have been paid for by unnecessary back surgery? Of course, if there is a specific bone problem then a surgeon may be able to do something useful. But for the majority of back pain sufferers surgery is probably about as practical a solution as a trip to the moon.

Self-help

Backache gets commoner as we get older. But it is not inevitable. Exercise regularly (and carefully), keep your weight under control and make sure that your posture is good – particularly while sitting – and you will reduce the risk of developing back trouble.

If you develop back pain also study the section on 'Pain' in this book.

1. You can strengthen your back with exercises

Most of us live our lives as though we are deliberately trying to develop back trouble.

We sit in badly designed seats, we lift and carry heavy objects without thinking of the damage we are doing, we stand for long periods and in the evenings we slump on soft sofas in front of the television.

As a result, most cases of back trouble are caused by muscle and joint problems.

The good news is that most cases of backache can be prevented (and even cured) by doing exercises which either improve flexibility or which increase the strength of the lower back muscles and the abdominal muscles.

Naturally, before trying any exercises you must check first with your doctor. And you should never do any back exercises if you are in pain, receiving treatment of any kind or if you have had or are awaiting surgery. Perhaps most important of all, you should always stop immediately if an exercise causes pain.

If you want to find out which exercises would help you, talk to a qualified chiropractor or osteopath. Ask around locally to find a practitioner who is trustworthy.

If you are looking for a general back strengthening exercise programme that you can try, consider swimming (though if you have backache, or any other health problem, you must obtain your doctor's approval before starting any exercise programme). You will need to swim regularly (aim to get into the pool at least three or four times a week) for 30 minutes or so at a time. Swimming will provide your body with an almost perfect exercise programme. It will improve the efficiency of your heart, it will help improve your muscle strength and it will improve your general flexibility. Swimming is one of the very few types of exercise that helps in these three important different ways.

Swimming is particularly good for back sufferers because it enables them to exercise without putting any stress or strain on their spines. The water will support the weight of their bodies and so they can exercise with the minimum of risk. The best and most effective strokes are the front and back crawl which will give the whole body a good, general work out.

If you swim breast stroke wear goggles and try to learn to swim without keeping your head lifted out of the water all the time. Extending your neck to keep your head out of the water can put a strain on your neck.

It is vital to remember that although the right type of exercise is essential for a healthy back the wrong sort of exercise can cause problems. Your back consists of scores of separate joints and all of those joints can be put under a tremendous amount of strain by any repetitive exercise. As a result, backache is a common problem among sportsmen and athletes who do not take care.

Warming-up before exercise, resting or even stopping when you feel tired, and cooling down gently after an exercise programme are all important.

Running is one of the sports most commonly associated with back injury. Running tends to tighten the lower muscles of the back, causing low back pain and increasing the risk of serious damage. Runners who exercise for too long on hard surfaces are particularly likely to suffer from backache. Every one hour's running means that the back gets 10,000 vibrations it doesn't want. Running on cambered roads means that the strains on the back are particularly bad because one leg is always running lower than the other.

But running is not, of course, the only sport that can cause back problems. Virtually any sport can cause trouble. Over enthusiastic swinging of a golf club, for example, can cause nasty strains that may take a long time to heal.

The most severe and potentially serious back injuries tend to occur in contact sports such as rugby and football where a sudden jolt can fracture a vertebrae, damage the spinal cord and produce permanent paralysis. Damage to the cervical spine – with resulting paralysis – is most common in some combat sports.

2. Strengthen your bones

Osteoporosis is one of the most fashionable modern diseases and there are many myths about it. It is widely believed that osteoporosis is a disease which almost exclusively affects women and that it can be prevented by swallowing calcium tablets or drinking lots of milk. These are fairy tales which would fit nicely alongside *The Three Bears* and *Red Riding Hood*. See the section on Osteoporosis in this book for more information.

3. Is your car seat creating backache?

Do you invariably get out of your car aching and feeling stiff? If so then your car may be wrecking your back.

Car seats are, in general, very badly designed and are responsible for millions of cases of backache.

Try to make sure that your car has a seat which can be adjusted in as many ways as possible. The seat should be firm (though not too firm – hard tractor seats cause lots of problems by transmitting vibrations directly up into the spine) and the backrest should give plenty of support.

Adjust your car seat so that you feel comfortable and can reach the controls easily and without stretching. If your seat doesn't give your lower back the support it needs, buy a cushion or support to put behind your back.

Try to make sure that you are relaxed while you are driving –

don't let yourself get stressed by traffic queues or badly behaved motorists. Learn how to relax your body and your mind. Stop frequently when driving on long journeys and when you do stop, get out of the car and walk around for a few minutes.

4. Try a rocking chair

One of the most effective ways to manage chronic low back pain is to sit in a rocking chair. Using a rocking chair stimulates the production of nerve impulses which provide effective and continuous pain relief. Rocking chairs are soothing, restful and relaxing.

5. Sleep on a firm bed

A soft, soggy bed may make your back worse.

If you don't want to buy a new (firm) bed try putting a board underneath your mattress to make it firmer. Alternatively, put your mattress, a sleeping bag or a quilt on the floor and sleep on the floor itself – using pillows and cushions to make yourself comfortable and to help keep your back straight.

Alternatively try a futon – a fairly thin, but firm mattress of the type which has been popular in Japan for several thousand years. A futon is rolled out on the floor or on a base frame to provide a comfortable but fairly solid bed that many backache sufferers find very suitable.

6. Lose excess weight

If you are overweight then you will put a constant extra strain on your back. If you try carrying a couple of bags of sugar around with you for ten minutes you may get an idea of just how damaging it can be to be dramatically overweight.

7. Rest when you need to

Exhaustion means strained, stressed and tired muscles. And backache is often one of the first symptoms which show that you need to rest.

8. When standing is better than sitting

Ernest Hemingway – a chronic back pain sufferer – wrote many of his books while standing up.

Many back sufferers are surprised by this and find it difficult to believe that standing up can be better for a bad back than sitting down.

But if the pressure within the intervertebral discs at the bottom of your spine is 100 per cent when you are standing up straight it will be 150 per cent when you are sitting up straight in an ordinary dining type chair and a massive 250 per cent when you are slouching or slumped forward in a chair. (In contrast it will be a modest 25 per cent when you are lying flat on your back in bed.)

In short, standing is much better for your back than sitting, and Ernest Hemingway knew what he was doing.

A writing slope – such as was popular a century or so ago in schools and offices – is much better for your back than a flat desk.

A horizontal surface creates back problems since it encourages too much bending of the back. A Victorian writing slope encourages the user to sit properly – particularly if used with a traditional stool.

We often think that we have improved our world since the nineteenth century but in many ways we have just made it worse. It is hardly surprising that backache now seems to be endemic.

9. Be careful with the shoes you choose to wear

Wearing the wrong sort of shoes is a frequent cause of backache. Women are particularly likely to develop backache as a result of wearing the wrong shoes because they are more vulnerable to the whims of fashion designers than men are.

High-heeled shoes can cause back trouble in four ways. First, they inevitably cause a certain amount of instability when you walk – however good your balance may be. And that instability leads to wobbling which leads to muscle strains and muscle tension. Backache is then almost inevitable.

Second, high-heels cause the Achilles tendons to tighten up – and that will lead to pain in your calves and, eventually, your back.

Third, and probably most important of all, high-heeled shoes offer no protection against jarring when you walk on hard surfaces. Shoes with some bounce in the sole provide a considerable amount of protection against jarring but high-heeled shoes usually transmit a shock up your spine every time you move.

Finally, high-heeled shoes tend to be rather narrow and tight fitting, and to produce bunions and other foot problems. People with bad feet tend to have some difficulty in walking – and that puts an additional strain on the whole of the back.

Try to keep high-heeled shoes for very special occasions and to wear low-heeled, well-fitting shoes with well-cushioned soles for everyday use.

10. Cold draughts can cause back trouble

This may sound obvious (and sound like something your mother used to warn you about) but draughts or winds cause trouble by making muscles cold and encouraging them to go into spasm. Avoid sitting or standing in draughts, and wear warm clothes if you have to go out into the cold.

Bowel cancer

After lung cancer, bowel cancer (the collective term for cancer of the colon and cancer of the rectum) is the biggest cancer killer in most parts of the world. Bowel cancer is a problem that is growing rapidly. The main cause? Diet. The evidence clearly shows a link between the consumption of meat (especially fatty meat) and the incidence of bowel cancer.

(Traditionally, Japan has had the lowest incidence of bowel cancer in the world. This was probably due to their low fat and high fibre diet. But in recent years, since a Western diet has been introduced into Japan, bowel cancer amongst the Japanese has risen.)

The colon (also known as the large intestine) consists of four parts: the ascending colon, transverse colon, descending colon and the sigmoid colon. The colon's main function is to absorb electrolytes and water from undigested food received from the ileum (small intestine). As it travels through the colon, the undigested food slowly forms into semi-solid faeces. The faeces then makes their way towards the rectum (the last part of the intestine) and stay there until defecation.

The colon makes up approximately the first six feet of the large intestine and the rectum makes up around the last eight to ten inches.

What is bowel cancer?

Bowel cancer is a malignant (life-threatening) tumour that has developed either in the colon or in the rectum or in both.

Cancer of the colon and cancer of the rectum are sometimes referred to collectively as colorectal cancer but most people know them both under the generic name 'bowel cancer'.

Studies have shown that most colorectal cancers begin as a polyp, which over a period of years, becomes malignant. A polyp is a non-malignant growth of tissue from the intestinal wall which protrudes into the intestine. Not all polyps turn into cancer of course, but having polyps does increase your risk of developing cancer. Polyps can sometimes be inherited and there is a hereditary condition known as familial polyposis which can inevitably increase your chances of developing bowel cancer.

Your risk of developing bowel cancer increases with:

1. Age. Your risk of developing cancer of the bowel rises after the age of 40.
2. A family or a personal history of bowel cancer or of familial polyposis. If this applies to you, then you should take extra care when it comes to looking after your health. (If a close relative developed bowel cancer before the age of 50, then you have a slightly greater risk than average of developing the disease. But don't worry too much as there is plenty you can do to help protect yourself against getting bowel cancer).
3. Ulcerative colitis, Crohn's disease and other inflammatory bowel diseases. People with any of these conditions have a higher risk than average of developing bowel cancer.
4. A diet high in fat, especially animal fat. If you consume lots of meat, greasy foods or dairy produce then you are markedly increasing your chances of getting cancer of the bowel.
5. Lack of exercise. You should take regular, gentle exercise to decrease your chances of developing the disease. Strenuous exercise has been shown to have no additional benefit whatsoever.
6. Obesity. Studies have shown that excess fat can influence the metabolism to increase cell growth in the colon and in the rectum.
7. Smoking.
8. Alcohol taken in excess. Alcohol is responsible for many illnesses so it is wise, therefore, to drink in moderation.
9. A diet low in fibre. Try eating more fresh fruit and vegetables

which are high in fibre. Besides, fresh fruit and vegetables are known to contain protective qualities which can help prevent against the development of cancer.

* * *

If you are exposed to any of the risk factors above, it doesn't mean to say that you are going to go on to develop bowel cancer. However, if any of the above risk factors do apply to you, then it is only sensible to take better care of your health. You might want to discuss preventative measures with your doctor, especially if you have a family or a personal history of bowel cancer or of familial polyps, or if you suffer from ulcerative colitis or Crohn's disease.

Remember, if caught early enough, bowel cancer can be cured. Some people feel embarrassed about discussing bowel problems with their doctor. By the time the patient seeks medical advice because he or she cannot cope any longer with his or her symptoms, it can sometimes be too late. Be sensible; don't die of embarrassment.

Symptoms of bowel cancer may include:

1. A recent change in bowel habits which has persisted for more than ten days such as: constipation, diarrhoea or a feeling that the bowel hasn't emptied properly.
2. Weight loss for no known reason.
3. Bloating or pain and tenderness in the lower abdomen.
4. Black, tarry stools (be aware that certain medications such as iron tablets can cause the stools to turn black).
5. Going to the toilet more often than usual, with possible loss of bowel control.
6. Anaemia.
7. Pain in the rectum which may make sitting down uncomfortable.
8. Either bright red or very dark blood on the toilet paper or in your stools (certain foods such as beetroot can cause redness in the stools which can look like blood loss).
9. Defecation may be painful.
10. Changes in the shape of your stools, especially if they are narrow or pipe-like.
11. Vomiting.
12. Constant fatigue.

Don't panic

If you have one or more of the above symptoms, it doesn't necessarily mean to say that you have bowel cancer. There are lots of less serious illnesses that can cause some of the above symptoms. However, to be on the safe side, you must always go and see your doctor if you are experiencing any of these symptoms – or any other unusual symptoms.

If you suspect that you may have bowel cancer, then you must make an appointment to see your doctor as soon as possible. If caught early enough, bowel cancer can be cured. Through embarrassment many people delay in seeing their doctor until the cancer is in its advanced stages by then of course, it may be too late.

Other reasons for blood loss

Haemorrhoids (commonly known as piles) can cause bleeding but there are usually other symptoms associated with haemorrhoids as well – such as itching and pain.

An anal fissure (a tear in the lining of the anus) can also result in bleeding. Straining too hard during a bowel movement, especially if you've been constipated, is the most common cause of an anal fissure.

If you think that you have haemorrhoids or an anal fissure and the bleeding persists for more than ten days, then you should still visit your doctor. It is dangerous to make this diagnosis by yourself because it may turn out to be something serious. Persistent blood loss or diarrhoea should always be investigated.

The one time when IBS can kill you is when you haven't got it

Bowel cancer is often mistakenly diagnosed for irritable bowel syndrome (IBS) because the symptoms can be very similar – especially the symptoms of bloating and diarrhoea. Patients regularly go back and forth to their doctor with bowel problems only to be told that they are suffering from irritable bowel syndrome. Much later on they find that they have bowel cancer.

The symptoms of irritable bowel syndrome usually come and go, whereas, the symptoms of bowel cancer are usually persistent. If you have persistent symptoms and your doctor says that you've simply got irritable bowel syndrome then you should ask for a second opinion.

With irritable bowel syndrome, a sufferer can go for days or even weeks without experiencing any symptoms at all, with bowel cancer, the symptoms are normally experienced every day.

It is also worth remembering that certain foods (and stress) can aggravate the symptoms of irritable bowel syndrome. Food or stress don't usually have much of an affect on the symptoms of bowel cancer.

If you have recently been diagnosed as having irritable bowel syndrome and you are not happy with this diagnosis, then you should ask for a second opinion as soon as possible. Normally, people instinctively know when something is seriously wrong with their bodies; always act upon your instincts because one day, they could save your life.

Remember: irritable bowel syndrome can kill you if you haven't got it.

What you can do to help protect yourself from bowel cancer

1. Nothing is more important for your health than eating a healthy balanced diet. You should cut out meat and fatty foods from your diet. If you can't stop eating meat or fatty foods then you should at least cut down on the amount you normally consume. You should also cut down on dairy produce and refined carbohydrates such as sugar. Eat plenty of wholegrain foods, fresh fruit and vegetables, especially cabbage, broccoli and Brussels sprouts. Vegetables tend to lose their goodness when they're cooked; lightly steaming vegetables is better as it tends to keep some of the goodness in. Lycopene, a chemical which is found in tomatoes is supposed to have powerful anti-cancer, protective qualities, but the benefits can only be gained by cooking the tomatoes.

2. If you don't take much exercise, then you should start exercising more. Walking is good exercise. You should aim to exercise a couple of times a week but you must do it in moderation (you should always consult your doctor before taking-up any form of exercise).

3. If you're overweight, then you should try and slim down. Following the above guidelines should help you to lose weight.

4. If you smoke, then you ought to give it up if you want to decrease your chances of getting bowel cancer or any kind of cancer.
5. If you drink alcohol in excess, then cut down.

Tests for bowel cancer

If your doctor wants to rule-out bowel cancer from being the cause of your recent symptoms, then he/she may refer you to a hospital for some tests. However, your doctor may want to carry out a simple examination first in his/her surgery, which involves feeling for any suspicious lumps. Having a finger poked up your rear end may sound rather undignified, but it's surely worth putting up with a few minutes of embarrassment if your life could be at stake.

If your doctor refers you to the hospital for further investigation then below are just some of the tests which you might expect to receive:

1. Barium enema – an X-ray examination of the bowel. The colon is filled with barium sulphate (a thick white liquid), which should be able to reveal any abnormalities in the bowel.
2. Flexible sigmoidoscope – a flexible thin tube with a camera on the end which looks inside the bowel. This procedure usually takes less than ten minutes to perform.
3. Colonoscope – the tube is very similar to the flexible sigmoidoscope except that it is longer. This means that it can look inside the whole of the colon whereas the flexible sigmoidoscope can only look inside the first 60cms of the bowel. This procedure takes a little longer to perform, and you will usually be sedated beforehand.

Treatment

Orthodox treatment normally depends on the location and the size of the tumour. Also, treatment depends on the patient's general health.

1. Surgery is the most common form of orthodox treatment for bowel cancer. The cancerous tissue is usually removed along with part of the surrounding healthy colon. The surgeon reconnects the healthy parts of the colon or the rectum by sewing them together. If it is not possible to reconnect the parts, then a temporary or a permanent colostomy may be necessary.

2. Radiation therapy may be used. These high-energy X-rays are used to kill cancer cells. Doctors may use radiation therapy after surgery to help kill off any remaining cancerous cells or they may use it before surgery to shrink the size of the tumour to help make it easier to operate.

3. To try and stabilise tumour growth, chemotherapy may be prescribed to kill off any cancerous cells in the body that remain after surgery. However, there is much doubt about the safety and effectiveness of radiation and chemotherapy and alternative approaches may be more effective. (See also the chapter on Cancer below.)

4. If you have been diagnosed with bowel cancer, then you are going to need lots of emotional support. Family and friends can only do so much to help. Most people feel that they need to talk to somebody who knows what they're going through and that's where joining a cancer support group might be helpful. There are plenty of cancer support groups around so do ask your doctor to help put you in touch with one. In a study published in *The Lancet* researchers studied two groups of women who had breast cancer. Half the women met one another informally to chat and offer one another support. The other half did not meet. The women who got together and supported each other lived twice as long. Those startling (and largely ignored) findings are just as relevant to bowel cancer patients as they are for women who have been diagnosed as having breast cancer.

Cancer

Cancer is one of the biggest killers of our time. One in three people will some day hear a doctor say the dreaded words: 'I'm afraid you've got cancer'. (Within a few years the figure will be one in two.)

But despite all the research which has been done there are more myths and unjustified fears about this disease than any other disease in the world.

One myth is that this disease always kills. It doesn't. Between a third and half of the people who get this disease recover – usually living long, perfectly healthy, perfectly normal lives.

But another, even more important, myth is that no one knows what causes this disease and as a result it is quite unavoidable.

That's a really dangerous myth because we now know a tremendous amount about what causes this disease. In fact, you may be surprised to learn that we know what causes a staggering 80 per cent of cancers.

It stands to reason, therefore, that if you want to cut your cancer risk by 80 per cent all you have to do is to try to avoid those things which are responsible.

'But surely,' you might say, 'if doctors know so much about the things which causes cancer we would have already heard about them – and been warned to avoid them by the government and the medical profession?'

Sadly, things aren't quite so straightforward these days.

It is difficult to avoid the conclusion that the truth about the causes of cancer has been deliberately suppressed – by businessmen and politicians.

The best way to avoid cancer

The top ten known causes of cancer

1.	Foods	50%
2.	Tobacco	30%
3.	Alcohol	3%
4.	Radiation (including X-rays)	3%
5.	Sunshine	2%
6.	Occupation	2%
7.	Medications (including prescription drugs)	2%
8.	Pollution of air and water	2%
9.	Tobacco (passive smoking)	1%
10.	Industrial and household products	1%

The figures in this table are 'estimates' but are based on the available research. Viruses which are known to cause cancer aren't included in this table – that is why the total doesn't add up to 100 per cent. The National Academy of Sciences in the USA, has concluded that: 'a little more than 40 per cent of cancers in men and almost 60 per cent of cancers in women in the United States could be attributed to dietary factors'. In 1981 it was estimated that dietary modifications might result in a one third reduction in the number of deaths from cancer in the United States – with a 90 per cent reduction in deaths from cancer of the stomach and large bowel; a 50 per cent reduction in deaths from cancers of the endometrium, gallbladder, pancreas and breast; a 20 per cent reduction in deaths from cancers of the lung, larynx, bladder, cervix, mouth, pharynx and oesophagus and a ten per cent reduction in deaths from other sites.

Many people who are aware that cancer is caused by environmental factors seem to believe that the causes are outside their control – regarding the pollution of air, water and food with chemicals as being the major risk factors. This table clearly shows that food and tobacco are by far the two most important causes of cancer and that, therefore, most people have far more control over their own risk of developing cancer than they realise. It is widely agreed that 80 per cent of all cancers are preventable – using knowledge which we have available at the moment. In other words, ignorance (sustained through political and industrial expediency) is responsible for 80 per cent of the millions of deaths caused by cancer each year.

The tips which follow show you how you can best cut your own risk of developing cancer. This section includes some simple tips designed to help you reduce the amount of damage that chemicals may do to your health.

Naturally, we cannot and do not guarantee that you won't get cancer if you follow our advice. But we do passionately believe your chances of developing cancer will be significantly lower than it will be if you take no action to protect yourself.

1. Do not eat meat
Researchers have linked eating meat to cancer – including cancers of the breast, prostate, uterus, colon, rectum, pancreas and kidney. Red meat seems the most dangerous type of meat – beef, for example, has been specifically linked to colon cancer. Women who eat meat are significantly more likely to develop breast cancer than women who rarely or never consume meat. Several studies have shown a relationship between the incidence of prostate cancer and the consumption of meat. If you don't want to get cancer – don't eat meat.

2. Control your weight
If you weigh just 22 pounds more than you did when you were 18

years old then you are probably at risk. Losing weight isn't just a matter of vanity. Women who are more than 40 per cent overweight are 55 per cent more likely to die of cancer – including cancers of the breast, uterus, ovary and gallbladder. Men who are more than 40 per cent overweight are 33 per cent more likely to die of cancer – with cancers of the colon, rectum and prostate the particular cancers they risk developing. Astonishingly, the cancer industry has done very little to educate people about the hazards of being overweight (perhaps there is little profit to be made out of simply offering advice as opposed to pills). A study in the USA showed that well over three quarters of American adults were unaware that excess weight is a risk factor for cancer. (In a country where obesity is endemic this is particularly alarming.)

3. Cut your intake of fatty food and avoid dairy products
There is evidence linking fatty food to cancer – including cancers of the breast, uterus, ovary, pancreas, stomach and colon. Avoid butter, milk, cream and other fatty foods. Keep down your intake of vegetable fats too. Fat intake and breast cancer are closely linked. If you choose a high fat diet you are making a conscious decision to increase your risk of developing breast cancer.

4. Eat plenty of fresh fruit and vegetables
Your chances of developing cancer – for example cancers of the lung, breast, colon, bladder, oral cavity, stomach and cervix – will go down if you eat plenty of vegetables. Fruit and vegetables contain plenty of fibre which can help to protect you against cancer – plus special anti-cancer ingredients. The best anti-cancer foods to eat include: apples, asparagus, baked beans, broccoli, Brussels sprouts, carrots, cauliflower, chick peas, corn, garlic, grapefruit, kidney beans, lentils, onions, oranges, pineapple, brown rice, soya beans, spinach and strawberries.

5. Keep away from people who smoke
It isn't enough not to smoke yourself. You are also at risk if you spend too much time inhaling other people's tobacco smoke. For example, the World Health Organisation has warned that: 'in marriages where one partner smokes and the other does not, the risk of lung cancer to the non-smoker is 20-50 per cent higher.' If you are travelling on public transport, eating in restaurants or going to the cinema choose

non-smoking areas whenever possible. Remember that tobacco smoke is still one of the most lethal cancer-causing agents known to man. Don't sit or spend time in smoke filled rooms and don't let people smoke in your home.

6. Avoid unnecessary X-rays

Many X-rays are unnecessary. Hospital doctors routinely send patients for routine X-rays but X-rays are not just extremely expensive and time consuming – they are also potentially dangerous. They can cause cancer. Check with your doctor that your X-ray is essential.

7. Beware of sunshine

Too much sunshine can cause skin cancer. Sunbathing is pointlessly reckless. Most cases of skin cancer are optional.

8. Beware of electrical appliances.

Don't sit closer than three feet to your TV set. Unplug your electric blanket before getting into bed. Don't sit within two and a half or three feet of a VDU. Don't sit or stand too close to electrical appliances – electricity is almost certainly more dangerous than you think. Try not to live within 150 yards of a major electricity supply line.

9. Minimise your consumption of food additives

If you eat a lot of packaged foods you almost certainly eat too many food additives. The average individual eats around 5.5 lb (2.5kg) of food additives every year. Food additives are potential hazards. You can minimise your consumption of food additives by eating a high proportion of fresh food.

10. Drink less alcohol

Alcohol can cause cancers of the mouth, larynx, oesophagus, stomach and pancreas. To minimise your cancer risk you should limit yourself to one or possibly two modest drinks a day.

11. Avoid chemicals

Try to have as few man-made chemicals in your home and your life as you possibly can. Take a look in your kitchen and your garage and you may be surprised to see just how many chemicals you have in your home. Whenever possible wash (and scrub) food before eating it. This will help remove surface chemicals. Buy organic food whenever you can.

12. Choose your toiletries with care

Use simple, unperfumed toiletries and use the simplest shampoo you can find. Be particularly careful if you use a hair dye. Some of the dyes used in these products may cause cancer. If you use aromatherapy oils make sure that they have been tested scientifically and have been shown to be entirely safe.

13. Avoid aerosols whenever you can

There is always a risk that you (or someone else) will inhale man-made chemicals.

14. Don't take medical drugs unless you really need them

This warning includes drugs which you have bought without a prescription. An increasing number of powerful drugs are now available over the pharmacy counter.

15. Avoid toxic fumes

If you decorate the inside of your house make sure that you keep the windows open. Paint fumes can be hazardous. Try not to spend too much time near to roads where there is a good deal of heavy traffic. Diesel fumes are extremely dangerous.

16. Avoid buying plastic toys

If possible buy unpainted wooden ones instead.

17. Consume plenty of vitamins and minerals

Make sure you eat a balanced and varied diet and if necessary take an appropriate supplement.

18. Listen to your body

Pay attention to symptoms which might suggest that your body doesn't like a chemical. If you develop strange symptoms make a note of when and how the symptoms first started, and precisely how they developed. And, at the same time, make a note of any new chemicals you may have tried. Common symptoms which suggest that your body doesn't like a chemical include: a skin rash, sneezing, nausea, tears for no reason. If you ignore these simple symptoms you may be making it easy for a chemical to do your body serious damage.

19. Stay safe at work

If you develop symptoms which you think might be linked to a chemical you could have encountered at work speak to your union representative, or to your employer, and find out if anyone else has reported developing similar symptoms.

20. Look at product labels carefully

If the small print tells you that a product can be dangerous then believe it. Companies don't issue warnings unless they have to. Virtually any product could cause problems these days. But medications (either ones which have been prescribed or ones which you have bought from the pharmacy) are near the top of the list. Many contain a whole range of ingredients – any one of which could possibly cause problems. Food additives. Detergents. Cleaning materials. The list is virtually endless.

21. Be careful when storing potentially dangerous products

Just because you know that the stuff in the old lemonade bottle is deadly it doesn't follow that everyone else will know that it is deadly. Children have a nasty habit of tasting strange looking brews. Every year thousands of children are poisoned – and many die – because dangerous chemicals were left lying around under sinks or in sheds or garages. Don't allow your home to become a toxic waste dump.

22. Improve your body's resistance to chemicals

Avoid foods which are high in fat. Fatty foods damage your body in several ways. If you eat fatty meat (and even lean meat may contain a good deal of 'hidden' fat) then you will almost certainly be introducing a number of chemicals into your body. Farm animals are fed a frightening selection of chemicals these days. Eat the meat from an animal and the residues of those chemicals will find their way into your body. It is because chemicals tend to collect in fat that breast cancer is so common among women. (Breast tissue contains a large proportion of fat.)

23. Try not to buy prepacked food which is wrapped in plastic

Paper makes a much safer wrapper. The chemicals from the plastic can 'leak' into the food.

How to spot cancer

When it comes to detecting a cancer which is developing, annual medical check-ups aren't much help. (Doctors like the idea of screening patients via annual check-ups because it's a way to make a lot of money for not doing very much work.) In our view, screening is of little value (and can do more harm than good). A growing number of doctors (including many of those actively involved in the screening 'industry') now agree that it is largely doctors, rather than patients, who benefit from screening programmes.

Instead you should try to be aware of the early warning signs that your body may show if a cancer is developing.

Many cancers are curable – especially if caught early. Here are some of the cancer signs you should watch out for:

1. Cancer of the large bowel: change in bowel habits (diarrhoea or constipation), unexplained weight loss, pain, passing blood.
2. Cancer of the cervix: unexplained bleeding or discharge, pain or bleeding after sex, weight loss.
3. Cancer of the breast: swelling or lump in breast, bloody discharge from nipple, enlarged glands in armpit, dimpling of the skin of the breast.
4. Cancer of the lung: persistent bad cough; blood in sputum, chest pain, wheezing, weight loss.
5. Cancer of the stomach: weight loss, persistent indigestion, vomiting blood, lump in abdomen, feeling full after very small meals.
6. Cancer of the liver: pain in abdomen, loss of appetite, weight loss, yellow eyes and skin, abdomen swollen.
7. Cancer of the ovary: irregular periods, hard lump in abdomen, pain during sex, bowel problems, excessive hair growth, voice gets deeper.
8. Cancer of the brain: headaches, vomiting, visual disturbances, weakness or paralysis, dizziness, fits, memory loss, personality changes.
9. Cancer of the skin: skin lesion that doesn't heal, bleeds, gets larger, changes shape, size or colour.
10. Cancer of the prostate: pain, urine retention, difficulty passing urine.
11. Cancer of the testicle: swelling in testicle.
12. Cancer of the blood (leukaemia): tiredness, paleness, bruising, bleeding easily, lots of infections.

13. Cancer of the womb: bleeding after sex, lump felt in abdomen.
14. Cancer of the throat: hoarseness, lump in throat, difficulty in swallowing, swollen glands in neck.

Remember: a patient with cancer may suffer from one, all or none of these symptoms. These symptom lists are not comprehensive. Patients may suffer from one or more of these symptoms without suffering from cancer. And a patient with a cancer may not have any of these symptoms. If you are at all worried see your doctor as soon as possible for advice.

Doctors and cancer

Doctors say that early detection is the only way to beat cancer. But this is a convenient lie. Doctors (inspired and paid by drug companies) want you to ask the wrong questions so that they don't have to worry too much about the answers they give you.

Cancer cells are normal cells which have become sick and have stopped listening to the brain's instructions. They are rogue cells. We all have cancer cells developing in our bodies at all times. You may find the thought rather alarming but the chances are that we all have cancer cells in our bodies today. We had cancer cells in our bodies yesterday and last week and we will have them there tomorrow and next week.

Despite the nonsense talked by doctors the best way for us to avoid cancer is not for us to wait until lumps have appeared and we have developed symptoms, and to then trot off to the doctor and ask him to chop out the lump, blast us with toxic radiotherapy or give us chemotherapy which will batter our weakened and threatened bodies with poison, but to give our bodies the best possible chance to ensure that they defeat those rogue cells (the cancer cells).

The fact that the concept of chemotherapy has survived at all is a tribute to the dishonest power of the medical establishment and the pharmaceutical industry. Chemotherapy has been a failure for decades and yet it still makes billions for doctors and drug companies. An increasing number of doctors – including some cancer specialists – now acknowledge that chemotherapy is often either no better, or worse than, no treatment at all, whereas alternative therapies may be and frequently are extremely effective.

Chemotherapy has repeatedly failed. The medical profession, the pharmaceutical industry and the cancer industry are so desperate to hide this fact that they now probably consider it a success if the survival rate of patients who take chemotherapy actually matches the survival rate of patients who don't take chemotherapy.

In order to kill the cancer cells (which are, after all, merely ordinary human cells which have got out of control) the drug must be so toxic that it inevitably causes a great deal of damage to other, healthy, cells. When chemotherapy is given by mouth (or by any other general, system route) the whole body may be affected – even though the drug is aimed only at one very specific site in the body. When chemotherapy fails to work (which it often does) the doctors usually respond by increasing the dose or making the chemotherapy even more toxic. The end result is that the chemotherapy may well kill the cancer cells but it will probably also kill the patient. (Thereby helping to perpetuate the old medical comment about the treatment being a success but the patient dying.)

Even when chemotherapy (or radiotherapy) does succeed in apparently 'killing' a cancer (and doctors like to give themselves a decent chance at a good cure rate by claiming that any patient who survives an extremely modest five years has been cured) there is a considerable risk that the cancer will recur. When you stop and think about it this isn't difficult to understand for chemotherapy (or radiotherapy or surgery) does absolutely nothing to alter the circumstances which led to the cancer developing in the first place.

For more information about cancer see Vernon Coleman's books *Superbody* and *How To Stop Your Doctor Killing You*.

Cataract

Cataract (a loss of transparency of the lens of the eye) most commonly occurs in the elderly and occurs so often that it is often regarded as simply due to the natural degenerative process of ageing. Most people over the age of 65 have some degree of cataract – usually confined to the edge of the lens and, therefore, not interfering much, if at all, with vision. Most people over the age of 75 have some visual deterioration resulting from cataract formation.

It isn't just the elderly that are susceptible to cataracts forming, people who suffer from diabetes mellitus are prone to them too. And it is possible for babies to develop 'congenital cataracts'. Infants who have a variety of rare genetic disorders such as galactosaemia are prone to having cataracts at birth. And cataracts can sometimes occur in infants who have Down's syndrome. Congenital cataracts may also be caused if the mother has an infection in early pregnancy, especially with the German measles virus.

If you've ever seen anyone with a cataract in its advanced stages, you might imagine that the sufferer must be totally blind in the affected eye. Not so. Light can still be transmitted by the densely opalescent (milky-white) lens. However, vision can be impaired (sometimes quite badly so) causing an increasing loss of clarity.

Cataracts usually affect both eyes but it is quite common for one eye to be affected more than the other.

Those who may be at special risk of developing cataracts include patients who:

1. Have been taking corticosteroid drugs for a long time.
2. Have been exposed to infrared radiation, X-rays and microwaves.
3. Have long-continued disorders of the eye/s such as uveitis and iritis
4. Have suffered an injury to the lens of the eye.
5. Are over 60.

Symptoms of a cataract may include:

1. Increased blurring of vision.
2. Halos around lights.
3. Colours may look different.
4. As the density of the lens increases, the person affected may become short-sighted. (One curious result of this phenomenon is that someone who was previously long-sighted may be able to read without using reading glasses for the first time in years.)
5. Milky-white lens (advanced stages).
6. There is no pain with a cataract.

Note: It is quite usual for cataract sufferers not to experience any of the above symptoms. The most common symptom that is often experienced is simply a progressive deterioration of vision.

Treatment

Although a change in the spectacles used can improve the sight in its early stages, as the cataract progresses and vision deteriorates sufferers may need surgery. Providing the eyes are otherwise healthy, the results of surgery are often excellent. Surgery involves the refractive power of the eye being replaced by a special, implanted lens.

Deafness: age-related hearing loss (a.k.a. presbyacusis)

Losing any one of your five senses is a tragedy; but hearing loss tends to be under-estimated and even ignored.

Age-related hearing loss, medically known as presbyacusis (derived from the Greek words for 'elder' and 'hear') tends to affect those over the age of 60. The condition is gradual, taking many years to progress. With presbyacusis it's not really a case of 'hear today and deaf tomorrow' but more a case of 'hear today, a bit hard of hearing next year and deaf in a year or two's time'. By the time we've reached 80, most of us will to a lesser or greater degree, experience some impairment to our hearing.

In the early stages, besides sounds being less clear, people with presbyacusis may have problems in hearing high frequency tones. Because speech is mainly made up of high-pitched tones understanding conversation can be very difficult, especially in the presence of background noise. Conversation may sound garbled as a result. As the condition progresses, lower frequency tones will also become less audible, thus causing a more general impairment in hearing.

Because presbyacusis is a slow but progressive condition, sufferers may not notice that there is anything wrong with their hearing to begin with. It is only when someone, who is usually close to them, points out that they have to keep repeating everything they say or that the television is often on too loud, that the sufferer becomes aware that he or she has a problem.

The causes of presbyacusis

Presbyacusis is an age-related condition. As we grow older, the delicate hair cells and nerve fibres of the inner ear slowly degenerate causing permanent hearing loss.

Certain drugs, a lack of blood supply to the inner ear due to high blood pressure, heart disease, arteriosclerosis and prolonged exposure to loud noises can all exacerbate the natural progression of presbyacusis.

Prevention

There are no preventative measures you can take to avoid getting presbyacusis because it is an age-related problem. However, you can try and stop it from getting worse by protecting your ears from loud noises and by being careful about which medicines you take. Some medicines can be toxic to the ear. In some (but not all) cases drug induced hearing loss is reversible – the hearing recovering when the drug is stopped. You must never stop taking any prescribed medication without consulting your doctor first. It may be dangerous to do so.

Symptoms of presbyacusis may include:

1. Difficulty in understanding speech, especially in the presence of background noise such as may be found in a noisy restaurant or pub even though those around you seem to be coping all right.
2. Sounds seem distorted.
3. Often being told that you've got the television or radio on too loudly.
4. Difficulty hearing on the telephone.
5. Having to constantly ask people to repeat what they've just said.

Diagnosis

If you are suffering from any of the above symptoms then you must make an appointment to see your doctor to have your ears examined. If you suddenly develop hearing loss, you must always see your doctor for investigation.

Your doctor may want to refer you to the Ear, Nose and Throat (ENT for short) department or to the audiology clinic at your nearest hospital for some hearing tests.

The audiologist at the hospital will carry out some tests which usually take around 20 minutes to complete. One of these tests may involve listening to a series of 'bleeps' over a set of headphones.

Treatment

Hearing loss caused by presbyacusis cannot be cured, but hearing-aids can make life for the sufferer just that little bit easier.

If you have been diagnosed as having hearing loss, then your audiologist may advise you to try a hearing-aid. Depending on the severity of your problem, lip-reading classes may also be recommended to you. It is usually some comfort to know that presbyacusis sufferers don't usually go completely deaf.

Hearing-aids are a lot more discreet today than they used to be. You can even buy hearing-aids now that are small enough to be worn inside your ear – so not even your best friend would know that you're wearing one.

A hearing-aid consists of a microphone to pick up sounds, an amplifier to increase their volume and a tiny speaker to transmit the amplified sounds.

Below, are a few brief descriptions of just some of the many different types of hearing-aids that are available today:

1. Behind-the-ear hearing-aids

A flexible plastic tube is connected from the ear mould, which fits inside your ear, to the hearing-aid which rests behind your ear.

2. In-the-ear aids

The actual hearing-aid is enclosed inside the ear mould which fits inside the outer part of your ear. People with limited dexterity may find its size and simple-to-use controls helpful.

3. In-the-canal aids

The ear mould of this particular type of aid is fitted inside your actual ear canal and the rest of the aid rests in the outer part of your ear. Although these are much more discreet than the behind-the-ear and in-the-ear aids they can, nevertheless, still be seen in the outer ear.

4. Completely-in-the-ear canal aids

These fit completely in the canal of your ear and cannot be seen, unless, of course, someone peers right inside your ear. These aids are not suitable if your hearing loss is severe or if your ear canals are too small.

5. *Digital hearing-aids*

Digital hearing-aids are the most recent kind of aid and are very expensive.

Digital hearing-aids contain a tiny computer which processes sounds in a certain way thus, making speech easier to understand even in the presence of background noise. These type of aids also last longer and whistle less than analogue hearing-aids.

6. *Body-aids*

These are the most powerful hearing-aids and are used by those suffering from profound hearing loss. The case is usually worn on a belt strapped around your chest. There is a wire from the case which is connected to a ear piece, which has a ear mould that fits into the ear canal.

* * *

If you have hearing loss, then don't be shy about seeking help for it, and certainly don't try to pretend that your hearing is fine when secretly, you're constantly having to struggle to keep up with conversations. It is not uncommon for people with presbyacusis to hide the fact that they have hearing loss. Deafness is definitely not something you should feel embarrassed about. If you request help, much can be done to help make your life easier, and hearing-aids are much more discreet now than they used to be. So don't suffer in silence.

Deep vein thrombosis

Deep vein thrombosis (DVT for short) affects hundreds of people every year. The risk of DVT is greater in those who travel on long-haul flights and an increased danger has also been linked to passengers travelling in economy class, simply because there is less leg room.

However, it isn't just long-haul airline passengers who are crammed into seats that would be a tight fit for an anorexic eight-year-old who are at risk of DVT – anyone can get it. Deep vein thrombosis can affect passengers who travel on shorter flights as well as people travelling in cars, trains and buses. Anyone who is immobilised for long periods of time is in danger of suffering from DVT – particularly if they are crammed into a small space and find it difficult to move around. DVT is, for example, a common hazard among bed-ridden patients.

Deep vein thrombosis is a blood clot that forms inside a vein which may completely block blood flow, or break free and travel to the lungs or heart where it can be fatal. When blood vessels are compressed (as they are when you are crammed into a seat which is too small) it is easy for clots up to a foot long to form.

Below are some tips on how you can prevent yourself from getting a DVT.

1. While seated, try clenching your calf muscles at regular intervals to stimulate blood circulation. Also, wriggle your feet and massage your lower legs and ankles.
2. Avoid socks and knee-high stockings with tight elastic. You must also avoid wearing garters.
3. Make sure that you drink plenty of water. Avoid caffeine and alcoholic drinks as these can dehydrate the body.
4. If travelling by aeroplane try to book an aisle seat on the plane to increase leg room. If you are unable to get an aisle seat, try to book one near an exit row or bulkhead.
5. Every hour, get up and walk about to help keep your circulation going. If you're in a car then stop in a safe place and exercise your legs.
6. Don't cross your legs or ankles whilst lying in bed or sitting down. Prolonged bed rest and sitting down for long periods all increases your risk of deep vein thrombosis.
7. When sitting for long periods, if you can, elevate your feet higher than your hips by resting them on something soft.
8. If you are bed-ridden, then raise the foot of your bed.
9. Some doctors recommend taking aspirin half an hour before travelling on a long-haul flight to help thin the blood, but you must consult your GP before doing this.

The risk of developing a DVT is greater among those who:

1. Are on the contraceptive pill.
2. Have varicose veins.
3. Smoke.
4. Take hormone supplements.
5. Are overweight.
6. Have recently had surgery.
7. Have heart disease or any other debilitating illness.
8. Are over 60.

The symptoms of DVT may include:

1. Pain and swelling which is normally felt in the calf, ankle or thigh.
2. Pain in the affected area when moving your foot or raising your leg.
3. Redness and tenderness.
4. Increased heartbeat and fever can sometimes occur.
5. Pain or soreness when walking.

Not everyone who has DVT suffers from all (or, indeed, any) of the above symptoms. And just because you have the above symptoms it doesn't necessarily follow that you have a DVT.

If you suspect that you may have a DVT you should get medical help as soon as possible. Don't be afraid to do so – it could save your life.

Diabetes (maturity onset)

Within a generation, diabetes will be commoner than indigestion.

Twenty years ago, one in every 50 people living in a developed country was a diabetic. Today, the incidence of diabetes is doubling every decade; within five years, ten per cent of the population will be diabetic. By the year 2020, nearly one in four people will be diabetic.

This section contains the facts everyone over 50 (whether a sufferer or not) should know about late onset diabetes.

What is diabetes?

Foods or liquids which contain sugar or carbohydrates are eventually broken down in the digestive system into a simple sugar called glucose. The glucose then enters the bloodstream, causing blood glucose levels to rise. In response to this rise in blood glucose, the pancreas produces a hormone called insulin which sends a message to the body tissues either to metabolise the glucose for energy or to store the glucose until it is needed; this causes the blood glucose levels to return to normal. In diabetes, either the pancreas, which lies partly behind the stomach, produces little or no insulin, or the tissues of the body becomes resistant to insulin. As a consequence, the glucose in the blood rises too much (this is hyperglycaemia) causing many unpleasant symptoms.

* * *

There are two types of diabetes. Type 1 diabetes (also known as insulin dependent diabetes mellitus or juvenile onset diabetes mellitus) and type 2 diabetes (also known as non-insulin dependent diabetes mellitus or maturity onset diabetes mellitus).

Type 1 diabetes usually occurs in childhood. In this type of diabetes, the pancreas produces very little or no insulin. Treatment always involves life-long daily insulin injections to help control glucose levels in the blood.

Type 2 diabetes begins later in life, usually after the age of 40 (although it can occur much earlier than that), and is the most common type of diabetes. In someone with type 2 diabetes, the pancreas usually continues to produce insulin, but the body's tissues do not respond to it. This is known as 'insulin resistance'. Treatment may involve one of the following: diet modification, exercise, oral medication, or insulin injections to help control glucose levels in the blood.

While the causes and the treatment of these two types of diabetes are different the fact is that if not kept under control both can cause the same long-term health problems. This section is concerned exclusively with type 2 diabetes.

Risk factors for type 2 diabetes may include:

1. Obesity. Obesity is a major factor in type 2 diabetes, and is present in up to 90 per cent of patients.
2. A sedentary lifestyle. Lack of exercise is also a major factor in type 2 diabetes.
3. Increasing age.
4. A family history of diabetes.
5. Certain types of medication (there are some drugs that can interfere with the production of insulin).
6. Stress.
7. Women who have had diabetes during pregnancy (this is known as gestational diabetes) have an increased risk of developing the disease later on.

Symptoms

Many people with type 2 diabetes do not know that they have the disease because the symptoms, which can be mild to begin with, often develop rather slowly.

Some people only find out that they have diabetes during a routine medical examination or because they have gone on to develop a health problem which is associated with the disease. Anyone over the age of 40 who is at risk of developing diabetes should be routinely tested for the disease. If you think that you are at risk, then you should discuss your concerns with your doctor.

Signs and symptoms of untreated diabetes may include:

1. Increased thirst (polydipsia).
2. Frequent urination (polyuria).
3. Blurred vision.
4. Weight loss.
5. Fatigue.
6. Tingling and numbness in the hands and feet.
7. Nausea.
8. Weakness.
9. Boils.
10. Irritability.

11. Cramps.
12. Extreme hunger.
13. Cuts and sores that are slow to heal.
14. Frequent infections, especially urinary tract infections and yeast infections of the vagina. Frequent infections are due to decreased resistance caused by elevated glucose levels in the blood.

Any of the symptoms listed above could relate to all sorts of illnesses: some very minor and some very serious. However, to be on the safe side, you should make an appointment to see your doctor for a medical examination as soon as possible if you have any of these problems. You should never, ever neglect any unusual symptoms.

Diagnosis

To check for diabetes, the doctor may use a simple blood test which usually involves drawing a small amount of blood from the thumb or fingertip and then transferring that blood onto a chemically coated strip. This chemically coated strip will probably be put into a machine that can measure glucose levels in the blood.

Alternatively, to begin with, the doctor may want a urine sample to see whether it contains glucose. If there is too much glucose in the blood, then it can spill over into the urine.

If the urine does contain glucose, then the doctor will probably arrange for a blood test, which will then be sent away to a laboratory for analysis. This analysis will determine how well the blood glucose levels are being controlled. Patients are usually told to 'fast' for eight hours before having this test.

Treatment

Treatment will depend on the amount of glucose that is present in the blood. A mild problem may be treated by a diet and exercise programme. A more serious problem may need oral hypoglycaemic drugs to help keep the glucose levels under control. Some type 2 diabetics may find that they need to have insulin injections later on, whereas, others may need to inject themselves with insulin from the onset of the disease.

Diabetes can be controlled through good management, which means: taking care of what you eat, checking your blood glucose levels regularly, exercising, taking medication for your diabetes if needed and having regular medical check-ups done by your doctor.

It has been shown that a strict low fat diet and exercise and stress control can reverse heart disease and researchers now believe that it may be possible to reverse diabetes with fairly dramatic diet changes. It seems clear that the best dietary programme for diabetics is one which is exclusively vegetarian or vegan. Even when a controlled diet doesn't reverse diabetes it will almost certainly help the patient minimise the need for medication and prevent some of the worst consequences of the disease (such as heart attacks and strokes).

Self-help

If you have diabetes don't just hand over the responsibility for your disease to your doctor. It's your responsibility too.

It's no good your doctor treating you if you are not willing to do anything to help yourself.

If you take drugs for your diabetes, then you mustn't rely on them to do all the work – they won't. It is up to you to make the effort to change some aspects of your lifestyle.

Too many diabetic sufferers continue to do the wrong things and eat all the wrong foods and then they wonder later on why they have become ill.

By managing your diabetes well, you can prevent or slow down the development of health complications. If you look after yourself, then there's no reason why you shouldn't live a long, normal and active life.

1. If you are overweight then you should try to slim down to an acceptable weight for your height and build. By losing weight, you are lowering your risk of developing long-term complications that are associated with diabetes. Before losing weight, however, you should discuss your diet plan with your doctor. If you don't diet sensibly, then you could be doing yourself far more harm than good.

2. You should try to avoid consuming too many sweet foods and sugary drinks as these can cause a rapid rise in blood glucose levels which can be too much for the insulin in the body to cope with. Over a period of time elevated glucose levels in the blood

can cause long-term health problems.

3. Because diabetes can cause high blood pressure, you should cut down on your intake of salt. Too much salt can exacerbate hypertension (high blood pressure).

4. If you should catch a cold or any other virus, then you must keep an eye on your diabetes even more carefully because viruses can interfere with blood glucose levels.

5. Foods that are high in fat are just as equally bad for your diabetes as foods that are high in sugar. So try to cut down on your intake of greasy foods, dairy products and meat. Meat can be very fatty, especially red meat. Research has shown that vegetarians are less likely to develop diabetes. (Vegetarians are also less likely to develop: anaemia, appendicitis, arthritis, breast cancer, cancer of the colon, cancer of the prostate, constipation, gallstones, gout, high blood pressure, indigestion, obesity, piles, strokes and varicose veins.)

6. You should make sure that you have regular medical check-ups by your doctor in order to look for any early signs of diabetic complications, and to also find out how well you are managing your condition.

7. Eat a healthy, balanced diet and spread out your intake of carbohydrates throughout the day to avoid fluctuations in blood sugar. Your doctor or a diabetic dietician will probably give you a nutrition plan to follow.

8. To try and reduce the rise in blood sugar levels that occurs after eating, you should try to include foods that are high in fibre in your meals.

9. All diabetics, regardless of what 'type' they are, should have their blood glucose levels monitored regularly. You will probably be taught how to do this at home. Maintaining strict blood glucose control is extremely important in the management of diabetes.

10. If you don't already exercise – then you should. Exercise plays a major role in helping to lower blood glucose levels and can have a positive long-term effect on your diabetes. It's obviously unwise to do five hours of aerobics every night or to swim across the channel twice a week. It is much healthier to exercise in moderation. You could try walking, cycling or even playing tennis; whatever you find enjoyable. However, before starting an exercise

programme, you should always consult your doctor. You could be putting your health at serious risk if you don't. If you take medication to control your diabetes, then you may have to adjust the dose according to how much exercise you do. Again, do consult your doctor about this.

11. Stress can increase the body's need for insulin so try to avoid as much stress as possible. Relax more and spend more time doing things that you enjoy.

12. Diabetes can reduce your resistance to infection, so if you injure yourself then make sure that you receive prompt medical treatment. If you have any wounds or ulcers on your body then do keep a close eye on them just in case they become infected.

13. If you smoke you should give it up. Research has shown that diabetics have an increased risk of developing heart disease, so smoking will only increase your risk even further.

14. Diabetics have an increased risk of developing eye problems, especially glaucoma, cataracts and diabetic retinopathy. So it is important to have your eyes checked annually. Diabetic retinopathy (degeneration of the retina) can lead to blindness, but early detection of the disease can usually be successfully treated with laser surgery.

15. If you are taking medication to help control your diabetes, then the timing of your meals is very important. Delaying or skipping meals can result in unhealthy fluctuations in blood glucose levels.

16. Read up as much as you can about type 2 diabetes. The more knowledgeable you are about your condition, the better equipped you are at knowing how to look after yourself.

17. Diabetes can lower your resistance to infections so you should take a good antioxidant to boost up your immune system and help your body fight off infections. However, before you start taking antioxidants, do consult your doctor first.

18. Foot infections are another complication of diabetes. To avoid problems, you must take great care of your feet and make sure that your toenails are cut properly. Foot infections are made worse by poor circulation to these extremities – foot massages might help improve the blood flow. If you develop an ulcer or an infection on your foot, then don't neglect it. Foot infections can develop into gangrene which can lead to amputation if you are not careful.

19. You should try to avoid alcohol because alcohol is high in calories, which is bad for your diabetes. However, if you have to drink, then at least make sure that you don't drink on an empty stomach, or consume too many drinks in one session. Excessive alcohol consumption, especially on an empty stomach, can cause the glucose in the blood to fall to abnormally low levels.

20. Being a diabetic does not mean that you are sentenced to live on lettuce leaves and carrot juice for the rest of your life. You can still eat some of your favourite foods provided that you do so in moderation. If you're stuck for ideas on what meals to have, then there are plenty of recipe books available which have been specifically written for diabetics. Some of them contain delicious recipes which require very little time or effort.

21. Diabetics should carry a card or wear a bracelet which has details of their condition.

Hypoglycaemia

Hypoglycaemia is a very serious complication of diabetes and if the symptoms aren't recognised, it can be fatal. Hypoglycaemia occurs when blood glucose falls to abnormally low levels. Medication to treat diabetes can sometimes cause blood glucose levels to fall very low and so can skipping meals. When blood glucose levels are extremely low the body releases a surge of adrenaline to stimulate the liver into releasing more glucose to help even-out the glucose levels in the blood. As a result of this internal activity, the sufferer may experience one or more of the following symptoms:

1. Nervousness.
2. Faintness.
3. Dizziness.
4. Hunger.
5. Sweating.
6. Shallow breathing.
7. Quivering.
8. Palpitations.
9. Headache.

If you are diabetic and you experience any of the above symptoms, you must check your blood glucose levels immediately. If you find that your glucose levels are too low, then you need to consume something to bring your glucose levels back up to normal. As a precaution, diabetics should always carry something sweet on them so that if they should ever have a 'hypo', they can treat their symptoms without delay.

Severe hypoglycaemia can often cause the following symptoms: irrational behaviour, irritability, fatigue, confusion, slurred speech, seizures and loss of consciousness.

If it isn't possible to give the diabetic patient something sweet to eat or drink because he or she has become unconscious, then medical help must be sought immediately.

The complications of diabetes

Maintaining strict blood glucose control is extremely important in the management of diabetes. Poorly controlled blood glucose levels can lead to many long-term health problems. These health problems may include:

1. Arteriosclerosis (hardening of the arteries).
2. Dupuytren's contracture.
3. Eye problems.
4. Heart disease.
5. High blood pressure.
6. Impotence.
7. Nephropathy (kidney damage) – your doctor should check for protein in your urine regularly as the presence of protein can indicate kidney damage.
8. Neuropathy (nerve damage).
9. Ulcers and foot infections – these can develop into gangrene if neglected.

Drugs (prescribed)

The half life of medical knowledge is getting shorter and shorter. By the time a young doctor has been in practice for five years much of the clinical information he was taught at medical school will be out-of-date. Most of what he was taught about drugs will be out-of-date too. In order to keep up-to-date doctors attend postgraduate courses and conferences. Many of these learning experiences are sponsored in some way by pharmaceutical industry companies. It is, therefore, hardly surprising if doctors regard drugs as pretty much the only answer whenever they are faced with a health problem which requires treatment.

But drugs are not, of course, the only answer. And they are frequently not the best answer.

There is no doubt that when used properly, and appropriately, drugs can – and do – save lives. But the medical profession's ongoing love affair with pills and capsules, and the communal tendency of doctors to encourage their patients to reach for the bottle whenever illness strikes, means that other, often safer and frequently more effective treatments may be ignored. In particular, the possibility of doing nothing at all (often one of the safest therapies of all) is frequently overlooked. Similarly, the ability of the body to heal itself (through 'bodypower') is often under-estimated. Serious, sometimes life-threatening health problems can sometimes be controlled very effectively without very much active intervention.

Today, it is common for patients (often perfectly healthy ones) to be given drugs which, according to their doctors, they will need to take for life.

Although providing drugs for patients suffering from chronic long-term problems (such as asthma, depression, high blood pressure or arthritis) is clearly a profitable area for pharmaceutical companies an even more profitable business is to sell drugs to perfectly healthy patients – the theory being that the drugs patients are given will stop them developing serious health problems in the future. This is an area where the drug companies are looking for huge growth in the future.

(If your doctor tells you that you are suffering from a long-term disorder for which you need to take long-term drug therapy – you should ask for a second opinion. Never forget that four out of ten patients who take pills suffer side effects.)

Never take any prescription drug unless you are convinced that it will improve your health and your life expectation.

Patients have a right to know what they are taking – and why.

Don't be shy. Here are some questions you should ask your doctor if he wants you to take a drug:

1. What is this medicine for?
2. How long should I take it? Should I take it until the bottle is empty or until my symptoms have gone?
3. What should I do if I miss a dose?
4. What side effects should I particularly watch out for?
5. Am I likely to need to take more when these have gone? Should I arrange another consultation?
6. Are there any foods I should avoid? Should I take the medication before, during or after meals?
7. How long will the medicine take to work – and how will I know that it is working?
8. How many times a day should I take it?
9. What side effects should I expect?

Of course, these days you might not have the choice over whether or not to take pills.

For years now it has been common for nurses – both in hospitals and in nursing homes – to hide drugs in food and drink. Sedatives, tranquillisers and sleeping tablets are among the drugs most commonly abused in this way.

Now this despicable practice has been made legal in many countries. Nursing staff are officially allowed to crush pills patients don't want to take and put them into food or drinks. One study showed that 'thousands of care home residents were being prescribed powerful tranquillisers for minor problems to make life easier for staff.' Another study showed that more than a quarter of pensioners living in nursing homes are on powerful sedatives which have turned them into 'zombies'. This report concluded that elderly people living in care homes are nearly three times as likely to be given 'chemical cosh' drugs as those in the community. Elderly folk living in the community get mugged by their young neighbours. Elderly folk living in nursing homes get mugged by their nurses. Doctors and nurses seem to have forgotten that everyone (including the elderly) has the right to refuse treatment they don't want.

Patients have a right to refuse drugs and tricking them into taking products which may kill them (and which will very probably reduce their quality of life) is well outside the traditions of medical practice. It is, to be blunt, immoral and unethical.

Drugs are already wildly overused in hospitals and nursing homes and this advice legitimises a practice which reeks of state control. Whatever happened to human rights – let alone patient rights?

Tips for any patient taking a prescription drug

1. Always follow any specific instructions that you have been given by your doctor. Read the label on your bottle of pills and take notice of what it says!
2. When you're not using them drugs should be stored in a locked cupboard out of reach of children in a room where the temperature will be fairly stable. The bathroom is probably the worst room in the house for storing medicines. Your bedroom – which probably has a more stable temperature – is much better.
3. Never take drugs which were prescribed for someone else. Return all unused supplies of drugs to your chemist.
4. It is wise to assume that all prescribed drugs can cause drowsiness. You shouldn't drive or operate machinery after taking a drug until you are sure that you are safe.
5. Drugs do not mix well with alcohol. If you want to drink while taking drugs ask your doctor whether or not it will be safe.
6. Do not take non-prescribed medicines while taking prescribed drugs.
7. Do not stop taking drugs suddenly if you have been advised to take a full course. Ring your doctor for advice if you need to stop for any reason. Some drugs have to be stopped gradually rather than abruptly.
8. Be on the look out for side effects and remember that if you seem to develop new symptoms while taking a prescription drug then the chances are high that the new symptoms are caused by the treatment you are taking for your original symptoms.

   Here are some of the commonest side effects associated with drugs:

   a) Drowsiness is a common problem with all drugs which have an effect on the central nervous system – these include: sedatives, tranquillisers, sleeping pills, most drugs used in the treatment of anxiety and depression and drugs used in the treatment of epilepsy. Drowsiness is also common with antihistamines (these are commonly used for allergies and so patients suffering from hayfever should be aware that their medication may make them feel sleepy).

b) Nausea and vomiting are caused by many different drugs including pain relievers, drugs used to treat infections, hormones and drugs prescribed for heart conditions.

c) Dizziness is commonly caused by aspirin but drugs used to treat high blood pressure, nerve disorders such as anxiety and depression and infections can also cause this side effect.

d) Drugs such as penicillin which are used to treat infection often cause diarrhoea – as do some drugs prescribed for intestinal disorders such as indigestion, gastritis and constipation.

e) Headache is a symptom that is associated with an enormous range of drugs.

f) Drugs used in the treatment of high blood pressure and in the treatment of nerve problems are particularly likely to produce a dry mouth.

g) Pain relievers, drugs used to treat infections and steroid drugs are the prescription products which are most likely to cause indigestion or wind.

h) Skin rashes are extremely common among patients taking drugs. Drugs used to treat infections – such as penicillin and sulphonamide – are commonly associated with this problem. A skin rash may suggest an allergy to a drug.

i) Itching associated with a skin rash means that an allergy reaction is almost certain.

j) Constipation is a common side effect with pain relievers, antacids, cough medicines and (naturally enough) drugs used in the treatment of diarrhoea.

k) Other side effects which are commonly noticed by patients taking prescription drugs include: confusion, hallucinations, tremors, fainting, wheezing, palpitations, blurred vision, depression, sweating, ringing in the ears and sexual problems such as frigidity and impotence.

9. Remember that patients who are over the age of 65 are more likely to suffer from side effects when taking drugs. This is because as the human body gets older it becomes less efficient at dealing with drugs – and more sensitive. Drug companies and doctors often recommend that older patients should be given reduced dosages of pills.

    a) Drowsiness and confusion are commoner among the elderly after taking sleeping tablets or tranquillisers.

    b) Dizziness, light-headedness and fainting and falling are commoner among the elderly when they take drugs to treat high blood pressure.

    c) Constipation after taking a painkiller is commoner among the elderly.

    d) Stomach upsets – including ulceration – are commoner after taking drugs for the treatment of arthritis.

    e) Problems in passing urine are commoner among the elderly when they need to take drugs.

10. Report any side effects to your doctor – and ask him if he's going to report the side effects to the authorities. The vast majority of doctors never bother to report side effects – with the result that potentially hazardous drugs remain on the market for far longer than they should.

11. If you need to see a doctor while taking a drug make sure he knows what you are taking – particularly if he intends to prescribe new treatment for you. Many drugs do not mix well together and may, indeed, react together in a dangerous way.

Gallstones

The gall bladder is a small bag (the size of a tiny purse) where bile is stored. Bile is a mixture of acids, pigments and cholesterol which help to absorb fats. Your gall bladder is tucked away under your liver (and under your rib cage) on your right hand side.

The most likely problem you'll get with your gall bladder is that you'll develop gallstones. These are usually made of cholesterol. But they can be made of calcium or pigment. By the time they reach their 50s one in five women and one in ten men have gallstones. As the years go by the occurrence of gallstones increases still further. By the time we're a couple of decades further down the line the vast majority of us will have gallstones. Since the majority of patients with gallstones never have any symptoms most gallstones are discovered by accident – often when X-rays are taken for some other, completely unrelated condition. At this point old-fashioned doctors (and surgeons looking for a way to finance their next skiing trip) will usually recommend action. Physicians will prescribe special drugs to dissolve the stones. Surgeons will want to fix a date for surgery.

The traditional operation is quite simple and relatively safe. The surgeon makes a cut in the abdominal wall and then reaches in and cuts out the gall bladder. Patients stay in hospital for a week or so and need up to six weeks sick leave. Some surgeons are now using lasers to cut out the gall bladder. They then suck out the bladder and stones through a tiny tube. This operation – through a keyhole sized scar – involves a hospital stay of no more than one or two days. And patients can be back at work within two weeks. But this operation does need a very skilled surgeon. Some surgeons are using a technique called lithotripsy – which shatters the gallstones. And some doctors are now prescribing drugs chenodeoxycholic acid and ursodeoxycholic acid which dissolve gallstones (though this technique was first tried back in 1937).

Gall bladder removal is the commonest abdominal operation surgeons do. You can manage perfectly well without your gall bladder. The gall bladder is just a warehouse and if it is removed bile just flows directly into your intestines.

But doctors still can't agree on when this operation should be performed or which patients need to have it done. We believe that drugs and surgery really are the last resort – to be used only when absolutely necessary. Literally millions of people have gallstones without knowing that they are there. Problems usually only develop when the stones get stuck moving out of the gall bladder.

We believe that gallstones which don't cause any symptoms can be left where they are. Gallstones (and the gall bladder) should only be removed when they cause trouble. One survey in Scotland showed that as many people die having their gall bladders removed as are killed by gall bladder stones. So the operation should only be done when it's really necessary (e.g. when the stones are causing pain).

You can reduce the pressure on your gall bladder (and reduce the risk of anything going wrong) by keeping your consumption of fatty food to a minimum.

That's it. That's all you need to do.

Cut your fat consumption to around 15 per cent of your food intake and the chances are good that your gall bladder, and your gallstones, will sit there quietly and cause you no discomfort.

(If you have gallstones look on the bright side: being forced to eat a low fat diet means that you will be far less likely to suffer from any one of the three big killers: cancer, heart disease and stroke.)

Glaucoma

Chronic, open-angle glaucoma

There are different types of glaucoma but the most common form, which tends to run in families, is called chronic (open-angle) glaucoma.

Chronic glaucoma is due to a gradual obstruction of fluid that normally drains into and out of the eye. Over a period of time, this blockage can cause a rise in pressure inside the eye. This can result in damage and possible loss of vision because the slow rise in intraocular pressure compresses the blood vessels which feed the fibres of the optic nerve.

Chronic glaucoma mainly affects those over the age of 40 and is one of the most common major eye disorders in the UK, affecting an estimated 250,000 people. It is a major cause of blindness. Glaucoma does not impair vision if treated early on. It's important, therefore, to visit your doctor or your nearest optician at the slightest change in your vision.

Owing to the fact that there are usually no symptoms with chronic glaucoma in its early stages (unlike acute glaucoma there is usually no pain) you should have regular routine eye-examinations (do make sure that the eye examination includes a glaucoma test). This is vital if you have a family history of the disease.

The symptoms of chronic glaucoma may include:

1. Blurred vision, particularly on one side towards the nose.
2. In small areas there is loss of peripheral vision.
3. Halos around lights.
4. Vision does not adjust well from light to dark.
5. Headaches.
6. Aching eye/s, pain.
7. Blind spots.
8. The eyeball may feel hard.

Usually there are no symptoms with chronic glaucoma until quite late on in the development of the disease.

The risk factors for chronic glaucoma may include:

1. Age (glaucoma is commonest over the age of 40).
2. Family history of acute or chronic glaucoma.
3. Smoking.
4. Tiredness.
5. Overwork.
6. Emotional stress.

Acute (closed-angle) glaucoma

Acute (closed-angle) glaucoma is caused by a sudden obstruction of the outflow of fluid in the eye.

The symptoms of acute glaucoma may include:

1. Severe, throbbing eye pain and headache.
2. Redness of the eye.
3. Blurred vision.
4. Halos around lights.
5. Nausea and vomiting can sometimes occur.
6. Dull but severe pain in and above the eye.
7. Swollen upper eyelid.
8. Fixed, dilated pupil.

Sufferers may experience only a few of the above symptoms. It is important that you see your doctor immediately if you experience any changes in your vision or any symptoms in or around your eyes.

Acute glaucoma requires urgent medical treatment. If left untreated, acute glaucoma can cause blindness.

The risk factors for acute glaucoma may include:
1. Age.
2. Smoking.
3. A family history of the disease (or of farsightedness).
4. Fatigue and emotional stress.

Treatment

It is important to treat glaucoma effectively. If untreated it can cause blindness. But the increased rise of pressure in the eye that occurs in glaucoma can normally be treated effectively. Treatment for glaucoma is usually life-long.

Eye-drops that help to reduce the pressure in the eye are normally prescribed by a doctor. The doctor may also prescribe diuretic drugs to help reduce the pressure. If the eyes refuse to respond to this kind of treatment surgery may be needed.

Acute glaucoma requires urgent medical treatment. Eye-drops or pills are normally given to help control the pressure in the eye and surgery may be necessary later on to help prevent another attack.

It's vital that anyone being treated for glaucoma should keep taking the treatment that has been prescribed otherwise the pressure inside the eye will just continue to rise. And this may result in permanent loss or impairment of vision. If the treatment produces unpleasant side effects you should see your doctor as soon as possible. You should also see your doctor promptly if you have an eye infection, pain in the eye, redness or any sudden changes in vision.

Haemorrhoids (aka 'piles')

Haemorrhoids are very common; affecting one in four people. It is usual for most people to get haemorrhoids occasionally and to experience only temporary discomfort, but there are some people whose lives are made miserable by haemorrhoids.

What are haemorrhoids?

The walls of the anal canal are very muscular. This helps to keep the anus closed until your next visit to the loo to open up your bowels. Owing to the fact that the anal canal contains lots of mucus so that waste matter can move along easier, there is an extra 'protection cover' to help prevent mucus from leaking out. This extra 'protection cover' is a mass of small veins which lies underneath the lining of the anal canal. Sometimes these veins can become varicose (this is what is known as haemorrhoids) and prolapse outside the anus looking like small grapes. There are veins just underneath the skin – lining the external part of the anus – and these can become varicose too.

There are three types of haemorrhoids: internal, external and prolapsing.

Internal haemorrhoids occur inside the rectum near the beginning of the anus. Generally, internal haemorrhoids are painless and the only symptom that is usually experienced is some bleeding.

External haemorrhoids are normally painful and occur underneath the skin around the anus. If the external haemorrhoid becomes thrombosed the pain experienced can be excruciating. If you find the pain intolerable and you cannot wait for the thrombosed haemorrhoid to go away of its own accord, then a tiny incision made by a doctor to remove the clot should immediately alleviate pain and swelling.

Prolapsed haemorrhoids are internal haemorrhoids that protrude through the anus outside the body, usually when a stool is passed. Normally, prolapsed haemorrhoids go back into the anus by themselves or if they don't, they can be gently pushed back up. However, in extreme cases, the haemorrhoid becomes permanently protruded. If this should happen, then your doctor may recommend surgery.

The causes of haemorrhoids

The main contributory factor is an increase in intra-abdominal pressure. As a result, the blood vessels swell and become engorged. An increase in intra-abdominal pressure occurs in:

1. The overweight.
2. Those who have to frequently strain whilst passing faeces (people

who suffer with constipation tend to have this problem).

3. People who lift heavy objects.
4. Pregnancy.

Diarrhoea, severe coughing and sitting or standing for long periods can also cause haemorrhoids. So can a congenital weakness of the veins in the anal canal.

Symptoms of haemorrhoids may include:

1. Loss of bright red blood. You may notice streaks of blood on the toilet paper. Prolonged loss of blood may lead to anaemia. Loss of blood from the anus should always be reported to your doctor as it can also be a symptom of bowel cancer.
2. Itching.
3. A painful lump or swelling around the anus.
4. Mucus from the anus (this can cause itching or exacerbate it).
5. Soreness or burning around the anus.
6. Pain.
7. Increasing discomfort when passing faeces.

In a majority of cases, haemorrhoidal attacks usually disappear within seven to ten days.

There are many anorectal problems which can cause haemorrhoidal-type symptoms. These include: fissures, abscesses, fistulae and itching or irritation around the anus.

Although haemorrhoids are not life-threatening, bowel cancer is. If you experience any sudden changes in your bowel habits or any unusual symptoms, especially blood loss, then you should see your doctor as soon as possible.

How to prevent haemorrhoids developing

Prevention is always the best treatment. Once the veins around or in the anus have been stretched, you are more likely to suffer another haemorrhoidal attack. The following are measures you can take to help prevent yourself from getting haemorrhoids, or to reduce your risk of them reccurring.

1. Constipation can cause haemorrhoids to develop because of the increase in intra-abdominal pressure caused by straining when

trying to pass a stool. Constipation can also aggravate already existing haemorrhoids. If you suffer from constipation, then you should try and increase the fibre in your diet and aim to drink at least eight to ten glasses of water a day to help keep your stools soft.

2. When lifting heavy objects, always exhale. You must never hold your breath as this increases intra-abdominal pressure. (And of course, you should never lift anything up without bending your knees and keeping your back straight.)

3. Try to lose excess weight. The overweight are more prone to getting haemorrhoids.

4. If you have a job which requires you to sit down or stand up for long periods at a time, then you should take regular five-minute breaks throughout the day to walk around.

Self-help

If you happen to be one of the 'one in four people' who has haemorrhoids there is plenty you can do to help ease your discomfort:

1. Itching is one of the symptoms that is often associated with external and prolapsed haemorrhoids. Sometimes the itching can be so profuse that the urge to scratch becomes irresistible. But whatever you do, leave well alone. By scratching, you are likely to damage the already delicate area around your anus, making things worse for yourself. You should be able to buy a good haemorrhoid cream, to help relieve any itching, from your local pharmacy or you can get one on prescription from your doctor.

2. After each bowel movement, clean the anal area gently with non-perfumed, soft toilet tissue. It is far gentler to the area around the anus to use a moist tissue rather than a dry one, but do make sure that you've dried yourself properly to avoid irritation.

3. Sitting in plain, warm water for 15 minutes several times a day should help relieve pain. The warmth of the water increases blood flow to the area which can help ease the swelling of the affected veins.

4. Constipation is a nightmare when you've got haemorrhoids. The pain of straining to pass a hard stool can be excruciating. So do

try to increase your fibre and fluid intake to help keep your bowel movements regular and to keep the stools soft.

5. You can help your stools to pass more easily by applying a little petroleum jelly to the anal area. You can use a cotton bud to do this.

6. If you have a prolapsed haemorrhoid, then try pushing it very gently back up into the anus. By doing this, you will reduce the risk of blood clots developing.

7. If the pain gets very bad, try putting your feet up on a footstool or a soft chair until the pain has subsided.

8. To help reduce swelling and inflammation in the area, try sitting on an ice pack (a packet of frozen peas will do) for five minutes. You must first wrap the frozen 'whatever it is' in a towel otherwise you'll get burnt.

9. To lessen pain and swelling, you might like to try an over-the-counter topical treatment or rectal suppositories, but you must not use them for longer than the duration stated on the packet.

10. Try to avoid alcohol and spicy foods if you can, as these are likely to aggravate haemorrhoidal symptoms.

If your haemorrhoidal symptoms have lasted for more than five days, or the pain becomes intolerable, then you must see your doctor. If you experience any bleeding from your anal area or you notice blood in your stools, then you should visit your doctor as soon as possible to rule out anything serious. Blood loss can be a sign of bowel cancer and if treated early enough, bowel cancer can be cured. If you suspect that you have haemorrhoids, then your doctor should make the diagnosis – not you.

Treatment

In a majority of cases, haemorrhoidal attacks disappear within seven to ten days. However, sometimes, haemorrhoidal attacks can be so severe that they may require surgery. The following are just a few of the medical procedures which may be used:

1. Sclerotherapy – a substance is injected around the blood vessel which causes the haemorrhoid to shrivel up and wither away.

2. Photocoagulation – a painless procedure using infra-red light to burn the haemorrhoidal tissue away.

3. Band ligation – tiny rubber bands are tied around the haemorrhoids, cutting off the blood supply and causing them to shrivel up and die away.
4. Haemorrhoidectomy – the affected part of the blood vessel is removed. A general anaesthetic in hospital is usually given for this surgical procedure.

Even with surgery, haemorrhoids are likely to return. So it makes sense therefore, to find out the underlying cause of your haemorrhoids and then to do something about it. Haemorrhoids can usually be controlled with a good healthy balanced diet, plenty of fluids and regular exercise.

Headaches and migraines

Four out of every five adults in Western societies suffer regularly, or occasionally, from headaches. Of those sufferers 88 per cent have tension headaches, ten per cent have migraines and all the other causes together make up the remaining two per cent. Headache is the commonest symptom requiring treatment or advice from a doctor, and muscle tension is by far the commonest cause of headache.

Tension headache

The word 'tension' in the phrase 'tension headache' doesn't refer to the stress or anxiety that so often causes this type of headache, but to the sustained muscle contraction which creates the headache. A tension headache develops when certain muscles of the head, neck and scalp are held too tightly for too long.

Some sources of muscle tension are fairly obvious. If you wrinkle your forehead with worry – or because you are squinting in bright light – then you will probably get a headache. If you sit or lie in an uncomfortable position then you may get a headache.

Strains caused by concentrating hard on something can cause a headache. If you have been crouched over the accounts or hunched over a steering wheel then you are likely to develop a tension headache.

You can see how the pains develop simply by looking at yourself in the mirror the next time you are worried about something. Look around your eyes – there will be lines developing in the skin there because you are frowning, squinting and screwing up your eyes. Look at the way your shoulders are hunched.

The nervous tension in your body produces muscle tension – and the muscle tension causes the headache.

Other sources of muscle tension may be less obvious. These include stress, anxiety, fear and anger. Worry about something that has happened can produce a nervous headache – as can worry about something that might happen in the future.

A tension headache will probably start in one place and gradually spread over the top of your head. It may be throbbing; it may feel as if you've got a hat on your head that is too tight; it may be a steady, pressing ache. The pain is often described as dull, nagging and steady (as opposed to sharp). It can last from a few minutes to a week or more and may slowly spread to the muscles of your neck and your jaw. The pain generally involves both sides of the head and terms such as 'pressure', 'vicelike' and 'tightening band' are often used to describe what the sufferer with a tension headache is experiencing. Every time you are upset or anxious or unhappy the pain may get worse.

(Incidentally, other terms may be used to describe this type of headache. 'Muscle tension headaches', 'muscle contraction headaches', 'psychogenic headaches' and 'depression headaches' are all synonyms for 'tension headaches'.)

It is important to see the role of nervous tension in the development of tension headaches as one cause among many. After all, many people suffer from prolonged exposure to stress without getting tension headaches.

It seems that in an individual whose head, neck and scalp muscles are already too tense, the addition of a tense situation may cause still more muscle tension, resulting in a tension headache.

We all have a 'weak point'. When under stress one individual may develop indigestion, a second may start to wheeze, a third may acquire a skin rash and a fourth may get a headache.

Most people try to deal with headaches of this sort with aspirin or paracetamol. Since both are excellent drugs they will probably work.

But taking a painkilling tablet to cure a nervous headache is rather like pouring water into a car that has a burst radiator hose – it is a very short-term solution to a potentially long-term problem.

Here are a few solutions that do not involve pills.

1. Since muscle tension will be helping to make your headache worse you can help yourself by deliberately relaxing the muscles of your head and neck. This is not as difficult as it sounds.

   Deliberately clench the muscles of your left hand. Make the muscles go as tight as you can get them. Hold your fist in that position while you count up to 20 and you begin to feel a pain developing. Then let your fist go loose.

   Much the same sort of thing happens in your head when you are under pressure. The muscles of your face, head and neck all become tight and so you get a pain.

   By learning how to relax the muscles around your head you can get rid of a headache, although you really need to practise this when you have not got a headache.

   Screw up your face really tightly. Try to tighten up every muscle in your face and neck. Now, slowly, relax all those muscles. Deliberately let them go all loose and floppy. You should be able to feel the tension and the potential pain pour out of them.

   If you practise this as often as you can then, next time you get a nervous headache you will be able to recognise the difference between tensed facial and neck muscles and relaxed face and neck muscles – and you will be able to combat your headache by deliberately letting your muscles go loose.

2. Next time you feel a tension headache developing try to look at what is happening as objectively as you can. Try to put everything into perspective. Often when things go wrong we panic and worry ourselves sick – when worrying really isn't going to help at all. If you are 20 minutes late, sitting frowning in your traffic jam isn't going to help at all. It is just going to mean that when you finally get to your destination you will have a stinking headache and feel absolutely rotten. Try to think of good things – things that you are looking forward to. Or try to remember good times in the past.

3. Try massaging the muscles of your face and neck with your finger tips. Start at the outside of your eyes. Make little round circular movements with your finger tips. Be slow and gentle. Then gradually work your way down the line of your jaw. Next, massage the bridge of your nose between your thumb and first finger.

Then massage your forehead. Finally, use both hands to massage the back of your neck. You will be amazed at how much difference it makes. Move your head forwards and backwards to get rid of some of the tension.

Migraine

Millions of working days are lost each year through migraine. The sufferers are said to have included: Lewis Carroll, Darwin, Freud, Joan of Arc, Rudyard Kipling, Nietzsche and Jefferson. It has been said that ten per cent of the population (women more than men) have migraine attacks from time to time. Migraine is frequently a warning that the stress threshold has been reached.

The symptoms vary a great deal but usually include some gastrointestinal signs in addition to a searing headache which may remain on one side of the head, switch from one side to the other or occur on both sides of the head. A migraine headache is frequently accompanied by stiffness and aching in the neck. (These are significant symptoms which, because they can be associated with other problems – such as meningitis – always merit an immediate consultation with a doctor.) The pain of a migraine seems to get steadily worse with each beat of the heart – this is because each beat of the heart pumps more blood, at higher and higher pressure, into the already strained and distended arteries. Nausea and vomiting, or one of these symptoms alone, is a common accompaniment. A single migraine may last anything from a few hours to days. The length of individual attacks varies as does the length of time between attacks.

Migraines usually begin in the sufferer's teens and may persist throughout the victim's life. They occur at irregular intervals, sometimes once or twice a week, usually less frequently.

Before the headache there is, in a classic migraine, usually a warning aura. Some sufferers see flaring lights. Visual disturbances are common.

Different sufferers have described a variety of aura experiences, including blind spots, visual zigzag patterns, flashing lights, tingling, not feeling sensations correctly on one half of the body, not being able to speak correctly and a vague feeling that a migraine attack is on the way. It is possible that the aura may be caused by the narrowing of the blood vessels which occurs before the vessel expanding – or pain producing – phase.

Migraines which do not come with an aura are known as 'common migraines' for the surprisingly appropriate reason that they are more common than classic migraines. Generally speaking, patients tend to get either one sort or the other.

The cause of migraine is still something of a mystery but it seems likely that the problem is largely a result of the body's response to stress. Misled into thinking that it can cope with the stress by preparing the muscles for immediate action, the body increases the blood supply to the muscles and closes down the supply to the brain. Then, when the threat seems to be lifting, the vessels open up again and the blood surges back through.

The initial constriction of the blood vessels causes the aura, the following dilation of the same vessels – and the renewed flow of blood – produces the pain. It is often the blood vessels on one side of the head that are affected; hence the result that the headache occurs on one side of the head.

Methods of dealing with migraine attacks include avoiding stress, learning to cope with pressures more effectively and limiting exposure to specific types of problems (or particular foods) which make symptoms worse.

It is vital to understand that migraine attacks may be triggered off by many different things. Sometimes a specific factor can be found which causes the attacks. Chocolate, cheese, oranges, lemons, shellfish, alcohol, bananas and fried foods have all been described as causing migraine attacks. A friend of ours had frequent migraine attacks until he gave up smoking cigars. Migraines can also be triggered by exercise, exhaustion, heat, sunlight, inhaled chemicals and hormone changes (about 70 per cent of female migraine sufferers of child bearing age report that a good number of their attacks occur regularly just before, during or immediately after menstruation). It is widely believed that genetic tendencies towards migraine are passed along within families.

The phrase 'migraine personality' is frequently used to describe a 'typical' migraine sufferer. Such an individual is said to be rigid and a perfectionist. Migraine sufferers are sometimes believed to be people who have to get everything done quickly and perfectly. However, although the concept of 'migraine personality' is still widely accepted by psychologists and doctors there are many sufferers who don't fit into this pattern – and many non-migraine sufferers who do match this description. To find out whether or not any of the known triggers are responsible for the headaches the migraine sufferer should keep a close record of all his or her activities for a month or two. Only then may a pattern be discovered showing some relationship between migraine attacks and a trigger. Making lists may be tiresome but it does frequently help pinpoint a cause.

When migraine attacks are plainly caused by distress they usually occur when the individual is relaxing. This is why migraine attacks often occur at weekends.

It is sometimes possible to use 'bodypower' to overcome a migraine. The technique which follows is taken from Vernon Coleman's book *Bodypower*. Since the symptoms of migraine are caused by a constriction of the blood vessels supplying the brain, it is clear that any effective treatment must help reverse that process. If you are going to stop the migraine developing, you have got to stop the blood vessels constricting.

At first thought it is difficult to see how it can be possible to do this. After all, you can't see or feel the arteries supplying your brain and so how can you possibly tell whether your efforts are working?

The solution to this problem was found when someone noticed that migraine sufferers often have cold hands and cold feet. This happens because when the vessels to the brain are constricted the vessels to the skin, and to the hands and feet, are also all constricted.

Now, although it isn't possible to tell whether or not you are succeeding in opening up, and keeping open, the arteries which supply your brain, it is possible to tell whether or not your attempts to open up the vessels supplying your hands are successful.

The 'bodypower' answer to migraine consists of making a conscious attempt to divert blood into the peripheral system which supplies your hands. If you can do this, and get your hands warmer, then you will also be diverting blood into the vessels supplying your brain – and thereby avoiding a migraine.

If you are a migraine sufferer who has been under a lot of pressure (and who, therefore, suspects that a migraine attack may be just around the corner), or if you have just had an aura suggesting that a migraine attack might be coming, try this technique:

1. Relax yourself physically and mentally.
2. Try to 'see' the blood vessels which supply your hands and try to see them getting wider and wider. See more and more blood flowing into the tissues. If you find that difficult, try to imagine that you are holding your hands up in front of a fire. Or imagine that you are lying on a warm beach.
3. You should slowly become aware of your hands getting warmer and warmer. As this happens so the blood supply to your brain will also be increased and your migraine attack will be aborted.

Brain tumours

People with headaches often worry in case they are developing brain tumours. The truth is that brain tumours are exceptionally rare. One expert recently surveyed 1,152 patients referred to a hospital specialist because of headaches. Only one of them had a brain tumour.

In the majority of patients with brain tumours there will be other very obvious symptoms (weakness, paralysis, eye problems etc.) in addition to a headache.

Caffeine withdrawal headaches

When an individual whose system is accustomed to a fairly steady supply of caffeine suddenly stops taking caffeine, a caffeine withdrawal headache may result. This headache may last for a week or more, and it can occur in individuals who do not normally suffer headaches, as well as those who do.

When caffeine is discontinued suddenly, many blood vessels that had been narrowed by the more or less constant vessel shrinking action of caffeine begin to stretch beyond their normal size, causing vascular headaches.

Since a dose of caffeine (usually obtained through taking a drink of tea, coffee or a cola drink) readily relieves the headache, it is easy to become trapped in a vicious circle of taking caffeine to relieve headaches that would never have occurred if caffeine hadn't been drunk in the first place.

Many early morning headaches result from caffeine withdrawal which has occurred during the night.

Anyone who drinks a lot of caffeine (a remarkably powerful drug) and who wishes to discontinue it is well advised to do so gradually in order to avoid caffeine withdrawal headaches.

Cervical spondylosis

Pain produced by problems involving the disks in the top part of the spine can sometimes produce headaches at the back of the head, and in the neck too. Sometimes this type of pain may spread into the shoulders. An X-ray of the neck is usually needed before a diagnosis blaming headaches on the bones of the neck can be made with certainty.

Chinese food syndrome headaches

Some people get headaches after eating a Chinese meal. In addition to the headache there may be other symptoms including a pressing pain in the chest, a sensation of burning over the trunk, neck and shoulders and a feeling of pressure and tightness in the face. This headache usually comes on about 25 minutes after eating Chinese food. The headache, frequently experienced as a band-like sensation over the forehead and a throbbing or pressure over the temples, usually lasts about an hour.

Chinese food syndrome has been shown to be due to monosodium glutamate (MSG) which is used widely in Chinese cooking and acts directly on blood vessels. The name MSG syndrome would be more appropriate since MSG is found in foods and additives other than those prepared and used by Chinese chefs.

For many people, MSG only causes headaches when eaten on an empty stomach.

Cluster headaches

The pain of a cluster headache usually centres around one eye. The pupil is contracted, the eye generally becomes red and weeps and the eyelid often droops. The nose blocks or runs on one side and vision may become blurred on the affected side. Eighty five per cent of those who get cluster headaches are male.

A cluster headache is accompanied by an extraordinarily severe pain (often described as burning, boring or tearing). Unlike the migraine sufferer, who usually wants to keep still, the cluster headache sufferer will often pace about with a hand pressed to the affected eye.

The term cluster headache is used because the headaches usually occurs in clusters during a six to 12 week period. Each attack usually comes on suddenly, lasting from ten minutes to two hours and returning two or three times in a 24 hour period. Alcohol and medicines which dilate blood vessels may trigger cluster headaches.

Cranial arteritis (temporal arteritis)

Cranial arteritis is an inflammation involving a specific artery. It usually affects men or women over the age of 50. The pain is usually superficial, boring in character and localised in the temple areas. The area involved will usually be very tender to the touch and the patient may complain of aches and pains in his or her shoulders too. There may, in addition, be some visual loss. The headache will probably be made worse by a range of movements including stooping, coughing and chewing.

Steroid drugs may help make the pain disappear quite quickly.

Dental problems

Tooth pains can produce headaches, and sometimes headaches can be caused by bad teeth without there being any obvious evidence of the source of the underlying problem.

Eyestrain

Eyestrain is a fairly rare cause of headache. But anyone who hasn't had an eye test for more than a year should visit an optician for a routine check-up.

To avoid headaches caused by eyestrain remember that adequate lighting is vital. The majority of headaches resulting from close work are caused by poor lighting. Anyone doing close work for long periods should use an adjustable reading lamp in conjunction with a good general overhead light. Papers which are being studied should be stood at an angle of about 45 degrees to the desk. Most good stationers sell book rests and stands. If you do a good deal of work on a computer make sure that the monitor is at a comfortable height and don't sit too close. Exercise your eyes regularly by moving them away from the screen every few minutes. Focus on something in the distance for a short while to help exercise the eye muscles. Finally, don't do close reading for more than two hours at a time. It is a good idea to take a break for half an hour every two hours.

Fasting headaches

Low blood sugar is a well known trigger of headaches. Headache sufferers who yearn for foods containing sugar, or whose headaches begin a few hours after eating, or who get headaches if they miss a meal, are likely candidates for low blood sugar problems.

The key to avoiding fasting headaches is to eat small, frequent meals rather than large three-times-a-day meals.

Glaucoma

In glaucoma the fluid pressure inside the eyeball builds up to very high levels. The result is a reduction in visual acuity as well as an often excruciating headache. Any patient who has a headache combined with eye problems and/or pain in or around the eye should seek medical advice urgently. Glaucoma can be treated with drugs but if it isn't treated the sight in the affected eye may be permanently damaged. (See also the section on glaucoma in this book.)

Hangover headaches

Alcohol is a potent dilator of blood vessels, causing vascular headaches. In addition some types of alcohol contain histamine which is also a potent dilator. Thirdly, alcohol is a diuretic which expels fluid from the body.

The pains associated with a hangover headache can usually be minimised (and in many cases avoided completely) by drinking one or two pints of water while, or immediately after, drinking alcohol.

Hot dog headaches

Meats may contain nitrites to give them an entirely fake 'natural' blood red colour. But nitrites dilate blood vessels and susceptible individuals may develop vascular headaches after eating quite small amounts of food containing them. Hot dogs, bacon, ham, luncheon meat, salami and other varieties of meat are the most likely causes of this type of headache. The obvious solution is to avoid the cause.

Ice cream headache

Some people get headaches after eating cold substances such as ice cream (or even just holding them in their mouths). The pain may be felt in the throat, on the forehead, at the temples and behind the ears. This is all due to referred pain.

Ice cream headaches can be avoided either by not eating cold substances or by eating them slowly and in small quantities (rather than gulping them down).

Injury

Any headache which follows an injury to the head or spine obviously merits immediate medical advice. It is worth remembering that severe head pains caused by bleeding within the skull can sometimes develop weeks after an injury.

Meningitis

The headache of meningitis is caused by an infection and inflammation of the sheath covering the brain. This is a potentially lethal condition. Patients with meningitis usually complain of, or exhibit, vomiting, drowsiness, neck stiffness, fever and a hatred of bright lights.

The possibility of meningitis being the cause of a headache is one of the most important reasons for always consulting a doctor when a severe headache develops.

Sexual headaches

Apart from the headache that means 'no' there are several types of head pain known to be associated with sex.

Pre-coital headaches, occurring just before sex, are probably the commonest. These are a type of tension headache and are produced when an individual worries either about whether or not a particular encounter is going to be successful, or about the possible consequences (this type of headache is most likely to be a problem if the relationship is an illicit one).

The commonest type of headache that occurs during intercourse is usually associated with contractions of the neck and face. The pain usually affects both sides of the head and is dull and aching. The patient's brow will be furrowed, his or her jaw will be clenched and there may well be tender areas on his or her scalp and neck. Again, these headaches are usually caused by tension (either because of anxiety about performance, guilt about the type of practice being enjoyed or guilt about the identity of the partner) and to stop this type of headache developing the patient needs to make sure that he or she can relax properly, and needs to be aware of any specific stresses which can be dealt with.

Occasionally, people suffer from sharp headaches which develop either just before an orgasm or some time afterwards. These headaches are usually violent, sharp, quite explosive and one-sided. They usually start slowly and build up as sexual excitement mounts. There is a theory that this type of headache may be caused by a rise in blood pressure but other experts have noted an association between these one-sided headaches and migraine. It has been suggested that heavy breathing during intercourse may be the cause of this type of headache. One solution, therefore, may be to try and breathe a little more normally.

Sinusitis

Headaches which develop after a cold may be a result of sinusitis. Cold air often makes thing worse, as does bending down. A steam inhalation, with or without the addition of a menthol crystal, is probably the best and simplest remedy.

To identify and control your headache

Here are some practical tips that should help all headache sufferers.
1. Anyone who suffers from headaches should keep a 'headache diary' – detailing the type of headache, when it started, how long it lasted, when it ended, whereabouts the pain was worst, whether there were any other symptoms (such as nausea or vomiting), what food had been eaten beforehand and so on.

   A 'headache diary' may help by showing a pattern. For example, headaches may always develop after a particular type of food is eaten, after a stressful type of meeting at work, at weekends after troublesome business problems or after trips to friends or relatives. The 'headache diary' is also a good way to check out the effectiveness of remedies you may have tried out.

Your 'headache diary' should enable you to spot if your headaches are being caused by an allergy or a sensitivity to any food you eat.

2. Learn to relax your mind and your body. Stress is a common cause of headaches. Stress can create headaches and it can make headaches worse.
3. When keeping your 'headache diary' make a note about any drugs you have taken (including both prescription and non prescription medicines).
4. Watch out for sympathomimetic drugs – these are drugs which imitate or mimic the action of the sympathetic nervous system. The sympathomimetics (and medicines which contain adrenalin) can cause headaches. Some of the medicines especially likely to include sympathomimetic agents include sinus, cold, allergy, asthma, decongestion and weight loss medicines. Many of these are available from a pharmacy without a prescription.

When to see a doctor

Most headaches are not life-threatening. The commonest headaches – tension headaches and migraines – may be painful but they are not lethal.

But headaches can sometimes be important warning signs that need attention. A headache may be the only warning of a brain tumour or an aneurysm. And so any new headache, recurring headache or change in headache pattern should be immediately reported to your doctor.

You must always seek medical advice if:

1. There is any change in your headache pattern.
2. You have a recurring headache.
3. You have any headache (however mild) that continues for 24 hours or more.
4. You develop any new or unexplained headache.
5. The headache has developed after a head injury.

6. Your headache has developed after starting medical treatment.
7. Your headache is accompanied by any neck stiffness.
8. The headache is severe and/or has developed suddenly and without warning.
9. You also have a temperature/fever.
10. You are worried.

Treatment

Doctors don't usually treat headaches very well. The main reason for this is that although headaches may be crippling and excruciating they aren't usually life-threatening. Headaches can wreck your life but they don't usually kill you. And doctors have a nasty habit of dismissing problems which aren't defined as 'life-threatening'.

Go and see your doctor with something impossible rare and threatening and you will quickly find yourself in a hospital, surrounded by men and women wearing white coats. You will probably be wired up to lots of equipment that needs electricity to make it work.

But turn up at your doctor's surgery or clinic with a skull numbing headache and you'll probably stagger out a minute or two later clutching a prescription for the latest wonder painkiller or for some exotic new tranquilliser.

Nevertheless, all headache sufferers should visit their doctor. This is not only to make sure that a correct diagnosis is made (and to ensure that there is no serious, underlying problem requiring treatment) but also to take appropriate advantage of any appropriate remedy which may be available.

The drugs your doctor is likely to prescribe will probably fall into these categories:

1. Painkillers

Aspirin and paracetamol are probably the two best simple painkillers available but most doctors are reluctant to prescribe them – they much prefer to prescribe the latest, most expensive and most complicated products. This is largely a result of the fact that because drug companies can't make big profits out of these two drugs they prefer to promote their own branded (and often highly expensive) products. Doctors succumb to temptation (and the entreaties of the drug company representatives) because they like to be able to offer their patients something more sophisticated and esoteric than a bottle of aspirin tablets. Drug companies will often claim that their painkillers are safer than aspirin. This isn't usually true, of course, but drug companies don't usually allow inconveniences like the truth to interfere with marketing propaganda. If you are a rich drug company it isn't difficult to find a doctor prepared to set up a trial to show that your latest superproduct is safer than aspirin.

(It would not be difficult to set up a trial which would prove conclusively that boiled sweets are safer and more effective headache remedies than aspirin tablets. Rely upon the placebo effect and a little positive encouragement and the boiled sweets will prove to be magnificent painkillers. Use high dosage ordinary non-soluble aspirin which burns holes in the stomach and it would be easy to show that aspirin is far too dangerous to be used.)

Caffeine is found in many headache medications. However, caffeine is a stimulant and it can add to some tension headache problems – despite an initial feeling of relief. Caffeine can increase both nervous tension and muscle tension, thus increasing the probability of more headaches when the medication wears off. This often starts a vicious circle with more and more caffeine containing medication being required to control more and more headaches. The treatment may turn a short-term, acute problem, into a long-term chronic problem.

The biggest hazard associated with the use of painkillers in the treatment of headache is that the patient will become addicted. Aspirin and paracetamol are not addictive drugs (although some patients may become hooked on the habit of taking them – which is a rather different thing) but some of the most popularly prescribed painkillers are addictive. It is no coincidence that the painkiller co-proxamol (also known as Distalgesic) is usually at or near the top of any list of the most popular prescription drugs. When taken in higher than recommended doses over long periods of time this drug can produce drug dependence.

2. *Tranquillisers*

Encouraged by the fact that many headaches are caused by stress and anxiety doctors will often hand over a prescription for a tranquilliser when faced with a patient complaining of a headache.

The logic behind this decision is based upon the fact that some tranquillisers – for example the benzodiazepines – do have a muscle relaxing effect as well as a tranquillising effect. However, any doctor who prescribes a tranquilliser for a patient suffering from headaches is exhibiting the sort of pharmacological knowledge and general wisdom usually associated with a dining table. Tranquillisers do not eradicate stress – or help an individual to cope with it better – and they are neither a useful nor a safe solution to a stress induced headache.

3. Antidepressants

Antidepressant drugs are often prescribed for headache sufferers, sometimes because it is believed that such medications may help, but more often because the doctor assumes that any patient with any headache must be depressed. This is nonsense and is little more than a sign that the prescribing doctor is woefully ignorant and really should find some other, more suitable form of employment. It is difficult to have much faith in doctors who prescribe these drugs for patients who aren't genuinely depressed.

Heart attacks and heart disease

If you die between 45 and 65 there is a one in three chance that you will die from a heart attack. If you're over 65 then your chances of being killed by a heart attack are even greater.

Heart disease is alongside cancer as one of the two major killers of our time. And yet, like cancer, heart disease is usually avoidable.

Doctors, hospitals and drug companies will tell you that the best ways to prevent and treat heart disease are to take drugs or to have surgery. That's self-serving nonsense. A money-making lie.

Drugs are neither the best way to prevent heart disease nor the best way to treat it. And surgery is a crude, potentially lethal and often ineffective way to tackle a delicate and curable problem. More than one third of all patients who have bypass surgery have measurable brain function loss that persists for many years after surgery. A study published in the *New England Journal of Medicine* showed a 20 per cent drop in mental ability of 53 per cent of bypass patients when they left hospital. By the fifth year after surgery there was still a significant decline in mental ability. It is believed that tiny blood clots form and go to the brain during the surgery while the heart-lung machine pumps and oxygenates blood during surgery. Dietary and lifestyle changes are much safer than surgery. Artery blockages can be reversed without surgery.

Coronary atherosclerosis (a.k.a. coronary-artery disease; coronary heart disease; ischaemic heart disease)

Atherosclerosis is a disease of the arteries in which fatty plaques build-up on the inner walls causing narrowing and loss of elasticity of the blood vessels. Blood flow is then impaired as a result.

The fatty plaques, medically known as atheroma which tend to accumulate at artery junctions, are mainly made up of cholesterol. That's why it is very important to cut out as much cholesterol as you can from your diet.

Owing to the fact that atherosclerosis can reduce blood flow to major arteries such as; the heart, brain, kidneys, intestine and the legs, it's a cause of a great number of serious illnesses. For instance, if blood flow to the brain is impaired, then a stroke is likely to occur.

Atherosclerosis kills more people in the UK than any other condition. The most common form of atherosclerosis is heart disease involving the coronary arteries, better known as coronary-artery disease.

There are two main coronary arteries which supply blood to the heart muscle and if they should become narrowed or blocked, adequate oxygen can no longer be provided resulting in damage or malfunction of the heart. Angina pectoris and myocardial infarction (heart attack) are the two most common features of coronary-artery disease.

Angina pectoris

Angina pectoris is a pain in the chest due to an insufficient supply of oxygen via the blood to the heart muscle.

Pain is often brought on by exercise or stress. This is because of the increased demand of oxygen required by the heart. In severe cases, sufferers experience pain at the slightest exertion, such as getting out of a chair.

There are many causes of angina pectoris but one of the main causes is coronary-artery disease due to atherosclerosis.

Symptoms of angina pectoris may include:

1. Frequent pain in the centre of the chest (similar to indigestion) which can sometimes radiate to the jaw, throat, left arm, back and between the shoulder-blades.
2. The pain usually feels like a mild ache and may be accompanied with numbness, tingling or heaviness in the left arm.
3. Dizziness, nausea, sweating and breathing difficulties can sometimes occur.
4. Pain can be brought on by exercise, stress or extreme temperatures.
5. Pain is relieved by resting.

Post menopausal women and men over the age of 35 are most affected by angina pectoris.

How to prevent an angina attack

1. Avoid activities that usually trigger off attacks of angina.
2. If you can, try not to go out when it's extremely cold or when it's very hot as this has been known to induce an angina attack.
3. Try to avoid stress.

Apart from refraining from doing any form of strenuous exercise, some people with angina pectoris are able to lead relatively normal lives. However, it all depends on what the underlying disease is and the effectiveness of treatment.

If you suspect that you have angina pectoris, then you must see your doctor straight away.

If you have angina pectoris and the pain does not go away after 15 minutes of rest or after you have taken your prescribed medicine then you must seek medical help as soon as possible because you may be having a heart attack. Also, if your attacks of angina become more frequent or increase in severity then you must see your doctor.

Heart attack (a.k.a. myocardial infarction)

Heart attacks are one of the commonest causes of death in developing countries.

A heart attack is caused by a complete or partial blockage of the coronary arteries causing death to part of the heart muscle.

Symptoms of a heart attack may include:

1. The most characteristic symptom is sudden unremitting pain in the chest (severity of pain depends on how bad the heart attack is).
2. The pain may feel like a squeezing or crushing feeling in the chest.
3. Pain may radiate to the neck, jaw, left arm or between the shoulder-blades.
4. Shortness of breath.
5. Nausea or vomiting.
6. Sweating.
7. Cold clammy skin.
8. Restlessness.
9. Feeling apprehensive.
10. Loss of consciousness (sometimes).

You do not have to experience all of these symptoms to be having a heart attack. Some heart attack victims experience very little pain and hardly develop any of these symptoms. This is known as a 'silent infarct' and the victim may be completely oblivious to the fact that he/she has had a heart attack.

If you suspect that you may be having a heart attack, call emergency services immediately. Chew one aspirin tablet (as this helps to thin the blood to stop it from clotting) and if you're at home alone, leave your front door open just in case you lose consciousness, this saves valuable time because life-saving minutes could be lost due to the ambulance crew having to force their way into your home.

If you're having a heart attack and you're in too much pain to call for emergency services, then do try your best to alert your next door neighbours.

After a first heart attack, the risk of having another one is dramatically increased. So it is important, therefore, to do your very best to look after your heart. Listen to what your doctor tells you and try to reduce any risk factors (see the 'risk increases with' section) that could lead to you having another heart attack.

After a heart attack, it is advisable to have regular medical assessments throughout your life to check that all is well with your heart.

The risk of having a heart attack, coronary-artery disease and angina pectoris increases with:

1. Age.
2. Smoking.
3. Too much fat in the diet, especially dairy produce, meat, poultry, fried foods and greasy chips. (You should always check the fat content of any of the foods you buy).
4. Obesity.
5. Family history of heart disease.
6. Lack of exercise.
7. Excessive alcohol intake (however, research has shown that drinking no more than two to three glasses of wine a day may help prevent heart disease).
8. Too much stress.
9. Atherosclerosis.
10. Previous heart attack or stroke.
11. Diabetes.
12. High blood pressure.

How to prevent a heart attack, coronary-artery disease and angina pectoris

1. Eat a low-fat and low-salt diet.
2. Eat more fruit and vegetables.
3. Don't smoke.
4. Try to reduce stress (you can try taking up forms of relaxation such as meditation or yoga. Alternatively, take up a hobby or spend more time doing something you enjoy).
5. Exercise sensibly and regularly but you *must* consult your doctor first (and get his permission).
6. Lose weight if you are overweight.

7. If you have diabetes or high blood pressure, try to keep whichever you have under control.
8. Drink alcohol in moderation (heavy alcohol consumption can seriously damage the heart).
9. Take antioxidants such as vitamin E (always consult your doctor before taking vitamin supplements of any kind).
10. Garlic is reputed to help prevent heart disease.
11. If you have to use oil for cooking, then try to use extra virgin olive oil as this is less harmful to your health.

Diagnosis

The official diagnosis of heart disease is usually done by having special tests in hospital. One of these tests involves having an electro-cardiogram (ECG for short) to measure the electrical activity in the heart. Other tests may include: an X-ray examination of the blood vessels, known as coronary angiography, and blood tests to see whether there is any underlying cause such as hyperlipidaemia or thyrotoxicosis.

Treatment

The official medical treatment of heart trouble depends on what form of heart disease you have, and the severity of it. Treatment can involve a wide number of things such as taking: nitroglycerin to help widen the arteries so that more blood can reach the heart, anti-coagulants to help prevent blood clots, calcium channel blockers or beta-blocker drugs to help stabilize an irregular heartbeat. Diuretic drugs may be given to clear the accumulation of fluid in the lungs which can sometimes be caused by heart failure. In severe cases, coronary-artery bypass surgery may be considered to re-establish blood flow to the heart muscle.

However, there is now convincing evidence to show that it is possible to 'cure' as well as 'prevent' heart disease with a simple regime including a low fat vegan diet, a modest exercise programme and a stress control programme. For more details see Vernon Coleman's book *How To Stop Your Doctor Killing You*.

All patients should visit their doctor if they suspect that they have (or might have) any form of heart disease.

But patients who are willing and able to take steps to improve their own health are less likely to need outside intervention. It is worth remembering that intervention (whether in the forms of surgery or drugs) is not without risks.

Even if you're 103, or you've suffered from a heart attack, it's never too late to start looking after your heart.

As well as adhering to all the above preventative measures, diet is extremely important when it comes to avoiding heart disease. The best diet is one which is low in fat, especially animal fats.

Before Western foods were introduced into their diet, the Japanese had the lowest rate of heart disease in the world. This was because they had a diet which was low in calories, meat and fat.

Heartburn

Under normal circumstances the acid mixture that helps to digest food in the stomach is kept away from the oesophagus by a sphincter which allows food to travel down into the stomach but doesn't allow food and acid to travel upwards into the gullet. The acid in the stomach is strong enough to dissolve steak (or burn holes in your carpet) and the oesophagus simply isn't made to cope with it. The sphincter is important. If the sphincter which usually divides the oesophagus from the stomach in this way doesn't do its job properly acid can sometimes splash upwards and irritate the oesophageal mucosa. The technical term for this is gastro-oesophageal reflux and the word 'heartburn' is very descriptive. The burning sensation rises up from the stomach and radiates to the upper chest – sometimes producing such a vicious pain that it can be confused with a heart attack.

Even when the sphincter is in good working condition acid can irritate the oesophagus when you lie down or bend over. Naturally enough, therefore, individuals who have a weak sphincter will find that they suffer far more when they are lying flat or bending over than they do when they are standing up straight. Being overweight can increase the risk of heartburn, as can eating a diet which contains too much fat. And despite the fact that heartburn usually has a solid physical cause there are many individuals who suffer from this symptom purely as a result of stress.

As many as one in ten adults has reflux symptoms on a daily basis. Nearly half get symptoms at least once a month. Pregnant women are particularly at risk and around three quarters of pregnant women suffer from heartburn at some point in their pregnancy. Heartburn is a widespread and major problem. If it persists, heartburn can be associated with ear pain, asthma, sinusitis and chronic laryngitis.

There are a number of things that you can do to protect yourself from heartburn (whether you've already got it or not). Avoiding smoking is a good start. Losing excess weight helps.

Coping with heartburn

Here are our top tips for dealing with heartburn.

1. Avoid coffee and tea.
2. Avoid fatty foods.
3. Avoid spicy foods.
4. Avoid chocolate.
5. Avoid peppermint.
6. Avoid drinks which are too hot or too cold.
7. Avoid alcohol and fizzy drinks
8. Don't lie down within three hours of eating a meal.
9. Try sleeping on an extra pillow.
10. Eat small meals.
11. Avoid unnecessary stress – and learn to deal with the unavoidable stresses in your life more effectively.
12. Antacid preparations will neutralise the acid in the stomach and provide a fairly instant relief. *Liquid* preparations coat the oesophagus effectively. The snag is that the stomach can react by producing more acid – meaning that the relief provided by the antacids can be short-lived. The stomach is likely to respond to *tablet* form antacids by producing a lower level of acidity – the desired effect may take more time but the effect should last longer.

Hiatus hernia

A hiatus hernia occurs when part of the stomach pushes through the diaphragm and into the chest cavity.

Most people who have a hiatus hernia experience no symptoms at all, but for some people the sphincter which lies between the stomach and the oesophagus becomes weakened by the hernia and this can allow a back-flow of acid from the stomach to escape up into the oesophagus. This back-flow of gastric acid is commonly known as acid reflux.

Acid reflux may cause inflammation of the oesophagus (oesophagitis), heartburn or indigestion– all of which can be quite distressing to the sufferer.

No-one knows the underlying cause of hiatus hernia, but it tends to be more common in adults over 50 (although it can affect anyone at any age), in those who smoke and in the overweight. Sometimes a hiatus hernia can be congenital. If this is the case, the condition is quite evident shortly after birth because the newborn baby will have difficulty in feeding. Depending on how large the hiatus hernia is, surgery is normally performed on the newborn soon after birth.

A hiatus hernia can also be caused by a rupture in some part of the diaphragm which allows part of the stomach to slip up into the chest. This may be caused by an abdominal injury such as a blow to the stomach or as a result of lifting heavy objects.

Risk of a hiatus hernia increases with:

1. Pregnancy.
2. Obesity.
3. Smoking.
4. Straining during bowel movements caused by chronic constipation.
5. Age (it is commoner over 50).

Symptoms of a hiatus hernia may include:

1. Indigestion.
2. Heartburn (this painful burning sensation may sometimes be felt at the back of the throat)
3. Acid-regurgitation, especially when lying down or when bending forwards.
4. Belching.

130

5. Feeling full and bloated after very small meals.
6. Flatulence.
7. Nausea.
8. A feeling of food being stuck in the oesophagus.
9. Swallowing difficulties (rare).
10. Pain on swallowing hot liquids.

It is, however, important to remember that many people with a hiatus hernia experience no symptoms at all.

How the diagnosis is made

1. Your own observation of symptoms and a medical examination by your doctor.
2. A barium X-ray in a hospital.
3. A type of endoscopy, called an oesophagoscopy may be performed. This involves a viewing instrument being passed down the throat into the oesophagus. A biopsy sample of tissue may be taken from the oesophagus for analysis.

There are many disorders (ulcers, angina, gall bladder disease) which can mimic a hiatus hernia. That is why it is important to see your doctor as soon as you suspect that you have a hiatus hernia. As always, you should not try to make the diagnosis by yourself.

Indigestion can sometimes be so severe with a hiatus hernia that the pain can be mistaken for a heart attack. If the pain (which is usually felt like a crushing feeling) comes on suddenly and radiates to your jaw or down your left arm and is accompanied by sweating or vomiting then there's a risk that you may well be having a heart attack. Call the emergency services immediately. You don't have to experience all of these symptoms to be having a heart attack.

Seventeen ways to relieve the symptoms caused by a hiatus hernia

1. If you are overweight then you should lose weight. This has been known to dramatically improve symptoms.
2. Lying down can cause acid reflux to occur, so to help combat this try raising the head of your bed four to six inches off the floor. You can do this by putting blocks underneath the two top

legs of the bed. The gravity should then keep the acid away from your oesophagus.

3. Avoid eating large meals and instead, eat smaller meals regularly throughout the day. Overfilling the stomach can push the acid upwards into the oesophagus.

4. Bending forwards or lying down straight after a meal can cause acid reflux to occur.

5. When acid indigestion occurs, some people reach for a glass of milk to help alleviate their symptoms but this only gives temporary relief. Milk can actually encourage acid production therefore, exacerbating the problem. You are much better off eating a plain slice of bread or even a plain biscuit to help mop up the acid.

6. Do not eat anything that is likely to be too heavy on the stomach for at least two hours before bedtime.

7. During bowel movements, try not to strain as this can make problems worse. Avoid constipation.

8. Drink plenty of water to help keep the stools soft. Water also helps to dilute the acid in the stomach.

9. High-fat foods, spices, alcohol, coffee, fizzy drinks, chocolate, sugar are all acid-forming and therefore, best avoided. Do keep a food diary as this will help you to find out what foods aggravate your symptoms.

10. Tomatoes and other fruits can irritate an already inflamed oesophagus. So can drinking fruit juice.

11. Sit up straight whilst eating meals as this helps to aid digestion.

12. Eat slowly and chew your food well.

13. Try not to eat or drink anything that is either too hot or too cold, as this can irritate the oesophagus.

14. Do not wear anything tight around the waist such as belts, girdles, etc.

15. Stress can make symptoms worse, so take up some form of relaxation or spend more time doing things you enjoy.

16. Avoid straining while lifting heavy objects.

17. If you suffer from acid regurgitation where the acid actually comes up into your mouth, then you should rinse your mouth out immediately with water because the acid from your stomach is so strong that it can corrode your teeth.

Treatment

If none of the above self-help measures work then a simple over-the-counter antacid remedy might be all that is needed to help alleviate your symptoms. However, if over-the-counter antacid remedies fail to relieve your symptoms, your doctor may prescribe drugs that help to reduce the amount of acid your stomach produces. These acid-suppressing drugs are known as proton pump inhibitors and are very powerful. They may have to be taken on a long-term basis because as soon as they are stopped, your symptoms may return.

It is far better for your health to follow self-help measures than to rely on medication.

Because acid-suppressants can reduce the amount of acid your stomach produces, the 'bad' bacteria in your digestive system which are normally killed off by gastric juices may thrive. This can increase your chances of getting gastroenteritis, especially if you travel abroad. So it is important to eat lots of natural live yoghurt which contain good bacteria called acidophilus. Alternatively, if you are not keen on the taste of natural yoghurt, then try taking acidophilus supplements which you should be able to buy from health food shops.

High blood pressure

If it wasn't under pressure the blood in your body would just stay where it was. Tissues would not receive the oxygen they need and waste products would accumulate.

Normally, a complex physiological process ensures that your blood is pumped out to the tissues through a network of arteries and back through your veins.

If your blood pressure falls dramatically for any reason (because you have lost a great deal of blood for example) you will feel faint.

Much commoner is the problem known as high blood pressure – when the blood which is being pumped around is under too great a pressure. This can cause serious trouble – with small vessels bursting and the blood leaking out into the tissues.

High blood pressure is one of the commonest, most dangerous

and most poorly controlled disorders in the developed world. It is the underlying cause of two of the biggest killers: heart disease and stroke. And although between one in four and one in five people has high blood pressure (in America alone there are said to be 50 million people with high blood pressure) only half of them know it.

Vast areas of the drug industry and the medical profession have got rich out of selling drugs designed to control high blood pressure but the benefit of those drugs to patients has been often questionable, frequently marginal and, on too many occasions, non-existent. Billions of dollars have been spent on drugs which are ineffective and which produce side effects which have had a devastating effect on the lives of the people who have taken them.

There aren't usually any symptoms associated with high blood pressure (a.k.a. hypertension) and many people don't know they have got high blood pressure until they have a stroke or a heart attack.

When high blood pressure is discovered in an otherwise healthy individual it is usually found as a result of a routine examination – performed either because it has been requested by an insurance company, or because it was conducted as part of a medical screening check-up.

Getting your blood pressure checked is by far the most useful aspect of a medical check-up. Everyone over the age of 50 should have their blood pressure measured once a year. If for some reason you can't get your doctor to do this you can buy a blood pressure testing machine from any decent pharmacy. Make sure that the product you buy comes with easy-to-follow instructions.

Yet another health care scandal

For decades the official answer to high blood pressure has been to attempt to deal with the problem with the aid of drugs. Moreover, millions of patients have been told by their doctors that, once having been diagnosed as suffering from high blood pressure, they will need to take drugs for the rest of their lives.

It is true that some people with high blood pressure will need long-term drug therapy. But it is certainly not true that everyone who is diagnosed as suffering from high blood pressure will need lifetime medication.

The claim that drug therapy is the only way to control high blood pressure is a massive fraud designed to keep doctors and drug companies rich.

The truth is that huge numbers of people who have high blood pressure can bring down their blood pressure without drugs (and without any vitamin, mineral or 'wonder' supplements).

Over the years, the obsession for attempting to deal with high blood pressure with drugs has probably done far more harm than good. Side effects – often serious – are relatively common with the drug therapy favoured for high blood pressure. (It is because the drugs used to treat high blood pressure so often cause serious or unpleasant side effects that many people abandon their treatment.)

If a perfectly healthy man visits his doctor for a routine medical examination prior to starting a new job, and, after being told that he has high blood pressure, is given a drug which makes him impotent, can anyone really be surprised if he stops taking the prescribed drug and decides to take his chances?

The real scandal (and it is a scandal) is that it has been known for years that many patients with high blood pressure can completely or partly control their blood pressure not by taking drugs but by making fundamental lifestyle changes.

For example, the first report showing a link between meat eating and high blood pressure came out of California in 1926. Those researchers showed that if vegetarians started to eat meat their blood pressure rose by as much as ten per cent in two weeks.

So, why, you might ask, has the medical profession persistently continued to insist that drug therapy is the only answer?

It is, sadly, the usual one word answer: money.

Doctors can't make money out of patients simply by telling them to change their lifestyles. And drug companies certainly can't make any money that way.

The drug industry and the medical profession have got away with the massive lie that the best (or, indeed, the only) way to deal with any illness is to take a drug.

A trial, called Dietary Approaches to Stop Hypertension, sponsored by the National Institutes of Health in the USA, showed that a diet which is rich in fruits, vegetables and low fat dairy products can reduce blood pressure as much as the most commonly used anti-hypertension drugs.

This study involved 459 people, of whom almost half were women. Two thirds of the individuals in the trial had moderate hypertension but none of them were taking any drugs. The participants in the study stayed on their diet for 11 weeks but the effects of the diet were obvious within just one week.

The research showed that this dietary change alone could reduce the risk of heart disease by 15 per cent and the likelihood of a stroke developing by 27 per cent.

Add to those percentages the improvements likely to be produced by losing excess weight, reducing salt consumption, keeping alcohol consumption down, learning to deal with stress more effectively and initiating and following a simple exercise programme (such as regular walking) and it becomes clear that doctors could (if they really wanted to) turn high blood pressure into a relatively uncommon disorder.

Reducing salt consumption

It has long been known that a diet which includes a great deal of salt can be dangerous to individuals who have high blood pressure, who have a family history of high blood pressure or who are for any other reason susceptible to high blood pressure.

Salt gets rid of calcium – and a low calcium level can mean a high blood pressure – so if you reduce your salt intake you will cut the amount of calcium which your body loses. Because salt pushes calcium through the kidneys and into the urine simply reducing your salt intake is likely to have the same sort of effect as taking a calcium supplement.

(There are two other important reasons for keeping your salt intake to a minimum. By cutting your salt intake and maintaining your body's calcium levels you will increase bone strength and bone density and, therefore, reduce your risk of suffering bone fractures. Second, cutting back on the amount of salt you consume could easily result in an almost immediate three pound weight loss.)

With this evidence available you might imagine that doctors would be keen to tell all their patients to minimise their salt intake and to eat foods such as broccoli, spinach, cabbage, chick peas, dried figs and beans which provide good supplies of calcium. These are better sources of calcium than dairy products such as milk and cheese.

(Incidentally, is it a coincidence that the six things which you can do to minimise calcium loss (avoiding tobacco, caffeine, too much alcohol, animal proteins and salt and taking regular, gentle exercise) have all, for some time now, been acknowledged as techniques for lowering the blood pressure? Or could it be, perhaps, that these things help bring down blood pressure, at least partly, because they help to keep calcium levels at a good level?)

It is, however, doubtful if one doctor in 100 spends any time at all telling his patients how to get more calcium in their diet – or how to stop the calcium their bodies do have from leaking away.

How depressing it is that most doctors prefer to respond to a diagnosis of high blood pressure by simply reaching for a pen and a prescription pad and scribbling out the name of the latest 'miracle' prescription drug. It is hardly surprising that in most developed countries around the world high blood pressure drugs take many of the top places in lists of the most frequently prescribed drugs.

(Drug companies adore high blood pressure. It is a disease which can last for many years. And so the potential for profit is vast.)

How to avoid developing high blood pressure

Whether or not you have a family history of high blood pressure there is a good chance that you will, at some stage in your life, be found to have a raised blood pressure.

This is particularly true if you enjoy a largely sedentary life and are regularly exposed to large amounts of stress.

To reduce your chances of developing high blood pressure you should take the following action:

1. Make a positive effort to learn how to relax your body and mind.
2. Minimise your exposure to stress. It is impossible to avoid stress completely but you can reduce the amount of stress in your life by refusing to take on unnecessary responsibilities and by walking away from potential problems which are not truly significant to you.
3. Do not smoke tobacco – and keep away from other people who smoke.
4. Eat a low fat diet. (Cut out fatty meat, high fat dairy products and other fatty foods.)

5. Do not eat meat – or, if you are unwilling to become completely vegetarian – eat as little meat as possible.

6. Take regular, gentle exercise (though not before getting your doctor's approval of course).

7. Reduce your consumption of salt and foods which contain a great deal of salt.

8. Eat plenty of calcium rich foods (such as leafy, green vegetables).

9. Eat foods such as apples, apricots, asparagus, bananas, beans, Brussels sprouts, cauliflower, dates, grapefruit, oranges, peaches, peas, pineapple, prunes, rhubarb, spinach, sunflower seeds and tomatoes which are rich in potassium.

10. Lose any excess weight.

11. Control your intake of alcohol.

12. Reduce your caffeine intake.

If you have high blood pressure

If you have high blood pressure and are taking one or more prescription drugs then we obviously do not suggest that you stop taking those drugs – or even reduce the dosage – before you talk to your doctor. Such action would be foolhardy (modern drugs are so powerful that they often need to be stopped slowly and always under medical supervision).

But talk to the doctor who prescribed the drugs. Ask him if he thinks that you would benefit from changing your diet, or making other changes to the way you live.

If he says yes then that is wonderful. Ask him to monitor your blood pressure while you alter your lifestyle. (Your blood pressure will need regular monitoring because if it drops, as a result of the changes you have made, your dosage of drugs may need to be reduced accordingly.)

If he says 'no' then, unless he convinces you that you have a type of high blood pressure which is unusual and which cannot therefore be altered by lifestyle changes, we suggest that you find another doctor.

And it may well be wise to purchase a blood pressure measuring machine which you can use at home. Taking your own blood pressure is relatively simple.

Taking your blood pressure yourself (or getting a relative or friend to take it with your machine) can have two advantages over having your blood pressure checked by a professional.

First, the machines which doctors use are very rarely checked. Most doctors use a sphygmomanometer for years (or even decades) without making sure that the machine is giving an accurate reading.

Second, there is clear evidence to show that when a doctor checks your blood pressure it is likely to be higher than it really is. The simple act of having a blood pressure measurement taken by a doctor pushes up most people's blood pressure.

Indigestion (dyspepsia)

This isn't a word that doctors use a great deal when describing stomach problems because it is a particularly vague sort of word which doesn't really mean anything definite. In literal terms the word indigestion simply means that there has been a failure of digestion and so it can theoretically refer to a small intestine problem as well as a stomach problem.

In practice, the word is used to describe the sort of symptoms which occur when a meal is eaten too quickly, or after an unusually spicy or fatty meal.

Sufferers usually complain of some pain in the centre of the chest and they may also feel slightly bloated. It's common for indigestion sufferers to complain of excessive wind and nausea. Occasionally an indigestion sufferer will actually vomit. Very few people who have indigestion will be interested in food for the pain tends to be accompanied by a full feeling and a loss of appetite.

Indigestion can be caused by smoking too much, by drinking too much alcohol or by taking too much tea or coffee. Other drugs, such as aspirin, can also cause indigestion.

However, although these specific causes are significant many of the individuals who suffer from indigestion do so directly as a result of stress.

Coping with indigestion – ten tips for sufferers

Most sufferers simply head straight for the bathroom cabinet or the local chemist's shop and take a few slugs from a bottle of white medicine. Traditional stomach remedies usually work well because they contain a substance which counteracts the powerful acid that is causing the pain. But swallowing a few gulps of white medicine after your symptoms develop only provides an immediate and short-term answer. There is a real risk that if you don't do something to stop your indigestion developing you will eventually end up with a stomach ulcer.

So, here are some tips on exactly how you can reduce your chances of developing indigestion. Even if you're not already a sufferer you'll benefit by following this advice.

1. Remember that eating regular meals is better for you than going for long periods without food. If you eat regularly then the acid that accumulates in your stomach will have nothing to work on – except your stomach lining.

2. Eat slowly. Put down your knife and fork between mouthfuls – that should slow you down.

3. Put small amounts into your mouth. If you stuff huge amounts of food into your mouth then you'll swallow without chewing. Chewing is an essential part of the digestive process.

4. When you've finished a meal have a short rest. Give your stomach time to finish its job before you start rushing around again.

5. Don't read or watch TV while you're eating. If you concentrate on what you're doing when you have a meal then you'll be much more likely to know when you've had enough to eat. Overeating is a common cause of stomach problems.

6. Don't let other people push you into eating more than you want. Be prepared to leave food on the side of your plate if you've had enough.

7. Avoid any foods which upset your stomach. The sort of foods that can cause upsets are: all fried foods, fizzy drinks, alcohol, strong tea or coffee, fatty foods, spicy foods, unripe fruit, very hot or very cold foods, tough food that can't be chewed easily, pickles, sprouts, radishes, cucumber, coarse bread, biscuits or cereals, nuts and dried fruit.

8. Some people believe that drinking water with a meal dilutes the digestive juices and adversely affects digestion. We don't think this is true. Water (or wine) taken with a meal stimulates stomach

acidity and triggers the digestive process in the small intestine. Sipping water with a meal should actually help the digestive process. (And if you really, really feel that drinking interferes with your digestion you should drink a glass or two of water at room temperature half an hour before a meal.) Other drinks worth trying include fennel tea and peppermint tea.

9. Try charcoal tablets.
10. Eat honey. A spoonful of honey or a honey sandwich may help.
11. Remember that tobacco smoke will irritate your stomach too.

If you suffer from recurrent or persistent indigestion (lasting more than five days) then you must see your GP.

Irritable bowel syndrome (IBS)

The three symptoms most commonly associated with IBS are colicky bowel pain, wind (usually causing bloating) and either diarrhoea or constipation, or some combination of the two. IBS sufferers often also complain of indigestion and heartburn.

When the bowel is full of wind (because of irritable bowel syndrome) there is, inevitably, a great deal of back pressure on the stomach. And that's what often causes the indigestion, the heartburn, the flatulence and the other stomach problems. IBS is now one of the commonest primary causes of these stomach disorders.

Irritable bowel syndrome is one of the commonest and most troublesome of all diseases. At one time or another as many as one in three people suffer from it. IBS is also one of the most commonly misdiagnosed of all diseases – and one of the most badly treated. Once it has developed it hardly ever disappears completely.

That's the bad news.

The good news is twofold.

First, irritable bowel syndrome is not, by itself, dangerous or life-threatening; it doesn't turn into anything more serious, it won't turn into cancer and it won't kill you.

And second, although it does tend to hang around – once you have got it you've probably got it for life – irritable bowel syndrome, or IBS, can be controlled. There is no quick, simple, reliable cure because there is no clearly defined cause. But although you may not be able to make the symptoms of irritable bowel syndrome disappear for ever – you *can* control it.

The symptoms of IBS

Most important are the primary symptoms which involve the bowel itself and what goes on inside it. Pain is probably the most obvious of these symptoms – though it is also one of the most variable. It is often a colicky, spasmodic sort of pain which comes and goes in waves; it can affect just about any part of the abdomen and it frequently fades a little when the sufferer goes to the toilet.

Most sufferers complain of diarrhoea – which can sometimes be quite sudden and explosive – but, oddly enough, constipation is also a common symptom. Sometimes the two problems alternate.

The third very common bowel problem associated with this complaint is wind and this really is typical. Most sufferers complain that their tummies swell up so much that their clothes don't fit them properly. Many complain of embarrassing rumblings and gurglings and other noises and of the social problems associated with escaping wind.

Most IBS patients have these three problems.

Next, there are the secondary symptoms which affect a lot of sufferers but which don't affect all patients. If you have IBS you're almost certain to have the three primary symptoms but you are unlikely to have all of the secondary symptoms.

One or two of the secondary symptoms are caused by the wind that is so widely associated with irritable bowel syndrome and these will probably come and go as the wind comes and goes. Symptoms in this category include a feeling of being full all the time and not being able to eat very much, a constant feeling of nausea, heartburn and indigestion. Back pains of one sort or another are also fairly commonplace and these too are frequently a result of wind accumulating in the intestines. It's even quite common for irritable bowel syndrome sufferers to complain of urinary frequency and other bladder problems caused by pressure produced by wind in the intestines.

Last, but certainly not least, there are the mental symptoms which aren't in any direct way related to the intestines or what is going on inside them. Anxiety, depression and irritability are all common but the one mental symptom that really seems to affect irritable bowel syndrome patients more than any other is tiredness.

Even though you may be quite convinced that you are suffering from irritable bowel syndrome you shouldn't make the diagnosis by yourself without visiting your doctor. Although IBS is probably the commonest of all bowel problems today there are other problems which can cause bowel symptoms and only by visiting your doctor can you be absolutely sure that you have got the diagnosis right.

What causes IBS?

There are two main causes.

The first is stress.

The word 'stress' has been used a lot in the last few years. And you may feel that it has been overworked. But the plain fact is that all muscles can be tightened up when you are under too much stress. Tension headaches are a good example of what happens when the muscles around your head are tightened by worry and anxiety. The muscles in your bowel walls are no exception – they are as vulnerable and as susceptible to stress as any other muscles – and in some individuals it is these muscles which suffer first when stress starts to get out of control. Lots of people who don't suffer from irritable bowel syndrome do get diarrhoea or cramping pains in their tummies when they are under too much pressure or when they are anxious.

The second explanation for the current epidemic of irritable bowel syndrome lies in the type of food we tend to eat these days.

Most of us tend to eat a bland over-refined, fatty diet that contains very little natural roughage. And our bowels can't cope very well with this.

Coping with IBS

There is no single wonder cure for irritable bowel syndrome but there are a good many ways in which you can help yourself. You will, of course, have visited your doctor and he may well be treating you. You should tell him if you decide to follow any of the advice which follows.

First, you should take a good, hard look at the amount of stress in your life. Try, for example, to make a list of all the things which worry you, which make you feel uptight, which keep you awake at night, which give you butterflies in your stomach or which you know upset you. Try to decide what things are really important to you. Decide how you are going to allocate your time. And make sure that every week you take some time off. If you want to relax properly you're going to have to work at it – and that will take a little effort and a little time.

Next, you probably need to take a long, cool, careful and critical look at your diet.

You may benefit if you *very* gradually increase the amount of fibre that you eat. To do this start eating wholemeal bread or high bran cereals. Eat wholewheat pasta, brown rice, oats – in porridge for example – and more fresh vegetables and fruit, though if you suffer a lot from wind you will probably be wise to avoid any vegetables – such as sprouts – which seem to cause you a lot of wind. Nibble fruit and nuts instead of chocolate and sweets and eat plenty of pulses – such as baked beans.

Try to cut down your fat intake too.

If you eat meat then cut off the visible fat and avoid red meats as often as you can. Drink skimmed or semi-skimmed milk rather than the full fat variety – though many IBS sufferers find that they benefit by cutting out dairy produce completely. Make low fat pastry, don't add fat when cooking and grill, bake, steam, poach, casserole and boil rather than roasting or frying.

You may find that it helps if you drink more fluids. Good, clean water is the best drink.

Next, try to do more exercise – but do get your doctor's approval first. Don't make the mistake of adding stress to your life by trying to run faster than anyone else. But if your doctor approves try to take more exercise that you enjoy. Walk, swim, dance, cycle or work out in the gym – all those things will help you because gentle, regular exercise seems to have a soothing effect on the bowel.

Eleven things every IBS sufferer should know

1. IBS affects three times as many women as men (though this may be because men are reluctant to own up to these symptoms – or

are more likely to blame them on drinking too much or eating unwisely).

2. IBS sufferers have an especially sensitive gastrointestinal tract – sensitive to stress, food, drugs, hormones or any other irritations. These stimulants cause the gastrointestinal tract to contract abnormally and they also seem to increase the sensitivity of the pain receptors in the large intestine.

3. Contractions within the gastrointestinal tract become stronger and more frequent during an attack of IBS – resulting in cramp-like pains and diarrhoea.

4. The pains and discomfort of IBS only rarely wake a sufferer. They nearly always occur when an individual is awake.

5. A high fat diet may cause symptoms. Other causes (or aggravations) include dairy produce, coffee, tea, citrus fruits and wheat. Avoid foods such as beans and cabbage which are difficult to digest. Artificial sweeteners and fructose may cause problems.

6. The 'spastic colon' pain often comes either as cramps or as a continuous dull ache in the area of the lower abdomen. Bloating, anxiety, difficulty in concentrating, nausea, headaches and tiredness are other common symptoms. Opening the bowels often relieves the pain. Sometimes there is relatively little pain with IBS – just diarrhoea (sometimes sudden and urgent) or constipation.

7. There is often some tenderness over the lower part of the abdomen.

8. Avoid particular types of stress which trigger the problem.

9. Regular physical activity (gentle exercise) often helps.

10. Some IBS sufferers benefit if they eat more fibre. Others (particularly those who suffer from flatulence or bloating) find that this makes things worse. Numerous drugs are prescribed for IBS. Their value seems to vary.

11. Three types of bacteria which may prove helpful are bifidobacteria, lactobacillus acidophilus and lactobacillus bulgaricus. These three may be helpful in creating a healthy bowel and can probably be best obtained by eating yoghurt. (If you don't want to eat dairy produce you can eat soya yoghurt.) The three help digest proteins, help digest lactose, help keep the bowels mildly acidic (which keeps the bowel healthier), manufacture

some useful vitamins (notably B and K vitamins), stimulate the contraction of the bowel walls and kill harmful organisms (thereby helping to prevent food poisoning and diarrhoea).

Low acid levels

Hydrochloric acid is produced by your stomach to help digest food. If you have too little of this acid, it can make proper digestion difficult. Low stomach acid can cause bloating and wind because the food lies undigested in the bowel. This can increase the production of gasses. Low stomach acid can also cause indigestion because there isn't enough acid in the stomach to digest the food properly. It is quite common for people with low stomach acid to assume that they suffer from too much acid and because of this, at the first sign of indigestion or bloating, they reach for an antacid. This of course, only exacerbates the condition.

As we get older our stomachs produce less acid so therefore, low stomach acid tends to be more common in the middle-aged and in the elderly.

If you suddenly develop symptoms of indigestion, wind or bloating, then you should visit your doctor as soon as possible to rule out any serious underlying health problem. If you suspect that you may suffer with low stomach acid, go and see your doctor for confirmation. Only your doctor can make that diagnosis.

If it has been confirmed to you that you suffer from low stomach acid, then follow the tips below:

1. Do not eat foods that are renowned for being hard to digest. Fried foods can be difficult to digest.
2. Cut down on your alcohol consumption.
3. Avoid caffeine or at least reduce your intake.
4. Try not to rush your food.
5. Chew your food properly to make digestion easier.
6. Eat smaller meals regularly.
7. Regular gentle exercise such as walking helps aid digestion.
8. If you suffer from bloating after meals, try drinking fennel tea.

Low blood pressure

Thousands of men and women suffer from a problem which doctors rarely recognise (and hardly ever take seriously), partly because drug companies don't have a cure for it and partly because in its mild, common form it rarely leads to death.

Every time your heart contracts it puts the ten pints of blood lying in your arteries and veins under pressure. It's that pressure that pushes fresh oxygen carrying blood to your brain, stomach, arms and legs.

If your blood pressure is too high there's a risk that a blood vessel will burst – giving you a stroke. But if your blood pressure is too low you'll feel tired and dizzy because your brain and muscles won't be getting the supplies they need.

It is thought that low blood pressure is sometimes caused by a weakness in the adrenal glands. These glands rest on top of your kidneys and are responsible for producing adrenaline and corticosteroid hormones.

Drugs can also cause low blood pressure and if you are taking any medication ask your doctor if your drug(s) could cause low blood pressure. Remember that you should always consult your doctor before stopping any medication.

Although there is plenty written about high blood pressure (hypertension), there appears to be very little written about low blood pressure (hypotension).

Low blood pressure can be more debilitating to the sufferer than high blood pressure. However, unlike high blood pressure, low blood pressure is usually quite harmless to the person affected. Because of this, it doesn't seem to be taken that seriously by orthodox doctors.

It is the failure of the drug companies to find a profitable cure that has really made low blood pressure an unfashionable diagnosis. Neither doctors nor drug companies feel comfortable with illnesses that can't be cured by pills.

But low blood pressure can cause devastating and disruptive symptoms that can ruin a sufferer's life. The vast majority of sufferers are women – thin and rather 'delicately' built.

The symptoms of low blood pressure may include:

1. General weakness and lack of stamina.
2. Cold hands and feet.
3. Difficulty in getting up and 'getting going' in the morning.
4. Persistent, mild depression.
5. Dizziness, particularly when getting up or moving around.
6. Light-headedness on getting up from lying in bed or from sitting down, especially when getting up suddenly.
7. Tiredness.
8. Fainting.
9. Headaches.

If you suffer from any of these symptoms, don't just automatically assume that it's due to low blood pressure without having seen your doctor first. Only your doctor can make that diagnosis and rule out any other medical problem.

Treating low blood pressure

In Germany and Austria doctors are now taking low blood pressure very seriously. They realise that it is one of the commonest diseases to affect women. And they believe that patients can treat themselves in three ways. First by taking exercise. Firming up the muscles and making your tissues demand oxygen seems to help. Ideally you should join a gym where you can try mild weight lifting and gentle aerobic exercises such as jogging and cycling. Start gently to begin with or you may feel dizzy and faint. But after a week or two you should notice that you have more energy and 'get up and go'. Only start exercise with your doctor's approval.

Second by taking cool showers. Your circulating blood responds quickly and dramatically to the temperature of your skin. One way to stimulate your circulation is to take a cool shower after a hot one. If you find the idea of a cool shower horrifying you can compromise by running cold water over your legs after a warm shower or bath. You should find that this makes you feel livelier.

Thirdly, put more stress into your life.

Stress and pressure can push up the blood pressure of an ordinary individual to dangerous levels. But if your blood pressure is normally low you may find that you benefit – and feel fresher – if you deliberately add a little more stress to your life.

If your job is relatively quiet and undemanding try taking up a hobby or sport that challenges you. Instead of slumping down in front of the TV go to an evening class or for a swim.

Below are some of the things you can do to help alleviate the symptoms that low blood pressure can cause:

1. Try and get up from bed or from sitting down – slowly.
2. Throughout the day, try eating smaller meals regularly.
3. Try making a fist several times with each hand before getting up. This can momentarily raise your blood pressure.

Low blood sugar

Low blood sugar, medically known as hypoglycaemia is something that most of us experience from time to time. Ever skipped breakfast, only to feel weak and faint by late morning?

The commonest cause of low blood sugar is skipping meals. If we go without food for too long, our blood sugar levels drop and we soon develop some of the symptoms of hypoglycaemia. Your brain's only food requirement is glucose. And so when your blood sugar levels decrease, the hypothalamus area in your utterly selfish brain makes you crave sweet foods.

This is not good. If you skip breakfast you are probably more inclined to gorge on high-calorie rich foods for lunch so that you can have the quick sugar fix that your brain is desperately crying out for. Far too many people eat lots of fatty sugary foods and end up putting on weight, which can cause their blood sugar levels to become unstable. This can lead to diabetes. And don't kid yourself into believing that you can stabilise your blood sugar levels by eating something sweet to help compensate for that meal you missed earlier on – because you can't and you won't. Eating something sweet can actually cause your blood sugar levels to drop because the body has to produce more insulin in order to cope with the sudden high sugar intake. To help keep your blood sugar levels stable, it is far better for your health to eat small nutritious meals frequently throughout the day.

The symptoms of low blood sugar may include:

1. Irritability.
2. Feeling weak.
3. Difficulty in concentrating.
4. Memory problems.

If your symptoms are severe (such as trembling, extreme weakness or blackouts) then you need something sweet inside you quickly to help boost your sugar levels. You could try drinking a high glucose drink or you could eat a chocolate bar. It is important to note that this should never be used as a long-term solution.

It is sensible to visit your doctor if you have any of the above symptoms so that he/she can rule out any other medical problem which you may have.

How to keep your blood sugar level stable

1. Eat a good breakfast such as low-sugar cereal, wholemeal toast with low-sugar jam, fruit, or grilled tomatoes on toast.
2. Eat plenty of fibre as this helps to release sugar into your blood more slowly.
3. Increase your water intake.
4. Eat more pasta, brown rice, spinach and wholemeal bread.
5. Eat more protein at lunchtime, such as tofu.
6. Eat smaller meals more frequently.
7. To help reduce your sugar cravings eat low-sugar health bars or fresh fruit.

Ménière's disease

Ménière's disease (named after the French physician, Prosper Ménière, who described the disease in 1861) is caused by an excess of endolymphatic fluid in the cochlear duct of the inner ear, which helps to maintain balance. In 80 to 85 per cent of cases, Ménière's disease affects one ear. Although there are many theories, no one really knows what causes the excess of fluid. It is thought that it may be due to food intolerances, salt retention, nutrient deficiency or even spasms of the blood vessels to the inner ear.

The disease mainly affects adults over the age of 50. Experts say that the disease is slightly more common in women but they don't understand why. (We suspect it's because there are far more women than men among the over 50 population.)

Ménière's disease is one of the commonest causes of dizziness, tinnitus and deafness. If you suffer from any combination of these symptoms you should consider carefully whether you might have this problem.

The symptoms of Ménière's disease may include:

1. Vertigo (a sensation of spinning or moving).
2. Tinnitus (ringing or buzzing in the affected ear).
3. A feeling of 'fullness' in the affected ear.
4. Fluctuating but progressive hearing loss in the affected ear.
5. Fatigue.

Vertigo

Vertigo is the main symptom of Ménière's disease and possibly the most distressing. Vertigo is the symptom that prompts most sufferers to seek medical help from their doctor.

Vertigo occurs in periodic episodes and is often called an 'attack'. A vertigo 'attack' may occur over a period of weeks or months and is interspersed by periods of remission. The duration of remission is variable. Although the sufferer may experience some warning just before an attack, those afflicted with the disease usually never know when the next vertigo attack will occur.

The vertigo can be mild and only cause unsteadiness or it can be so bad that it leaves the sufferer totally incapacitated, at least until the symptom subsides. The sufferer may find that lying down helps. The slightest movement of the head can exacerbate the vertigo.

Nausea and vomiting are often experienced with vertigo and sometimes the vomiting can be so severe that the sufferer cannot even keep down fluids. The doctor may be able prescribe anti-emetic drugs to help prevent vomiting and to lessen nausea.

Sweating can accompany vertigo just like the sweating that is often experienced by severe motion sickness. Nystagmus (jerky eye movements) may also accompany the vertigo.

It is not unusual for vertigo attacks to become less frequent over the years and, in some cases, to disappear altogether. However, although the vertigo attacks may become less frequent the tinnitus and hearing loss still persists.

Tinnitus

Sufferers may experience a slight noise or they may be unlucky enough to experience a loud buzzing or ringing in the affected ear which may interfere with daily life by making concentration and sleep difficult.

Tinnitus usually persists in between attacks of vertigo and may be constant or intermittent. Tinnitus may worsen before, during or after an attack of vertigo.

Unfortunately, treatments to cure tinnitus are usually unsuccessful, but there are techniques which can make the condition tolerable.

Hearing loss

As well as affecting the vestibular nerve of the inner ear causing vertigo, Ménière's also affects the auditory nerve. This causes impairment of hearing.

Hearing loss only occurs in the affected ear. The sufferer may find that they have difficulty in hearing low frequency sounds to begin with. They may find that certain sounds appear distorted, and that loud sounds become intolerable. Although hearing loss fluctuates from time to time, it can get progressively worse as the years pass by. Eventually, sufferers may have difficulty in hearing all sound frequencies and in some cases, hearing in the affected ear may be lost altogether.

Feeling of 'fullness' in the ear

Periodically, the sufferer may experience a feeling of 'fullness' in the affected ear. The experience of 'fullness' is rather like the feeling you get when you go up a hill and your ears go 'pop', except it cannot be cleared by swallowing.

Fatigue

Many sufferers of Ménière's complain of fatigue as being one of the symptoms of the disease.

Diagnosis

There are many diseases that can cause some of the symptoms of Ménière's. So if you suddenly develop vertigo or tinnitus you must not automatically assume that you have Ménière's disease, only your doctor can make that diagnosis.

Treatment

Anti-emetic drugs may be prescribed by the doctor to help reduce nausea and to prevent vomiting. Diuretics may be given to try and decrease the fluid in the inner ear. In extreme cases, where the vertigo is so disabling that the sufferer has difficulty coping, surgery may be an option. As with many operations, there is a risk that the condition may worsen as a result.

For obvious reasons, there are certain activities that sufferers of Ménière's disease should refrain from doing, so as not to endanger themselves and the lives of others. These include: driving, climbing ladders and operating machinery.

Self-help

Follow the guidelines below to help keep symptoms under control:

1. In some sufferers, external stimuli such as loud noises can trigger or exacerbate attacks of vertigo.
2. Avoid cigarettes and alcohol as they can make symptoms worse.
3. Sticking to a low-salt diet may lessen symptoms.
4. Food allergies have been known to trigger attacks of vertigo or make it worse. So keep a diary for a couple of months. Note down what you have had to eat each day and how bad your symptoms were. Some people find that dairy produce can make their symptoms worse.
5. Stress can make the condition worse. Try and make time to relax during the day. Spend more time doing the things that you enjoy.
6. Caffeine can make symptoms worse. Coffee, tea, chocolate and cola drinks all contain caffeine.
7. During an attack of vertigo, you should rest quietly until the dizziness disappears and try to avoid any sudden head movements.

8. Wristbands designed to help relieve sea-sickness have been found to be very effective at reducing the nausea that accompanies vertigo. These wristbands can be bought from any good pharmacist.

9. Visualisation can help Ménière's disease sufferers. Ménière's is caused by excess fluid in the inner ear, so visualise the excess fluid being drained away. There is advice about visualisation in Vernon Coleman's book *Mindpower*.

Osteoporosis

Osteoporosis has become one of the most fashionable diseases of the late twentieth century. There are probably more myths about it than about any other disease. (The biggest myth – deliberately created – is that it is exclusively a female problem. It isn't.)

Osteoporosis has become a major source of income for three massive international industries. The solutions offered by these three industries often do more harm than good. But you can protect yourself against osteoporosis simply by making lifestyle changes which cost nothing.

* * *

The international pharmaceutical industry first began to profit from the sale of female hormones in the early 1960s when the contraceptive pill was introduced.

After that it was only a few years before drug companies dramatically increased the potential number of consumers for hormones by offering oestrogen supplements to menopausal women.

For about ten years from the middle 1960s onwards oestrogen pills were heavily promoted as a 'miracle' solution for the many physical and mental problems which were widely described, by both doctors and journalists, as being an inevitable consequence of the menopause.

The symptoms of the menopause are known to be caused by a reduction in the body's natural production of female hormones – particularly oestrogen. When a woman goes past her days of potential motherhood those hormones are no longer required and so production falters.

Suddenly, now that there was a 'remedy' available, the menopause began to merit much more serious attention from doctors.

Relatively minor symptoms which would, a few years earlier, have been ignored both by menopausal women themselves and by their medical advisers were now regarded as potentially life-threatening – or at least life-destroying.

There had, of course, always been some women who had suffered serious and troublesome symptoms during the menopause. But the availability of a commercially profitable treatment for menopausal symptoms meant that all women reaching the menopause were now encouraged to regard themselves as 'patients' and to regard treatment with oestrogen not as a last resort but as a simple, safe and essential way to avoid potentially troublesome symptoms.

* * *

The drug companies were enthusiastic about treating menopausal women because all women who live long enough eventually become menopausal – and that is a lot of business (particularly if women are encouraged to keep taking their hormone therapy for a decade or two after they reach the menopause).

Doctors were enthusiastic partly because oestrogen therapy gave them something positive to offer their patients and partly because doctors, on the whole, are now little more than a marketing arm of the pharmaceutical industry.

And many radical feminists were uncritically enthusiastic because here, at last, there seemed to be a solution to a problem (or potential problem) that only affected women.

There was something of a hiccup in the 'let's stop all menopausal symptoms by automatically giving all women oestrogen therapy' campaign in the mid 1970s when it was discovered that women using oestrogen had a dramatically increased chance of developing endometrial cancer. The figures showed that women who used oestrogen for seven years or more were 14 times as likely as other women to develop endometrial cancer. Cancer records in the USA showed that there had been an 80 per cent increase in the incidence of endometrial cancer among white women aged 50 or over during the late 1960s and early 1970s – the very years when women in that group were taking oestrogen therapy to prevent menopausal symptoms.

Soon, it seemed that endometrial cancer wasn't the only problem associated with oestrogen. Evidence appeared suggesting the possibility that oestrogen therapy might also be linked to breast cancer, cancer of the ovary, diabetes, liver disease and gall bladder problems.

This news badly damaged public confidence in the idea of routine oestrogen therapy for women going through the menopause.

Naturally, however, the drug companies were not going to be defeated by this. They added progesterone to the oestrogen and argued that the new addition would protect the uterus from the oestrogen. The new combined product was known as hormone replacement therapy (HRT).

It was not considered necessary to perform long-term clinical trials to find out if the new twin hormone approach would prove to be safer, as safe or less safe than the progesterone only approach. Such long-term trials would, inevitably, have delayed the time when women would be able to benefit from this new therapy. (There would, of course, also have been a similar delay in the revival of drug company profits.)

There was, however, a snag affecting the launch of new, improved hormone replacement therapy.

The problems associated with the use of oestrogen to treat and prevent menopausal symptoms had created considerable anxiety and mistrust among women.

The drug companies knew that they had to find some way to make women believe that the menopause posed a real threat to their health and, indeed, to their lives.

In order to sell hormone replacement therapy the drug companies had to find a way to convince women that any risks associated with this double hormone cocktail were worth taking. They had to find a disease that could be associated with the menopause, that could be described as deadly and dangerous and that, it could be argued, could be effectively treated with hormone replacement therapy.

They chose a disease called osteoporosis which fitted the requirements almost perfectly. However, one of the first things that had to be done was to redefine the disease.

Osteoporosis used to be a disease in which bones had become

thin and weak and had fractured. But the number of people suffering from this condition was relatively small. And so, in order dramatically to increase the target audience, osteoporosis was redefined as a disease characterised by the fact that low bone mass and increased bone fragility had increased the risk of bone fracture. (This is something of a nonsense since evidence from non Western countries shows that low bone mass does not necessarily increase the risk of bone fracture. Indeed, half the population in the West have 'thin' bones which never fracture.)

According to the original definition of osteoporosis only around one million people a year develop osteoporosis in the USA But according to the new definition the number of people suffering from osteoporosis can be measured in tens of millions.

One expert has claimed that redefining osteoporosis in this way is rather like redefining heart disease in such a way that a man who has a high blood cholesterol level (but hasn't actually had a heart attack) will be defined as a heart attack victim.

* * *

In order to balance the hazards known or suspected to be associated with hormone replacement therapy it was also necessary to put a great deal of emphasis on the risks associated with osteoporosis.

The drug companies knew that if women perceived osteoporosis as offering only a modest danger to their health they would not be prepared to take HRT to prevent it. Osteoporosis had to be built up into a significant life-threatening disorder.

And so the lobbyists, public relations experts and industry spin-doctors put a great deal of effort into turning osteoporosis from a relatively little known disorder into a scary and significant disease.

Women who were targeted as good HRT consumers were warned that hip fractures among women in the danger age group exceed the incidence of cancer of the cervix, breast and uterus and that half of all patients who have a hip fracture will need long-term care while one in six will die within six months.

Pretty frightening stuff.

What the spin-doctors didn't tell women was that most of the women who have hip fractures are in their seventies, eighties and nineties – and are, therefore, likely to need long-term care (or to die) because of other health problems.

Women were also shown pictures of women with 'dowager's hump' – which is created when vertebrae collapse causing shrinkage and, eventually, a hump – and warned that this was what awaited them if they did not take immediate action to protect themselves.

This was scaremongering on a massive scale because only a tiny fraction of women with osteoporosis – perhaps around five per cent of 70-year-olds – ever develop collapsed vertebrae. Only about one in five of these develop symptoms.

By the time they are 80 years old virtually all women in the USA (and other Western nations) are officially suffering from osteoporosis. And yet only a tiny proportion of those women will suffer bone fractures.

* * *

The other strange thing about choosing osteoporosis as a menopausal risk was that osteoporosis had never before been regarded as a disease of 'women' as opposed to a disease of 'human beings'.

One man in three over the age of 60 gets osteoporosis and so it can hardly be argued that this is because their circulating levels of female hormone have dropped. Men are more likely to die as a result of fractures which have developed because of osteoporosis than women are.

But when the drug industry public relations people got to work osteoporosis was quickly redefined as a serious menopausal problem.

Doctors were hired to spread the news about osteoporosis, the menopause and hormone replacement therapy and journalists eagerly passed the news on to their readers. Television viewers, radio listeners and newspaper and magazine readers all learnt that hormone replacement therapy is the best way to prevent osteoporosis – a disease which would, without the miracle of HRT, be a major threat to the health of all menopausal women.

By the early 1990s, the campaign to link osteoporosis and the menopause had been completely successful. Women were by then so terrified of osteoporosis, and the associated bone fractures and dowager's hump, that they were pouring into their doctors' surgeries and demanding HRT – regardless of the possible consequences.

The drug companies had once again succeeded in creating a disease, and a fear, that would enable them to market a potentially hazardous product.

The plain, unadulterated fact is that the alleged relationship between osteoporosis and the menopause is an entirely artificial one which was created for purely commercial reasons.

Even more significantly, perhaps, the marketing of HRT to prevent osteoporosis developing, had turned a product which had been originally designed, and thought of, as a treatment into a form of prevention.

In commercial terms this was, of course, a highly significant move and it is now a typical approach for the pharmaceutical industry to take.

The drug companies know, for example, that their profits will be far higher if they can sell drugs to *prevent* heart disease, depression or asthma than if they can only sell drugs to *treat* heart disease, depression or asthma. The commercial potential for a drug which can be recommended as a preventative is infinitely greater than the potential for a drug which only has a therapeutic use. By no means all individuals actually develop heart disease, depression or asthma but most individuals are keen *not* to develop those problems.

* * *

Once the drug companies had established osteoporosis as a dangerous but avoidable consequence of the menopause a number of other groups jumped onto the rolling bandwagon.

Dairy farmers – and their marketing experts – quickly recognised that they could sell milk as a natural 'medicine' designed to help prevent osteoporosis.

The dairy industry was, of course, in a great deal of trouble at the time when osteoporosis was artificially linked with the menopause. Millions of people had cut down their milk consumption, or had stopped drinking milk completely, because they were worried about the associated fat consumption (not to mention the serious allergy problems known to be associated with milk).

But once they had realised that milk contains calcium – the most significant ingredient of bone – the dairy industry wasted no time at all in creating a new myth: that drinking milk leads to strong, healthy bones and a reduction in the risk of developing osteoporosis and bone fractures.

Parts of the dairy industry even started to add extra calcium to milk to enhance its value as a preventative against osteoporosis and to substantiate the threat made to women that their bones would become frail and brittle and would fracture more easily if they didn't drink milk.

There was no clinical evidence to support the claim that a diet rich in milk would help prevent osteoporosis or fractured bones. However, that small problem was not allowed to stand in the way and milk was vigorously promoted to women as an essential and healthy source of bone strengthening food.

The manufacturers, distributors and retailers of vitamin and mineral supplements also benefited from the drug industry's success in scaring millions of women about the newly established link between osteoporosis, fractured bones and the menopause.

By the mid 1980s, American women were spending over $150 million on calcium supplements which they believed would help prevent osteoporosis.

Naturally, there was no clinical evidence to support the claim that taking calcium supplements did or could prevent bone loss, osteoporosis or bone fractures.

The three myths about osteoporosis

The marketing programmes developed by the pharmaceutical industry, the dairy industry and the mineral supplement industry had, by the early 1990s, successfully established several important myths as fact.

Myth 1: Osteoporosis is a disease which exclusively or largely affects women.

Myth 2: Osteoporosis is directly caused by, or is an inevitable consequence, of menopausal changes in circulating hormone levels.

Myth 3: Osteoporosis (and the risk of developing bone fractures) can be safely prevented and/or cured by swallowing large quantities of calcium – ideally either in the form of dairy produce or calcium tablets.

These myths are well established as apparent facts but are relatively easy to disprove.

Myth 1: *Osteoporosis is a women's problem*

Osteoporosis has been described as a problem largely affecting women. It was traditionally simply a bone disorder which affected both men and women but was given its special status as a major menopausal symptom in order to counteract the risk known to be associated with hormone replacement therapy. The fact that men are more likely to die of bone fractures than women are is ignored because it doesn't fit into the scheme of things – and certainly doesn't help drug companies sell HRT. Most men aged 75 and over have lost enough bone to put them within the definition of osteoporosis or to put them at significant risk of developing osteoporosis and the alleged sequelae. (The fact that most of those men never fracture any bones is proof that osteoporosis does not necessarily lead to fracture rather than that men don't develop osteoporosis).

Myth 2: *Osteoporosis is caused by the menopause*

If osteoporosis really were caused by the menopause (or even associated with it directly) then it would be fair to assume that the incidence of the disease would be much the same among women everywhere.

But it isn't.

There are many parts of the world where osteoporosis and bone fractures are almost unheard of among post-menopausal women (and certainly little or no commoner than among pre-menopausal women). Many women in Africa, Asia and South America live many years beyond the menopause without developing an increased tendency to bone fracture. Oestrogen levels among such women are not higher than among Western women – and bone density loss is comparable – but bone fracture rates are much lower.

Previous theories about bone density levels being linked to hormone levels have been disproved by studies which have shown that some women lose comparatively little bone when they go through the menopause while among other women bone loss actually starts before the menopause.

Particularly convincing is research which shows that sex hormone levels are more or less identical in women with and without osteoporosis. If bone loss was triggered by hormone loss one would rationally expect a dramatic fall in hormone levels to result in a big bone loss: that doesn't happen.

It is also important to remember that bone density loss, osteoporosis and a tendency to bone fracture also occurs in white males – as well as white females. Once again this seems to provide convincing evidence that there is no link between the menopause and osteoporosis.

The truth is that all the evidence shows that the alleged link between the menopause and osteoporosis simply does not exist.

We do, however, have evidence showing that vegetarian and vegan women have higher bone density (and a smaller likelihood of developing fractures) than meat eating women. This is true for vegetarian women even when they have lower oestrogen levels than meat eating women.

The conclusion has to be that women who want stronger bones and a smaller fracture risk should give up eating meat.

This evidence has never been widely publicised. Readers with a slightly cynical or sceptical streak might ask themselves whether this could be because drug companies, doctors and the dairy industry could not possibly gain anything by encouraging patients to stop eating meat. Indeed, the meat industry has a huge interest in suppressing such evidence.

Myth 3: Osteoporosis can be prevented by taking extra calcium (as milk or as supplements)

The fact that bone is largely made up of calcium has encouraged many people in the belief that a good calcium intake is essential for healthy bones.

However, although it is obviously true that some calcium is essential for healthy bones the evidence shows that a high calcium intake alone will not necessarily prevent osteoporosis or ensure strong bones.

Countries where people have a high calcium intake (such as Sweden or Finland) tend to have higher fracture rates than less 'well-developed' countries (such as those in Asia) where calcium intake is not high and dairy consumption is low or non-existent.

There is no group of people in the world with a lower incidence of osteoporosis than the Bantu of Africa. But the average Bantu consumes less than a quarter of the amount of calcium consumed by the average Westerner. (Western women are encouraged to consume between 1,000 and 1,500 mg of calcium a day but the Bantu take in as little as 175 mg of calcium a day). The Japanese daily intake of calcium is around 500 mg daily but fracture rates there are much lower than in the USA. People living as far apart as China and Peru have a low calcium intake and a low osteoporosis rate. It may seem surprising but there simply isn't a link between calcium intake and bone loss.

On the contrary it now seems clear that bone loss and osteoporosis are problems which are much commoner in white women than in black women. And although there may be some genetic component in this, diet and lifestyle are probably most significant.

In 1996, a study of over 500 women showed that white women are twice as likely to have fractures as are black women. This confirmed the results of a previous study, conducted in Texas, USA in 1988, which showed that hip fractures were much less common among African American women and Mexican American women than among white women. This strong racial difference was confirmed by a third study, conducted in 1992, which showed that black South African women, who have a low intake of calcium in their daily diet, have a fracture rate which is only about five per cent that of white women.

Since black women are obviously just as likely to have a menopause as are white women it is perfectly clear from all this that there can be no direct relationship between the menopause and osteoporosis or bone fracture.

* * *

It is a part of this myth that dairy products (such as milk) are a safe and vital source of calcium. Indeed, a high intake of milk doesn't appear to help avoid bone loss, osteoporosis or fractures.

The Harvard Nurses' Study, which involved 77,761 women aged between 34 and 59, showed that women who drank three or more glasses of milk a day had no fewer hip or arm fractures than those who drank little or no milk. Indeed, the dairy industry must have been shocked by the results which showed that fracture rates for milk drinkers were significantly *higher* for those women who consumed three or more glasses of milk a day.

Those countries around the world where dairy produce is consumed most enthusiastically are also the countries where osteoporosis is at its commonest. Osteoporosis is at its rarest in countries where dairy produce consumption is low. The evidence points strongly to a vegan, rather than a vegetarian, diet being the healthiest option for anyone wanting strong bones in old age.

Dairy products (such as milk and cheese) are sometimes thought of as standard or irreplaceable sources of calcium. However, this isn't true. For example, only about 30 per cent of the calcium in milk is absorbed by the human body – possibly less than for typical green, leafy vegetables. Dark green leafy vegetables (such as kale and broccoli) are good plant sources of calcium and some experts believe that calcium is more readily absorbed from kale than it is from milk.

The main problem with milk seems to be that although it does contain calcium it also contains protein and eating protein derived from animals results in an increased rate of calcium excretion. It is significant that osteoporosis is most common in countries (USA, UK, Finland, Sweden) which have the largest consumption of dairy products.

Human beings are the only animals in the world who routinely drink milk obtained from another species. And it isn't a wise thing to do. Milk is not the 'safe' food it is often made out to be. Even if milk were a good source of calcium (which it is not) it would not be a safe source of calcium.

It has been known for some time that cow's milk may cause a number of allergies and digestive troubles. Asthma, eczema, irritable bowel syndrome, migraine and sinus problems are just five extremely common disorders which may be associated with drinking milk.

Clinical studies have also shown that there may be a link between cancer of the ovary and dairy products.

The original studies showed a higher than normal risk of ovarian cancer in women who consumed more lactose (foods which contain a lot of lactose include skimmed milk, ice cream, yoghurt and cottage cheese) and had less of an enzyme which helps to eliminate the galactose component of lactose.

Ovarian cancer is more common in Northern Europe than in Asia and the consumption of cow's milk products may be one reason for this difference. And there has been a report suggesting that there may be a link between milk (even skimmed milk) and breast cancer. In one study a researcher described cow's milk as a cocktail of cancer-causing chemicals.

There are two other worries about milk.

First, no one knows the consequences of the fact that many farmers give their cows hormones in order to increase the milk yield. Inevitably, those hormones get into the cow's milk and so anyone who drinks the milk is likely to be getting an unwanted blast of hormones. Other drugs – such as antibiotics – which are routinely given to cattle are also likely to find their way into milk.

Second, there is a very real risk that cow's milk (and, quite possibly, the milk from other animals) could be contaminated with the factor which causes Mad Cow disease.

None of this need be a problem since cow's milk contains nothing that cannot be obtained in other foods and is nowhere near as good a source of calcium as the dairy industry would have us all believe.

* * *

Just as the theory about milk helping to prevent osteoporosis has been exposed for the sham it is, so some studies have shown that calcium supplementation doesn't lower the incidence of fractures. Indeed, there is evidence to show that individuals who take large quantities of calcium supplementation have a 50 per cent increased risk of developing bone fractures.

A good calcium intake in childhood, and during pre-menopausal years, will help build strong bones (and, therefore, help reduce the risk of thin, weak bones in later life) but that good calcium intake can best be obtained from a good varied diet rather than from supplements. And cow's milk is not a good source of bone strength at any age. Drinking cow's milk during the teenage years does not provide protection against osteoporosis.

The real problem with calcium supplements is that some are not well absorbed while too much calcium supplementation can lead to calcification of the joints and to kidney stones.

* * *

Clearly, there are a number of lessons to be learned from the way that these myths have been deliberately created. And make no mistake about it: these myths did not develop by accident. The myths about osteoporosis, the menopause, milk and calcium supplements were manufactured, quite cold bloodedly, for very specific commercial purposes.

* * *

It is clear that without the link to osteoporosis the hazards posed by the menopause are considerably less significant. An American study which began in 1976 and which involves 122,000 nurses, suggests that any life extending qualities which HRT possesses depend largely upon the hormones helping to reduce a woman's chances of developing heart disease. This survey shows that HRT has little positive or useful effect on mortality rates when it is taken by women who have a low risk of heart disease.

The significance of this is, of course, the fact that if a woman wants to reduce her risk of developing heart disease she doesn't have to take HRT; she can cut her risk of developing heart disease by avoiding tobacco, cutting down her fat consumption, learning how to relax, losing excess weight (preferably gradually through a change in diet rather than through an artificial dieting programme) and taking regular, gentle exercise.

The hazards associated with HRT are real and for many women the disadvantages outweigh the advantages. It is still not precisely clear exactly what the risks are of a woman on HRT developing cancer. But it seems unlikely that anyone would disagree with the statement that a woman who takes HRT has a greater chance of developing cancer than a woman who doesn't. Studies have shown that HRT increases the incidence of breast cancer by ten per cent a year for each year that the HRT is used. That is, surely, a significant level of hazard. And there are other risks too. According to a major study of 23,000 female nurses, menopausal women who take HRT are 50 per cent more likely to develop asthma.

The evidence supports the contention that HRT should only ever be considered as a treatment and never as a preventative. If a woman has menopausal symptoms which are causing her great distress then she may consider that the largely undetermined risks associated with

HRT may be worth taking. On the other hand the mass market long-term treatment of millions of healthy women with HRT cannot possibly be justified.

Other, safer (and probably more effective) products are available to alleviate menopausal symptoms. For example, women who suffer psychological symptoms (such as irritability and a decline in sex drive) have been helped by taking St John's Wort (which should be available through good local health food stores but which should, like all remedies, only be taken under the advice and recommendation of a professionally trained health care professional). One trial showed that menopausal women taking St John's Wort were dramatically less likely to suffer from low self-esteem, irritability and other associated problems. The same trial showed that most of the women who had complained of a lack of sexual desire recovered their enthusiasm for sex after taking St John's Wort.

* * *

It should also now be clear that we all have to be constantly on the look out for new myths and new attempts to manipulate our natural fears of ill health and death purely for profit.

Drug companies, doctors, the dairy industry and the supplements industry have conspired to encourage women to take HRT, to swallow calcium supplements and to drink vast quantities of milk when the evidence shows that all these alleged remedies are of far greater benefit to those who manufacture, sell or prescribe them than they are to women themselves.

Women want to trust doctors and still often tend to believe what they read in magazines and hear on television. But, sadly, women have been lied to, misled and deceived by doctors and journalists for years. HRT can almost certainly cause cancer. Calcium supplements aren't necessarily effective at helping to build bone but they can cause kidney stones and other health endangering problems. And drinking milk may actually cause bone loss and the development of bone fractures.

International pharmaceutical companies, and other exclusively profit orientated organisations, employ thousands of public relations executives, press officers, lobbyists, researchers, doctors and journalists who are paid to create new fears and to build up demands for products which might otherwise have a small or even non-existent commercial value.

The bottom line is that none of us can trust the pharmaceutical industry, the food industry, the politicians or the medical profession to tell us the truth about what is good or bad for our health or to protect us from those who are inspired solely by greed.

The truth (and for many people it is an unacceptable and unwelcome truth) is that osteoporosis, loss of bone strength and an increased tendency to bone fracture are, like so many other health problems of the twenty-first century, a result of our poor lifestyle and our poor dietary habits.

Attempting to combat these problems by taking hormones or drugs does not tackle the problem at source and is likely to make matters worse by creating new health problems on top of the existing ones.

The great failing of our modern society is that we are constantly searching for the magic solution. Even when the answers to our problems are clear and simple we still prefer to look for solutions in a bottle.

Weak bones and bone fractures are, like cancer and heart disease, problems which we can have some control over. We cannot avoid them completely, of course, but we can dramatically improve our odds of avoiding them.

We are constantly encouraged to put our faith in drugs. But we are encouraged to do that because the people who make the drugs want to sell them to us – not because they want to make us well again.

The truth about how to build strong bones and avoid osteoporosis

The myths now exposed were, of course, developed quite deliberately for very specific commercial purposes. The truth about maintaining strong bones (and avoiding osteoporosis) is quite different to these myths.

One study has shown that vegetarians absorb and retain more calcium from foods than do non-vegetarians and other studies cite lower rates of osteoporosis in vegetarians than in non-vegetarians. Vegetarian and vegan diets may actually protect against osteoporosis. The wisest course is to obtain dietary calcium from a wide range of sources. Possible calcium sources include: broccoli, molasses, chick peas, dried figs, tofu, endive, cabbage, kale, spinach and many different types of beans (including soya beans and vegetarian baked beans). Probably the simplest way to make sure you get plenty of calcium is to eat plenty of dark green leafy vegetables.

Many factors in addition to, and other than, the consumption of calcium play a significant part in the development and maintenance of healthy bones. These factors have not been widely discussed or promoted in recent years and it is difficult to avoid the conclusion that this has been because these other factors have not been promoted by individuals working for or on behalf of commercial organisations. Put quite simply, it is easy to make money out of selling calcium (either in the form of milk or calcium tablets) but not easy to make money out of offering good advice which does not involve the sale of a product.

It is, for example, vital to remember that there are, in addition to calcium, around 20 other essential nutrients – including a variety of vitamins and minerals – which are required before the body can build and maintain healthy bones. If the diet is deficient in any of these nutrients then the bones will become weak. You don't need to take supplements to obtain these essential nutrients: all you need is a good, balanced diet that includes plenty of fruit and vegetables (preferably organically grown and genetically unmodified).

It is also important to remember that apart from ensuring a reasonable intake of calcium (best done without dairy produce) it is also necessary to reduce the loss of calcium from your body.

There are a number of things you can do to minimise calcium loss.

First, you should avoid tobacco (smokers have a hip fracture risk 40 per cent higher than non-smokers).

Second, don't drink more than two cups of coffee or tea a day and keep your intake of alcohol down.

Third, you should be aware that a sedentary lifestyle may lead to calcium losses so take regular, gentle exercise which you enjoy. Exercising just three times a week will help to strengthen bone density noticeably. The best forms of exercise for strengthening the bones include weight training and walking uphill or cycling uphill. (Remember that you should not exercise if it is painful and you should always consult your doctor before starting an exercise programme or altering your exercise habits).

Fourth you should keep down your intake of salt.

Fifth, it is important to avoid constant dieting. The evidence shows that whenever someone diets and loses weight he or she will also lose bone. Since women tend to diet more than men this is a problem which affects women more than men. Clearly, therefore, women who have spent much of their lives dieting, regaining weight and dieting again will have lost a good deal of bone by the time they reach the menopause. (And the arrival of the menopause will be a mere coincidence). Could this possibly help explain why osteoporosis is commoner in the West?

It is also important to be aware that the human body needs vitamin D to make healthy bones. Obtaining vitamin D is easy: ten or 20 minutes of sun on face, hands and arms, taken just three times a week, should produce all the vitamin D the body needs. People with dark skin, or those who live in cloudy or smoggy areas or in Northern areas may need slightly more exposure.

Finally, and most importantly, you should be aware that eating animal protein results in withdrawal of calcium from the bones into the bloodstream. The calcium is then excreted in the urine and lost. Eating large amounts of animal protein can dramatically increase the rate at which the body loses calcium. This is probably the most important single secret in the battle against osteoporosis and bone fractures. It is a secret which has been deliberately suppressed and hidden by those industries which have a vested interest in selling their 'solutions' to this problem – and by the meat industry which is, not surprisingly, nervous about the long-term consequences to its own profitability once the secret becomes widely known.

The truth is that meat consumption is one of the most important factors in the development of bone loss, osteoporosis and fractures.

(Incidentally, meat protein is a very poor source of calcium. Strawberries contain more calcium than rump steak or corned beef).

A report which was published in the *American Journal of Clinical Nutrition* in 1994, showed that when volunteers switched from a typical Western diet to one which did not include animal protein, calcium losses were halved. A study of the health of 85,900 women aged between 35 and 59 showed that an increase in consumption of animal protein was associated with an increased risk of forearm fracture. No such association was found for the consumption of vegetable protein. Women who consume five or more servings of red meat each week have a significantly increased risk of forearm fracture when compared with women who eat red meat less than once a week.

Moreover, there is strong evidence to suggest that in those countries where calcium consumption is low and bone fracture rates are also low the key factor may well be the level of animal protein consumption.

For example, hip fracture rates in Beijing (China) are among the lowest in the world despite the fact that the mean daily intake of calcium in China is only 540 mg per person per day. (In the USA the comparable figure is 1140 mg). The big nutritional difference between the two countries lies in the amount of animal protein which is consumed. A staggering 70 per cent of the protein consumed in the USA is from animals. In China just seven per cent of the protein consumed is from animals.

In addition to all this, it is important to remember that environmental toxins and mental stresses can also interfere with the body's ability to function effectively – and, therefore, its ability to build new bone. And the surgical removal of the ovaries can have a damaging effect on the body's bone building ability.

Osteoporosis: the conclusion

Osteoporosis is a nasty disease. But it is a disease largely created and sustained by our way of life. As with so many other disorders our slick 'in a bottle' twenty-first century solutions often simply add additional problems to existing ones. The best way to avoid osteoporosis – and to deal with it – is to be aware of the real causes and to do something about them.

Osteoporosis is yet another twenty-first century lifestyle disease which can, not surprisingly perhaps, best be avoided (and conquered) through a change in lifestyle.

Pain

The gate control theory of pain, put forward by two scientists called Melzack and Wall, suggested that when body tissues are damaged messages carrying information about the injury travel towards the brain along two quite separate sets of nerve fibres.

The larger fibres carry messages about sensations other than pain and the smaller fibres carry the pain messages. The messages which travel along the larger fibres tend to arrive at the spinal cord before the messages travelling along the smaller fibres and, if there are enough non-painful sensations travelling, the pain messages won't be able to get through.

Once this theory had been accepted it was possible to explain all sorts of natural phenomena which had, up until then, been a mystery.

So, for example, it became clear that when we rub a sore spot what we are doing is increasing the number of non-pain messages travelling towards the spinal cord (and thence the brain). If you knock your elbow you will automatically reach to rub the spot because subconsciously you know that by rubbing the area you will be able to cut down the amount of pain that you feel.

Having realised just how rubbing a sore or painful place can relieve pain the next step for scientists was to come up with a way of stimulating the passage of non-painful sensations even more efficiently.

And doctors came up with the idea of using electricity to produce the necessary stimulus.

When the theory was first put into practice in the late 1960s doctors suggested that electricity should be introduced into the body through electrodes surgically implanted in the spine. Although that did work the fact that it involved an operation limited the usefulness and availability of the procedure.

Next, it was discovered that all nerves within an inch or so of the surface of the skin can be stimulated by electrodes which are simply stuck onto the skin.

And that encouraged medical researchers to start giving patients pocket-sized battery operated stimulators.

They worked!

More exciting still it was found that Transcutaneous Electrical Nerve Stimulation (it quickly became known as TENS) did not just stimulate the passage of sensory impulses designed to inhibit the passage of pain impulses; it also stimulated the body to start producing its own pain-relieving hormones: the endorphins.

Beg, buy or borrow a TENS machine

A TENS machine is a quite remarkable device which can help conquer pain extremely effectively at very low cost and with very few side effects.

During recent years an enormous number of research projects have shown that TENS machines are convenient, safe and effective. They are also cheap to buy and extremely cheap to run.

In a study conducted with patients suffering from rheumatoid arthritis it was found that TENS equipment produced pain relief in up to 95 per cent of patients with up to 50 per cent of patients getting long-term relief.

But it isn't just arthritis patients who benefit from using TENS machines – up to 90 per cent of patients get short-term relief from pain and 35 per cent of patients are still getting relief after two years of use.

TENS machines have been shown to be effective in the treatment of all kinds of pain.

With this sort of success available from a small, cheap, portable, long lasting machine that can be used at home without any training, and that does not seem to produce any side effects, you might imagine that doctors would be recommending TENS machines to millions of patients – and that shops would have different models stocked high on their shelves.

But if you try to buy a TENS machine you might have difficulty. Why?

Because drug companies don't want patients in pain to be able to deal with their symptom so easily and quickly and cheaply. Drug companies make huge amounts of money out of selling drugs to pain sufferers.

TENS machines would cost them a fortune in lost sales.

So, we believe that doctors and drug companies have conspired to keep TENS machines away from the public.

However, there is some good news. If you want to try a TENS

machine ask your doctor to refer you to the nearest pain clinic. You should be able to obtain one on loan and if you find that the machine works for you then you should be able to obtain one for permanent use. Alternatively, for details of a simple, portable tens device which works visit www.tenspen.com

(Incidentally, using electricity to treat pain isn't new. The ancient Egyptians used electricity to treat pain as did Hippocrates. One Roman physician cured headaches with the energy produced by electric torpedo fish. Another claimed that gout could be cured by putting the feet in a bucket of water along with an electric eel.)

Keep busy

The natural reaction to pain is to rest. When a pain is severe this is appropriate, sensible and healing. But it is possible to rest too much. And unless your pain is acute or you have been told to rest by your doctor you may be doing yourself more harm than good by resting. Physical inactivity can result in the weakening of muscles and the deterioration of many of the body's essential organs and can lead to the development of pressure sores. Mental inactivity can make pain worse simply by reducing the amount of sensory input going into your brain. If you have too little to think about then your brain will become ever more acutely aware of any pain sensations which might be around.

Have you ever come in from the garden, got into the bath and discovered that your arms and legs are covered in scratches and bruises?

Have you ever been busy in the kitchen and then suddenly noticed that there is blood everywhere – from a finger you didn't even know you'd cut?

Have you ever been for a long walk, arrived home tired but happy and then woken up next day feeling stiff and hardly able to move?

In all those instances pain impulses – telling you to stop – just couldn't get through because you were engrossed in what you were doing. Messages coming down from your brain were blocking the pathways and leaving no room for pain messages.

One of the earliest pieces of research to show the value of keeping your mind active was done by two researchers from the University of

Oregon Medical School. They took a number of volunteer students and divided them into several groups.

Members of the first group of students were told to sit still, to do nothing and to keep their hands in ice water for as long as they could. Members of the second group were also told to put their hands into ice water but were told that they could watch a nearby clock and use the clock to help set themselves goals and objectives. Members of the third group of volunteers were given access to a slide projector and a series of slides. They were allowed to operate the projector with their free hand and to look at as many slides as they liked.

The results of the experiment showed that when people in pain keep their minds busy they increase their pain tolerance level. The volunteers in the first group, the ones who were not thinking about anything in particular, managed to keep their hands in the ice water for an average of 174 seconds. The volunteers in the second group, the ones who were watching the clock, managed to last out for 196 seconds. But the volunteers who were allowed to look at the slides managed to keep their hands in the ice water for an average of 271 seconds.

Clearly, therefore, you should do everything you can to keep yourself busy.

You should, for example, try to take as little time off work as possible. Work can provide you with physical activity, mental stimulation and a target for your enthusiasm.

If your work does not provide you with the intellectual stimulation that you need then start taking evening classes or day classes at a local college. Try to find a subject that excites you and that you think you will enjoy. If it's useful as well then consider that a bonus.

When you need to distract yourself from your pain create mental games to keep your mind occupied if you don't have anything to read, watch or listen to. Try doing mental arithmetic or try concocting fantasies for yourself. It doesn't matter what you do as long as you keep your mind busy. In one experiment volunteers found that they could put up with extra pain if they listened to music they liked.

Factors which affect the pain you feel

There are a number of factors which can influence your awareness of your pain by hiding or stopping pain impulses on their way to your brain.

Most important of all is the fact that for a pain to be felt, the stimulus must exceed your personal pain threshold. If you are going to be aware that you have hit your thumb you must hit it with a certain amount of force. If you hit your thumb a light, glancing blow then you might be aware that your thumb has been 'touched' but you won't feel a 'pain'. If you don't hit your thumb hard enough your tissues won't produce the chemicals necessary to stimulate a nervous response.

Pain thresholds vary from one individual to another. Some of the variations are caused by factors which you will find difficult to control.

For example, women have much the same sort of pain threshold as men but they are less tolerant of pain than men. This is probably because men are taught to be 'strong' and not to cry out when in pain. On average men can tolerate pain for 20 per cent longer than women.

The number of brothers and sisters you have can also influence the way you react to pain. Children who grow up with at least three other brothers and sisters are likely to have much higher pain tolerance levels than children who grow up with fewer brothers and sisters.

Age is a significant factor too. Your ability to tolerate pain will change as you get older. You will become better able to tolerate superficial pains and less able to tolerate deep pains. And nationality and race can be significant too.

Finally, what you learned as a child can have a serious effect on how you respond to pain. If your parents made a fuss every time you got a knock or a bruise then you will have a comparatively low pain threshold and pain tolerance level. If, however, your parents took little notice when you complained of pain then you will have grown up indifferent to pain – with a high pain threshold and a great ability to tolerate pain.

Children can 'learn' pain behaviour from their parents. If you grew up in a household where one or both parents complained of back trouble you are more likely to suffer from back pain.

You can't do much about any of these things, of course. You can't change your age, your sex, your race or how you were brought up as a child.

But there are some factors which you may be able to control. Your pain threshold varies from minute to minute according to a variety of hidden factors. You might find that it helps to know some of the commonest.

For example, your attitude towards your pain is crucial. If you think a pain is trivial and harmless you will ignore it and it will probably go away. If you think a pain is serious and potentially life-threatening you will worry about it and it will not go away.

Your attitude towards the pain can, on occasion, be more important than the strength of the pain itself. If you have a headache and believe that it is caused by a brain tumour the headache will probably continue to get worse and worse. But as soon as you are assured by your doctor that the headache is simply a result of stress and tension it will probably start to go away. If you have a backache which you believe is caused by secondary cancer deposits then the pain will probably get worse and worse. But if you are convincingly reassured that the pain is caused by nothing more significant than a muscle strain you will probably find that it becomes less significant.

Where you are and what you are doing can be terribly significant. During a UK football Cup Final, one of the goal-keepers broke his neck. But he carried on playing. He was so wrapped up in the game that he ignored his pain until the match had finished. It was only when he collected his medal that he realised that he'd done something serious.

If you're busy with an important tennis match you won't notice the blisters on your hand. If you're trying to reach succulent blackberries in a hedge you won't notice the scratches you receive trying to reach them.

How frightened you are also influences the amount of pain you feel. Have you ever had toothache, booked an appointment to see the dentist and found that by the time you walked into the consulting room your pain had disappeared?

You aren't alone if you have. It's a very common phenomenon. When you are first aware of an aching tooth your threshold is low. You are worried by the pain and you don't know how long it is going to last. Fear lowers your pain threshold and pain tolerance levels.

As soon as you've got your appointment to see the dentist your anxiety begins to lift. You feel more confident. And because you know that relief will soon be available you suffer less from the pain.

Finally, your mental state can be crucial. Have you ever had a day when everything seems to go wrong? If you have then you know that by the end of it the smallest problem can become a crisis. A lost button, a missed bus or a mislaid pen can all seem horrendous. Small difficulties get taken out of all proportion when we feel low.

Your response to pain is influenced by mood in exactly the same way. If you are feeling unhappy and you hit your thumb then the pain will seem worse than if you are feeling happy when you hit your thumb. If you are a backache sufferer then your pain will almost certainly be more significant when you are feeling miserable.

How heat can help

Heat has been used to help relieve pain for centuries and just about every country in the world has a history of using spas, saunas, hot springs, baths and soaking tubs to help eradicate pain. Although heat can help just about any sort of pain it is particularly effective for backache.

Just how heat produces its useful effect is still something of a mystery although scientists have put forward several theories. It has been suggested that heat generates nerve impulses which help stop pain impulses getting through to the brain. Alternatively, it may be that heating the body may increase the rate at which pain disappears since heating the tissues increases the flow of blood and the blood removes products such as histamine and prostaglandins (chemicals which are produced by the body and which are responsible for the sensation of pain).

The truth is that both these theories are probably correct, although to a certain extent the question of just how heat relieves pain is rather academic since the important thing is that heat does relieve pain.

There are numerous ways of applying heat to your body. The best way is probably by having a warm bath or sauna. Millions of sportsmen and women and gardeners will confirm that nothing soothes sore and inflamed muscles quite as much as lying down in a bath full of warm water. As an alternative to an ordinary hot bath you could try visiting your nearest well-heated swimming pool, sauna or steam room. The heat of a sauna encourages the superficial circulation and this helps to get rid of mild aches and pains.

If you want to apply heat to specific areas of your body then you can try using heated towels, an electrically heated pad, a sun lamp or a hot water bottle. If you try using a hot water bottle do make sure that the rubber is not perished, that the stopper fits well and that the bottle is wrapped in a towel so that it does not burn your skin.

Use ice to treat pain

Few of us think of ice as being a useful remedy for pain but it is. Indeed, cold is often even more effective than heat at reducing pain.

After being massaged with ice, many patients get up to four hours of pain relief.

One theory is that the ice constricts the blood vessels and makes the area feel numb. Another theory is that ice produces endorphins – special internally produced pain relieving hormones – and interferes with the passage of pain impulses.

To avoid being cut by pieces of ice which are sharp edged, put the ice into a rubber ice bag or hot water bottle. Alternatively you can simply wrap ice cubes in a thin cloth such as a tea towel.

Whatever you choose you can best get relief by rubbing the ice all over the painful area in circular or backwards and forwards movements. Press fairly firmly. When you rub ice on your skin you should first feel the cold, then feel a burning and then a stiffness. Finally there is a numbness. You should not hold the ice in contact with your skin for more than five minutes at a time – you should remember that ice, like heat, can burn. You should keep the ice moving so that it doesn't remain in contact with one part of the skin for more than a few seconds. Once your skin *starts* to feel numb remove the ice and start to move the area immediately.

Use your imagination to beat your pain

If you watch a TV film with hot desert scenes in it you'll feel thirsty and there is a good chance that you'll go out into the kitchen to make yourself a cold drink. If you watch a film with cold, arctic scenes in it you'll shiver and turn up the fire. If you watch a scary, horror film on TV you'll check the doors and windows double carefully before you go to bed.

If you think you could be made redundant you will start to worry about the future and to create all sorts of terrible scenarios. You will create images and anxieties simply by worrying. Your fears may not come true but your body will still respond to them. Your imagination is powerful and your body will respond just as readily to things that you imagine as it will to reality.

Until fairly recently most of the evidence linking the human imagination to pain was evidence showing that by thinking about sad and unhappy things you could make yourself ill, create new pains for yourself or make existing pains worse.

But in the last few years a number of experiments have shown that the human imagination can also have a very positive effect. If you learn how to use your imagination in a positive way you can get rid of pain.

In one early experiment to show just how much pain can be controlled by the human imagination 36 volunteers were told to place their right hands in ice water and to hold their hands there for as long as they could.

This isn't as easy as it sounds. The human hand doesn't like being held in icy water – it hurts!

In a second experiment the volunteers were then told to put their hands into the ice water again but this time to try and imagine pleasant scenes. They were told to try to imagine that instead of sitting in a laboratory with one hand in freezing cold water they were sitting in the sunshine by the edge of a beautiful blue lake. The results were remarkable.

In the first experiment the volunteers managed to keep their hands in the water for an average of 69 seconds. The women in the group managed to keep their hands in the ice water for an average of a mere 34 seconds.

But in the second experiment, when using their imaginations to help them forget their pain, the volunteers did much better. The men managed an average of 117 seconds while the women managed an average of 176 seconds!

This experiment has been repeated on many occasions and every time the results are the same: if the volunteers taking part can convince themselves that they are somewhere else then they will be able to cope with far more pain.

In one almost identical experiment volunteers sitting with their hands in ice cold water were told to close their eyes and to imagine that they were sitting in the middle of a boiling hot desert and that the ice water was simply welcomingly cool and delightfully refreshing. The volunteers coped with the pain far, far better than they had been able to when they were simply sitting with their hands in ice cold water.

All these experiments show quite clearly that you can use your imagination to help you control pain. Your imagination can produce problems and create pain (or at the very least make it worse) but it can also solve problems and eradicate pain.

You can use your imagination to help control your pain in a number of quite different ways.

First, you can use your imagination to create pleasant and relaxing scenes that help to calm and soothe you.

Second, you can use your imagination in a much more aggressive way. In one experiment patients were asked to concentrate on the parts of their bodies where their pains were most intense. They were then asked to visualise the shape of their pain and to imagine that it had a vivid red line all around it. The patients were then asked to watch their pain slowly getting smaller and smaller. The researchers found that when patients could imagine their pain area getting smaller they also benefited as the intensity of the pain diminished.

By regarding your pain as an enemy and by developing a wide range of imaginative combative skills you can take an active part in controlling it. Here are some techniques that have been shown to work.

1. Imagine that you have left your body and that you are watching yourself from the other side of the room. Imagine that as you watch a nurse approaches and soothes your body. Imagine that you are surrounded by tender, loving, compassionate, people and that they are all helping to ease your pain. Only return to your body when you see that the pain has been banished from it.

2. Imagine that you can see the pain in your body as a small, invading army of dirty brown cells. The clearer you can see the 'evil' cells the more effective this technique will be. Imagine that every pain sensation in your body is produced by one of these cells. Now, imagine that your body's own fighting forces, your

white cells, are regrouping to attack the invaders. Imagine that your white cells have been quietly building up their forces for several hours and that they are ready to tackle the pain producers. Next, imagine that your white cells are fighting and destroying the dirty, brown invading cells. Imagine that the corpses of the brown cells are littering your tissues. Your white cells, your personal fighting force, are winning their battle.

3. Imagine that your pain is being transmitted around your body via a series of thin wires. Try to see wires connecting your brain to every single part of your body that hurts. Now, imagine that deep inside your body there is a small fighting force of miniature doctors. Each mini doctor is equipped with a strong pair of wire cutters. One by one your tiny army of doctors cut your pain transmitting wires. As each wire is cut you realise that your pain is being reduced.

Laughter – (possibly) the best medicine

It may be an exaggeration to describe laughter as the best medicine. But it is no exaggeration to describe it as one of the best ways to tackle and defeat pain.

Scientists still don't know exactly how laughter defeats pain. But there are several theories. Some argue that laughter reduces the amount of inflammatory change in the human body. Others say that laughter helps by improving respiration, by lowering blood pressure and by increasing the supply of internally produced hormones. It may be that laughter works by diverting attention away from pain.

Whatever the truth may be about how it works there is little doubt that laughter – and even smiling – is an effective pain control therapy. And it has several advantages over other pain remedies: most notably it doesn't cost anything and there aren't any side effects.

Conquering pain through laughter doesn't just mean watching funny films and reading funny books (though both those will help).

You will find that you will benefit enormously if you can surround yourself with people who are generally happy and cheerful rather than sad and miserable.

If you spend all your time with people who are always gloomy and pessimistic then you will inevitably begin to adopt their gloominess. Unhappiness is contagious.

And try not to take yourself – or everything in your life – too seriously. Of course, there will be some things in your life that you will want to take seriously. But that doesn't mean that you have to be serious all the time. It is good occasionally to watch a movie that has a message or to read a book that informs and educates. But it is also good to watch a movie that makes you laugh and to read a book that simply entertains.

And remember that it isn't always the expensive things in life which provide the most pleasure. When did you last read a children's comic?

If you are a naturally pessimistic individual try to suppress your pessimism and to replace it with at least a little optimism. Try to start each day in as cheerful and optimistic a frame of mind as you can. If you get up in the morning thinking of how your pain is going to restrict your life, and how your backache is going to spoil everything you do then it won't take much else to turn a potentially bad day into a terrible day. If you go through the day growling and scowling then everyone you meet will be depressed by your mood and will respond accordingly. By evening you will probably be in a deep, dark depression. Your pessimism will have rebounded and your susceptibility to pain will have probably increased.

If you truly find it impossible to be optimistic, or you find it difficult to smile or to laugh, talk to your doctor and tell him how you feel. Depression and pain often go together in a vicious and debilitating circle. Pain produces depression and depression makes pain worse. It can be difficult to break the cycle but your doctor may be able to help you.

Measure your pain

It is impossible to measure pain objectively. There are so many different factors involved that it is impossible for you to compare the pain you get in your back with the pain your neighbour gets in her womb.

But you can measure variations in a particular pain. You can tell whether or not a specific pain is getting better or worse.

And by doing this you can tell whether or not a pain relieving technique that you are using is working.

Look through the list of words which follow and pick out the four which you think describe your pain most accurately:

sore	(1)
dull	(1)
tender	(1)
annoying	(1)
troublesome	(1)
uncomfortable	(1)
tiring	(2)
hurting	(2)
heavy	(2)
distressing	(2)
miserable	(2)
sickening	(2)
exhausting	(3)
frightful	(3)
wretched	(3)
intense	(3)
horrible	(3)
punishing	(3)
terrifying	(4)
vicious	(4)
killing	(4)
unbearable	(4)
excruciating	(4)
intolerable	(4)

Add up the numbers that follow each of the four words you have chosen. The total is your pain score. Next time you want to measure your pain look through the list again and repeat the procedure, comparing your total score with previous total scores.

Periodontal disease (gum disease)

Periodontal disease (inflammation and infection of the periodontium: the tissues that surround and support your teeth) affects a staggering 90 per cent of the population and is a major cause of tooth loss in adults. It is responsible for more tooth loss than tooth decay and because periodontal disease is usually painless, you may not even know that you have it.

The main cause of periodontal disease is an accumulation of bacterial plaque (a clear sticky film that constantly forms on the teeth) which has deposited below the gum line. Periodontal disease can affect one tooth or many teeth. In the early stages of the disease, the bacterial plaque infects and inflames the gums; this is known as gingivitis. If left untreated, gingivitis can lead to periodontitis. With time, the inflamed margin of the gum starts to recede, forming pockets of empty space between the teeth and gums. These pockets quickly fill up with plaque and become infected causing further recession and destruction of gum tissue. Eventually, the alveolar bone that anchors the teeth becomes infected and that is destroyed too, causing the teeth to loosen so much that, even if they are healthy, they may start to fall out.

There is evidence to suggest that periodontal disease may increase your risk of developing heart disease and respiratory problems. It may also increase your risk of having a stroke.

Periodontal disease can be prevented with regular dental check-ups and good oral hygiene. And the disease can be halted or even reversed.

Symptoms of periodontal disease may include:

1. Red, swollen or tender gums.
2. Gums that bleed easily when you brush your teeth.
3. Receding gums (where the gums detach themselves away from the teeth, giving the teeth a longer appearance).
4. Teeth that feel loose.
5. Pus between the teeth and gums.
6. Aching teeth and gums, especially when eating hot, cold or sweet foods.
7. Spaces developing between the teeth.
8. An unpleasant taste in the mouth.
9. Persistent bad breath.
10. A change in your 'bite' (your bite feels different when you put your teeth together).

If you experience any of the above symptoms, then you should make an appointment to see your dentist as soon as possible. Remember, if caught early enough, periodontal disease can be successfully treated.

Diagnosis

If you suspect that you have periodontal disease, then your dentist will almost certainly want to give you a thorough examination of your teeth and gums. This may involve: checking your gums for any signs of inflammation or recession, examining your teeth to see if any are loose, looking at your overall bite to assess how your teeth fit together and using a small measuring device to determine the depth of the spaces between your teeth and gums. Your dentist may want to take X-rays to find out whether any damage has been done to the bone that anchors your teeth.

Treatment

A majority of patients with periodontal disease are usually referred to a dental hygienist for scaling. Scaling involves gently scraping off the plaque and tartar from the surface of the teeth and from just underneath the gum line.

Depending on how advanced the disease is, regular scaling by a dental hygienist and good oral hygiene practised at home, should help to stop the disease from progressing. If caught early enough, periodontal disease can be reversed. The commonest reason for continued activity of periodontal disease is a lack of good oral hygiene.

If your periodontal disease is advanced, then your dentist may recommend surgery to save your teeth.

Prevention and self-help

1. Before cleaning or flossing your teeth, rinse your mouth out with water because this helps to remove any food particles which may become embedded into your gums during the brushing or flossing process. (It is, incidentally, worth being aware that there is as yet no evidence that flossing is of any value. Most dentists say it is useful. But, perhaps surprisingly, we haven't been able

to find any clinical evidence *proving* that it is useful.)

2. Because periodontal disease is an infection, you need to give your immune system a boost. The best way to do this is by making sure that you cut out as much stress as possible from your life and that you eat a healthy diet which includes lots of fresh fruit and vegetables. Vitamin C helps promote healthy gums, so make sure you eat plenty of foods that are rich in this vitamin.

3. Some prescribed drugs can affect the health of your teeth and gums. If you are taking medication and you are worried about the side effects then have a word with your doctor. Do not stop taking any prescribed drug without consulting your doctor first.

4. If you have diabetes, you should be extra vigilant with your oral care because diabetics are more susceptible to developing periodontal disease.

5. If one or both of your parents had periodontal disease, then your chances of getting the disease are slightly increased.

6. Bacterial plaque entering below the gum line is responsible for periodontal disease. So in order to prevent or to treat periodontal disease, you must make sure that you brush your teeth regularly, taking particular care to gently brush your teeth near the gum line.

7. Visit your dentist for regular check-ups. Not only does your dentist look for cavities but he or she checks to see whether your gums are healthy too. You should also make an appointment to see a dental hygienist four times a year for a thorough scale and polish.

8. Try to avoid using a hard-bristle toothbrush and opt for a soft or a medium-bristle toothbrush instead. A hard-bristle toothbrush can easily damage the gums, making them more susceptible to infection. Research has shown that an electric toothbrush with a rotating head is very effective at getting rid of plaque.

9. After cleaning your teeth, you should gently brush the top of your tongue because the surface of your tongue usually harbours lots of bacteria. By doing this, you are reducing the amount of bacteria in your mouth and reducing your chances of getting periodontal disease.

10. If you have periodontal disease then you could try using a mouthwash to help combat the infection. However, do ask your dentist whether using a mouthwash is suitable for you.

11. Don't be shy about asking your dentist to show you how to floss your teeth properly because if you use dental floss incorrectly, you could infect your gums or make an existing infection worse. And remember, before flossing your teeth, make sure that all food particles are removed otherwise, flossing could drive food into your gums, causing infection.

12. Smokers are much more likely to develop periodontal disease than non-smokers.

13. Cut down on foods and drinks that have a high sugar content, as the bacterial plaque which is responsible for periodontal disease, thrives on sugar.

14. Change your toothbrush regularly. Some dentists recommend that you change your toothbrush every three to four months. You cannot expect to clean your teeth efficiently if the bristles on your toothbrush are worn or bent.

Polymyalgia rheumatica

Polymyalgia rheumatica, a relatively uncommon disorder, can affect both men and women but affects two or three times as many women as men. It doesn't usually affect anyone under the age of 50. The joints usually affected are the hips, shoulders and neck. The cause of the pain and discomfort associated with polymyalgia rheumatica is unknown but the main symptoms of polymyalgia rheumatica are tenderness and discomfort. The discomfort is usually at its worst early on in the morning. Many patients have difficulty in getting out of bed. Patients often also complain of tiredness, depression, weakness, weight loss and fever. The symptoms may develop gradually or suddenly.

Steroids usually provide dramatic relief. Indeed, the results are so spectacular that giving steroids is sometimes regarded as a diagnostic test for this disease.

Prostate disease:
(prostate enlargement and prostate cancer)

Prostate cancer is almost certainly the commonest type of cancer to affect men – and it is now believed to affect one in three men over the age of 50.

Half of all men who die (of anything) also have cancer of the prostate (though most of them don't know). Half of all men who die in their 60s already have prostate cancer developing. And even 40 per cent of men in their 50s who die from something else have prostate cancer that they probably didn't know about.

Twenty facts about the prostate gland

1. The prostate gland is one of the male reproductive organs. It contains 20-30 small ducts which open into the urethra.
2. Much of the bulk of semen comes from the prostate gland.
3. The prostate gland is three sided and roughly pyramidal in shape. Its base lies against the under surface of the bladder.
4. The first part of the urethra runs through the prostate gland.
5. The prostate gland contains fibrous tissue and smooth muscle and feels firm to the touch.
6. Prostate gland secretions are alkaline and buffer the ejaculate against the acidity of vaginal secretions.
7. Benign (non cancerous) enlargement of the prostate gland is very common in men over the age of 50. It is the pressing of the enlarged prostate against the urethra which is likely to cause urinary tract symptoms (such as having to pass urine more often).
8. A healthy prostate is roughly the size of a walnut. But there is considerable variation in size.
9. The prostate isn't clearly divided into lobes but doctors refer to 'lobes' as a way of defining the part of the prostate to which they are referring. There are, allegedly, an anterior lobe, a posterior lobe, two lateral lobes and a median lobe.
10. If the prostate gland becomes infected it usually becomes enlarged and tender.
11. From the age of nine onwards the prostate gland grows in response to increasing circulating levels of testosterone.

12. The prostate gland reaches adult size when its owner is in his late teens.

13. When the prostate gland becomes cancerous it usually feels very hard and often irregular.

14. The prostate gland may enlarge a good deal before its owner starts to notice any symptoms.

15. When an enlarged prostate gland presses on the urethra the urethra becomes narrower and the stream of urine becomes weaker. It then takes greater pressure to force urine out.

16. When the prostate gland is pressing on the urethra, and preventing urine from flowing out of the bladder, the bladder never really empties properly. At this point the owner of the bladder has to visit the lavatory frequently to pass small amounts of urine.

17. If the urethra becomes completely blocked the owner of the enlarged prostate will want to pass urine but will be unable to do so. Catheterisation may be necessary.

18. One possible cause of prostate enlargement in old age seems to be a less active sex life with few or no ejaculations.

19. The risk of obstruction seems to increase among men who smoke or drink excessively.

20. Some drugs (e.g. a variety of drugs obtainable on prescription) also increase the risk of obstruction. Men who have prostate enlargement and who are taking drugs of any kind (whether obtained on prescription or not) should ask their doctor if there could be a link between the two.

Prostate cancer and diet

There is a considerable amount of research available proving the existence of links between specific types of food and prostate cancer.

Way back in 1982 the National Research Council in the United States of America published a technical report entitled 'Diet, Nutrition and Cancer' which showed that diet was probably the single most important factor in the development of cancer, and that there was evidence linking cancers of the breast, colon and prostate to particular foods or types of food. But the evidence linking cancer and food goes back many years before 1982.

For example, since the mid 1970s there has been strong evidence to show a link between a high fat intake and prostate cancer. The National Academy of Sciences in the USA reported some time ago that an American study had shown a correlation between a high fat intake and a high risk for prostate cancer. Studies in 41 countries have shown a high correlation between mortality from prostate cancer and intake of fats, milk and meats (especially beef).

A ten year Japanese study involving 122,261 men aged 40 or older showed 'an inverse association between daily intake of green and yellow vegetables and mortality from prostate cancer'. (In other words the more green and yellow vegetables you eat the less likely you are to develop prostate cancer – and vice versa.) Another study showed that vegetarian men were less likely to develop prostate cancer.

In 1993 a study of 47,855 men, included in the *Medical Research Modernization Committee Report* revealed that men who had high fat diets had a relative risk of 1.79 for advanced prostate cancer compared to those on low fat diets. (Meaning that men eating a high fat diet are almost twice as likely to develop prostate cancer as are men on a low fat diet.) The investigators who produced this study found that most animal fats were associated with advanced prostate cancer, but fats from vegetables, dairy products (except butter) and fish were not.

In a paper entitled 'A Case-Control Study of Prostatic Cancer With Reference to Dietary Habits' which was published in the journal *The Prostate* in 1988, a team of authors from the Kyoto University, Kyoto University Hospital and Nagoya City University, all in Japan, and Erasmus University Rotterdam in The Netherlands, reported that in 1950 the incidence of prostatic cancer in Japan had been about 0.4 per 100,000 male members of the population but by 1963 it had increased to 2.0 per 100,000 and by 1975 it had grown to 2.5 per 100,000. Observers had suggested that this increase might be linked to the Westernization of Japanese eating habits. (During recent years the consumption of fat, animal protein, eggs, dairy products and oil have all increased considerably in Japan.) And so these authors studied sufferers from prostatic cancer and patients suffering from benign prostatic hypertrophy (non cancerous prostate enlargement) in order to identify the risk factors for prostatic cancer. They found that a 'low daily intake of beta-carotene...were significantly correlated with prostatic cancer development.' (Carrots and other orange and yellow-orange fruits and vegetables, and dark green, leafy vegetables are excellent sources of beta carotene.)

In an article entitled 'Cohort Study of Diet, Lifestyle and Prostate Cancer in Adventist Men', which was published in the journal *Cancer* in 1989, authors from the Department of Preventive Medicine, Lorna Linda University School of Medicine, Lorna Linda, California, USA reported how they had evaluated the dietary and lifestyle characteristics of approximately 14,000 Seventh-Day Adventist men.

The men completed a detailed lifestyle questionnaire in 1976, and were monitored for cancer incidence until the end of 1982. The authors concluded that 'increasing consumption of beans, lentils and peas, tomatoes, raisins, dates and other dried fruit were all associated with significantly decreased prostate cancer risk.'

In an article entitled 'A Prospective Study of Dietary Fat and Risk of Prostate Cancer', which was published in the *Journal of the National Cancer Institute* in 1993, authors from the Harvard Medical School and Brigham and Women's Hospital, Boston, Mass, USA, Harvard School of Public Health, Boston, USA and Mayo Medical School, Rochester, Minn., USA pointed out that 'the strong correlation between national consumption of fat and national rate of mortality from prostate cancer has raised the hypothesis that dietary fat increases the risk of this malignancy.'

By studying information relating to 51,529 American men between the ages of 40 and 75, and sending follow-up questionnaires to the men in 1988 and 1990, the authors examined the relationship of fat consumption to the incidence of advanced prostate cancer and to the total incidence of prostate cancer and found that 'total fat consumption was directly related to risk of advanced prostate cancer' and that 'this association was due primarily to animal fat ...but not vegetable fat. Red meat represented the food group with the strongest positive association with advanced cancer.'

The authors concluded that: 'The results support the hypothesis that animal fat, especially fat from red meat, is associated with an elevated risk of advanced prostate cancer.' They also noted that: 'These findings support recommendations to lower intake of meat to reduce the risk of prostate cancer.'

In an article entitled 'Risk of death from cancer and ischaemic heart disease in meat and non-meat eaters' published in the *British*

192

Medical Journal in 1994, authors from the London School of Hygiene and Tropical Medicine in the UK, the University of Otago, Dunedin, New Zealand and the University of Oxford, UK, investigated the health consequences of a vegetarian diet by examining the 12 year mortality of vegetarians and meat eaters.

The researchers reported that their results confirmed 'the findings of previous studies that have shown a reduction in all cause, cancer and cardiovascular mortality among people who do not eat meat.'

The researchers showed a 'roughly 40 per cent reduction in mortality from cancer in vegetarians and fish eaters compared with meat eaters' and also added that 'the fact that total mortality was about 20 per cent lower in the non-meat eating group than the meat eaters is perhaps of greatest clinical importance.'

In 1988, in *The American Journal of Clinical Nutrition*, authors from the Division of Cancer Prevention and Control, National Cancer Institute, National Institutes of Health, Bethesda, MD, USA reported that it had been estimated that 930,000 Americans would develop cancer in a single calendar year and that 472,000 individuals would subsequently die of their cancer.

It was reported that the National Cancer Institute (the NCI), which aims to reduce cancer incidence, morbidity and mortality, 'believes that the potential for dietary changes to reduce the risk of cancer is considerable and that the existing scientific data provide evidence that is sufficiently consistent to warrant prudent interim dietary guidelines that will promote good health and reduce the risk of some types of cancer.'

The NCI suggested reducing fat intake, increasing fibre intake, including a variety of fruits and vegetables in the daily diet, avoiding obesity, consuming alcoholic beverages in moderation if at all and minimising the consumption of salt-cured, salt-pickled and smoked foods.

The report stated that the NCI believed that if these guidelines were followed there would be a 50 per cent reduction in cancer of the colon and rectum, a 25 per cent reduction in breast cancer and a 15 per cent reduction in cancers of the prostate, endometrium and gallbladder.

Although the evidence showing that fat causes cancer is totally convincing (a United States Surgeon General has advised American citizens that: 'a comparison of populations indicates that death rates for cancers of the breast, colon and prostate are directly proportional to estimated dietary fat intakes') there is still a considerable amount of doubt about the mechanism whereby fat causes cancer.

One theory is that carcinogenic chemicals simply dissolve and accumulate in fatty tissues. If this is the case then people who eat animal fats will suffer twice for the chances are high that the fat they are eating already contains dissolved carcinogens.

According to the journal *Australasian Health and Healing* more than 177 organochlorines (synthetic chemicals created when chlorine gas is bonded to carbon-rich organic matter) have been found in the tissues of the general population of the United States and Canada. Organochlorines can cause infertility, birth defects, miscarriages, immune system suppression, metabolic dysfunction, behavioural disorders, hormonal abnormalities and cancer.

These chlorine based compounds can cause cancer in various ways. Some cause cancer directly. Others produce cancers by interfering with or mimicking human hormones. A third group suppress the immune system and then enhance the carcinogenic effect of other chemicals. These chemicals seem to strike first at the reproductive system – which is probably why a heavy fat consumption increases the risk of developing cancers of the breast, prostate, and uterus.

Another possibility is that fat may encourage the development of cancer by affecting the activity of sex hormones. Vegetarian and low fat diets reduce the levels of circulating female sex hormones such as oestradiol.

Despite the lack of clear evidence about exactly how fat causes cancer, the final message is quite clear – to reduce your cancer risk you should make a real effort to cut back your fat intake – and that includes cutting out vegetable fats too.

You should not make the mistake of assuming that you can avoid or cut down your fat intake noticeably by living on a diet of chicken and fish. Although it is widely believed that both fish and chicken are low in fat the truth is that even skinless white meat from a chicken is 23 per cent fat while most fish contain between 20 to 30 per cent fat and some are much higher – mackerel, for example, contains over 50 per cent fat.

The only truly low fat diet is a diet which is mainly composed of vegetables, fruits, and whole grain cereals. Rice contains only about one per cent fat and no plant foods contain any cholesterol (although frying potatoes and turning them into chips can add a lot of fat).

If you ignore this message then you are making a clear and conscious choice to accept a high cancer risk as the price for your high fat diet.

Incidentally, there is also evidence showing that men who have developed prostate cancer will be more likely to recover if they follow a low fat diet. Men in Hong Kong (where the usual diet is rich in rice and vegetables) are half as likely to have cancerous cells in their prostate glands as are men in, for example, Sweden (where diets are high in dairy products and meat). If cancer strikes men in these two areas the men in Hong Kong are eight times more likely to survive than the men in Sweden. Eight times more likely to survive! It is a disgrace that the medical profession still fails to share this vital information with prostate cancer patients.

In 1999, in Quebec City, researchers followed 384 men with prostate cancer over a five year period. The researchers found that the men who ate most saturated fat (the kind most likely to be found in meat and dairy products) had three times the risk of dying from their cancer, compared to the men who followed a low intake of saturated fat.

In 2002, Dr Dean Ornish presented early work showing that a low fat, vegan diet (together with regular exercise and stress management) has a healing effect on men with prostate cancer.

Other research has also shown that men who have advanced prostate cancer can also benefit from the right sort of diet. One study showed that prostate cancer sufferers who followed a macrobiotic diet (consisting mainly of whole grains, vegetables and legumes and avoiding dairy products and most meats) had an average survival of 228 months, compared to 72 months for a matched group of men who followed their 'normal' diet.

Why don't more men with prostate cancer change their diets? Partly because doctors don't know these things. A publication entitled *Prostate Cancer Risk Management Programme* published in the UK jointly by the NHS and Cancer Research UK (a large cancer research charity) in 2002 did not even mention diet in its list of treatments for prostate cancer.

Lycopene

Recent research has also shown that tomatoes and strawberries can protect against cancer. A nine year study of 47,000 men showed that those who ate lots of tomato-based foods (including tomato based spaghetti sauce and pizzas containing tomato) were much less likely to develop prostate cancer.

Men who eat four servings a week of tomato-based foods (particularly tomato ketchup, canned tomatoes, tomato soup, tomato based spaghetti sauce and the tomato sauce used in preparing pizza) reduce their risk of developing prostate cancer by 20 per cent while men who eat at least ten servings a week of tomato-based foods are up to 45 per cent less likely to develop prostate cancer. The reason is that tomatoes contain good quantities of lycopene, a powerful antioxidant, which helps provide protection against cancer – particularly prostate cancer. Lycopene may also protect against heart disease and other cancers. It is the heat processing which seems to increase the availability of lycopene in tomatoes. So frying tomatoes should also increase their lycopene availability.

Tomatoes are not the only foods to be rich in lycopene. Grapefruit is packed with vitamins (especially vitamin C) and rich in fibre and will help strengthen the immune system. But it is pink grapefruit which contains the lycopene which helps provide protection against cancer (particularly prostate cancer) and heart disease. Watermelon contains lycopene and melon with orange flesh (such as cantaloupe) is rich in carotene.

The benefit of losing weight

Any man who wants to avoid prostate cancer should do everything he can to make sure that he does not become overweight.

If you are already overweight then make a real effort to diet successfully – and to maintain an acceptable weight for your height. Heart disease, strokes, diabetes, gallstones and many types of cancer (including prostate cancer) are now all known to be made more likely by excess weight. One large study showed that the lowest overall cancer mortality was seen in men whose body weights were between ten per cent below and 20 per cent above the average for their age and height. Men who are more than 40 per cent overweight are 33 per cent more likely to die of cancer (with cancer of the colon, rectum and prostate the particular cancers they risk developing).

If you weigh just 22 pounds more than you did when you were 18 years old then you are probably at risk.

Other factors associated with the development of prostate cancer

1. Prostate cancer can be hereditary and so if there is a history of this disease in the family it is particularly important to eat wisely. If an individual's father or brother have prostate cancer then his chances of developing the disease are doubled. If a man has two close relatives with prostate cancer then he has four times the chance of getting the disease. The risk for any man who has three or more relatives with prostate cancer is increased by seven to ten times.
2. There is also a chance that men who work with or are exposed to radioactive substances may be at increased risk of developing prostate cancer.
3. A man who has suffered from a sexually transmitted disease may be at greater risk of developing prostate cancer.
4. Some doctors now warn that men who have a vasectomy may have a greater risk of developing prostate cancer.
5. Men who spend lots of time in strong sunlight seem to have a reduced risk of prostate cancer (but need to watch out for skin cancer).

Diagnosis

Prostate cancer can develop for several years without any symptoms developing. But the early signs may be similar to the early signs of ordinary prostate enlargement: discomfort or pain on passing urine or having to get up at night to pass urine.

A decade or so ago the only way to test for prostate cancer was for a doctor to put a finger into a man's anus and feel the prostate with a finger. This test was and is known as a Digital Rectal Examination (DRE). The examining doctor would be worried if the prostate felt large, uneven or unusually hard.

These days doctors sometimes regard DRE as primitive, old-fashioned, out-dated and rather hit and miss – and unlikely to pick up anything other than a well-developed cancer that may be too late for treatment.

The modern way of checking for prostate cancer is to perform a Prostatic Specific Antigen (PSA) blood test. This test measures the amount of a substance produced both by normal prostate tissue and by cancerous tissue. When the prostate is healthy the level is low – but when there is cancer within the prostate the level rises. Ultrasound imaging can be done to check the shape and size of any prostate cancer tumour.

There is still much doubt about whether or not screening for prostate cancer is worthwhile. Those in favour claim that regular PSA tests can pick up the disease early – when it is easier to treat. Those against claim that the test isn't all that reliable (it is possible for the PSA result to be high and there to be no cancer present) and that the test is just another example of unnecessary 'high tech' medicine which may result in the over-treatment of men who may have prostate cancer but for whom treatment may be neither necessary or appropriate. Approximately two thirds of men undergoing biopsy because of an elevated PSA are not found to have prostate cancer at all. Whether the anxiety, and additional hazards of being further investigated make PSA testing worthwhile is debatable. (It is also possible that a man might have a negative PSA test and yet have prostate cancer. False reassurance can be a major killer since a negative PSA test can encourage both a patient and his doctors to ignore other symptoms.) One of the test's most enthusiastic, and eminent, medical supporters claims that: 'I believe that a decision to be screened would increase my chance of being diagnosed ... and the diagnosis would come five to eight years earlier.' But, and it's a big 'but', he admits that: 'There is no good evidence that the greater likelihood of knowing, and knowing sooner, would reduce my chances of a prostate cancer death.'

PSA tests are now regularly performed on American men – a fact which probably explains why the incidence of the disease is increasing so rapidly in the USA – but there is still some doubt about whether having annual PSA tests makes any difference to life expectancy. (In just the same way that there is real doubt about the value of breast and cervical screening programmes).

In the UK, PSA testing is not routinely offered on the grounds that: 'screening would undoubtedly lead to some men (with indolent disease) suffering from impotence, incontinence and even death, who would not have done so had screening not been introduced.' In other words, even the Government and medical establishment (normally enthusiastic supporters of medical screening programmes) regard PSA testing as likely to do more harm than good. 'To date,' says the British Government, 'there is no good evidence to say whether or not screening healthy asymptomatic men would reduce mortality from prostate cancer.'

Treatment

There is a considerable amount of controversy about whether or not it is sensible to treat prostate cancer. (And if treatment is unnecessary then, clearly, trying to diagnose the disease is also a waste of time and effort). Only one in three men diagnosed as having clinical prostate cancer (as opposed to prostate cancer identified only with the aid of a blood test) die of the disease.

Surgery is the most popular form of treatment for prostate cancer and radical prostatectomy (the complete removal of the prostate gland) is now probably the surgical money spinner that radical mastectomy (the complete removal of breast tissue) in patients with breast cancer was a few years ago.

But just because it is popular that doesn't mean that surgery is the best option. Remember that the urologists who recommend prostate surgery also have most to gain – most of them remove prostates for a living. (If you visit a Ford garage the salesman will probably try to sell you a Ford motor car. He's unlikely to suggest that you try a BMW.)

Surgeons who advocate radical surgery point to survival figures which seem to suggest that patients who have a prostate removal operation for prostate cancer do live longer. But there is some opposition to this argument. Surgeons tend to operate only on youngish patients who have relatively small and undeveloped cancers – and these are the very patients who will live longest anyway.

What surgeons tend to underestimate are the side effects of surgery. Radical prostatectomy is pretty serious surgery and there is a significant mortality rate (the operation alone kills around one in 50 men aged 70 or more). It can take quite a while to recover from the operation and there is also a growing amount of evidence to show that complications and side effects are no where near as uncommon as they were once thought to be.

The two most significant after effects are impotence and incontinence. Roughly half of the patients who have radical prostatectomies become incontinent and between eight and nine out of every ten experience impotence. These are serious, life-destroying side effects.

In general, although surgery is usually regarded as the 'gold standard' treatment for prostate cancer, and although it may well occasionally be vital, life-saving and the 'best' solution, we haven't seen any convincing evidence suggesting that every man diagnosed as having prostate cancer should automatically have a radical prostatectomy. Death, impotence and incontinence are, after all, pretty severe side effects. Most doctors regard surgery as the first and main option but we haven't been able to find any analytical evidence to support this point of view.

If your prostate cancer has only just started to develop, and has not spread outside the prostate, then other forms of treatment – less destructive and less likely to produce horrendous side effects – may be more comfortable and just as effective.

If the prostate cancer has spread outside the prostate – and has affected other organs elsewhere in the body – then it is probably too late for surgery.

Apart from prostatectomy the other type of surgery that used to be commonly performed for prostate cancer was orchidectomy (removal of both testicles). This operation is not usually necessary now that hormone treatments can be used to reduce blood testosterone levels.

In a few years time radical prostatectomy will probably be regarded as usually unnecessary and barbaric – in much the same way that radical mastectomy is today regarded as usually unnecessary and barbaric.

Radiation therapy for prostate cancer usually gets a bad press. Surgeons will sometimes claim that patients who are treated with radiation have poor survival rates. But the patients who end up being treated with radiation are often the older patients or patients with more advanced cancers who are considered unsuitable for surgery. Under these conditions it is not surprising that patients who have radiation therapy may seem to have relatively poor survival rates.

One type of radiation therapy is particularly interesting. Called brachytherapy this form of treatment involves the use of radioactive seeds. The technique was first developed decades ago and then abandoned because of poor results but, by using ultrasound, modern doctors can place the seeds more accurately. The seeds emit radiation for six to nine months. External radiation is also sometimes used to make sure that the cancer is thoroughly attacked. Research has shown that patients who are treated with a combination of external radiation and radioactive seeds have much the same success rate as patients who undergo surgery. The big advantage of this new and very specific type of radiation treatment is that the side effects are less crippling and there is no dangerous, weakening operation to undergo.

Cryosurgery involves freezing the tumour. Unfortunately, the side effects with this type of treatment seem to be similar to those associated with surgery.

Drug therapy is used as a treatment method because prostate cancer seems to depend on testosterone – the male hormone. Testosterone suppressant drugs are sometimes used together with both surgery and radiation – and they seem to improve the results because they make the tumour shrink. The side effects may be uncomfortable and even hazardous.

Conclusion

Having prostate cancer doesn't necessarily always mean that you should treat it. Most prostate cancers are slow growing. At least four out of every five men with the disease live for another ten years. There are a number of doctors (and patients) who prefer to wait and see what happens. This passive approach seems particularly popular when the patient is over 70 years old. It is sometimes argued that most of the men over 70 who develop prostate cancer will die of something else and although we're not sure that this is true it is not an argument which is easy to dismiss.

The difficulty in deciding what to do with a patient who has prostate cancer is enhanced by the fact that not enough research has been done to compare different treatment methods or, indeed, to compare the treatment versus a passive 'wait and see' approach.

If treatment methods were without risk this wouldn't matter. But all treatments carry risks and so treating men unnecessarily can be unnecessarily dangerous. If surgery was performed on all the men in Britain who are likely to have prostate cancer at the moment then roughly 2,000 men would die of the surgery alone – approximately the same number of men as would be killed by the cancer.

We desperately need more research to compare surgery with radiation and to compare both with the 'wait and see' approach. But men don't push hard enough for money to be spent on diseases which affect them and the amount of research done into prostate cancer is minute compared to the amount done into breast cancer or AIDS. Medline, the computerised database of medical research recently contained details of 5,224 studies into prostate cancer, 34,216 studies into breast cancer and 85,536 studies into AIDS.

Benign (non-cancerous) prostate enlargement

One specialist in urology, a member of both the American Urology Association and the American College of Surgeons, recently admitted that when he was operating on men with prostate problems he knew that most of them would never have sex again.

American and British doctors commonly advocate surgery or powerful prescription drugs at the very first sign of prostate hypertrophy. But surgery on the prostate gland is frequently a pretty crude business. Readers have reported that after operations on their prostate glands their sex lives have gone. 'I have no erections and produce no semen,' wrote one unhappy man who had an operation on his prostate gland. 'Is this normal?'

You will probably not be surprised to hear that the drugs which are prescribed don't always work and may (gosh, sit down, you're going to find this difficult to believe) produce unpleasant side effects.

The unbridled and exclusive enthusiasm of so many doctors for drugs and surgery when confronted by patients with prostate problems is yet another twenty-first century health scandal.

But what makes the scandal worse is that patients in many other countries (particularly the Far East and much of mainland Europe) are usually treated effectively with herb products which have been proved to work in numerous published studies.

Orthodox, drug company trained doctors often dismiss alternative remedies as being unacceptable because they haven't been properly tested. But the herbal remedies for prostate enlargement have been tested and they do work.

There are over 30 plant derived compounds available in Europe as treatments for benign prostatic hypertrophy.

There really isn't any excuse (other than a pathetic reluctance to risk offending the medical establishment and the pharmaceutical industry) for doctors to still turn to prescription drugs and surgery as 'first choice therapy' when faced with men with hypertrophied prostate glands.

We can, in a way, understand surgeons not wanting to recommend alternatives to surgery. Many pay the payments on their houses and BMWs with the fees they receive for operating. It is immoral and dishonest but it is at least comprehensible.

What we cannot understand is the fact that so many doctors remain reluctant to recommend natural, herbal products – which have been proved to be both safe and effective – while they are at the same time enthusiastic about drug company products for which the most accurate adjective is probably 'expensive'.

How to reduce an enlarged prostate by natural methods

If you have a benignly enlarged prostate (or you want to avoid or delay developing an enlarged prostate gland) there are several products which seem to be worth trying. Keeping your prostate in good condition is very much about knowing what to eat and what to avoid.

Rye pollen extracts and the herb saw palmetto have both been used to help reduce the size of the prostate gland. There is evidence that both help to reduce prostate size and reduce the symptoms created by benign prostate enlargement. Regular intake of saw palmetto prevents or reduces the conversion of testosterone to dihydrotestosterone – a substance which can stimulate prostate cells to multiply at a faster rate than normal.

Zinc is also essential for a healthy prostate gland. A healthy prostate needs zinc because it is required for producing male hormones. And zinc helps to protect the prostate from the toxic effects of the metal cadmium (which can, even in quite small quantities, stimulate the prostate to enlarge). Zinc is found in whole grain cereals, wholemeal bread, soya beans and sunflower seeds.

Raynaud's disease

Raynaud's disease is a disorder of the circulatory system causing intermittent spasms of the small blood vessels that supply the fingers and toes (although this condition mainly affects the fingers).

Contractions of the smaller blood vessels means that the fingers, and occasionally the toes, receives an inadequate supply of blood. This may cause the affected digits to become pale, red or bluish in colour. Tingling or numbness may also occur. These symptoms are very common in those suffering from Raynaud's disease.

Below you will find a list of the signs and symptoms you should look out for; the factors which can increase your risk of getting the disease and some self-prevention measures you can follow.

Signs and symptoms may include:

1. Paleness of the fingers, especially when exposed to cold temperatures. Fingers turn pale because of lack of blood, but once the blood flow slowly returns to normal, the digits turn bluish in colour and then red.
2. Numbness, tingling or burning may be felt in the affected fingers or toes.
3. Ulcers on the fingertips and chronic infections around the nails can sometimes happen when the disease is in its advanced stages. However, these symptoms usually take years to develop and much can be done by then to help prevent them.
4. Painful ulceration and gangrene may occur as a result of permanent reduction of blood flow due to the gradual thickening of the arteries. It is very rare for this to happen.

The risk of Raynaud's disease increases with:

1. Exposure to cold temperatures.
2. Stress.
3. Smoking (the disease is uncommon amongst non-smokers).

Self-help

1. If you smoke, then give it up. Smoking impairs blood circulation to the extremities.
2. Avoid caffeine as this can constrict the blood vessels. Caffeine can be found in coffee, tea, cola drinks, etc.
3. You should try and cut down on saturated fats which can be found in dairy produce, hard margarines and fatty meats.
4. Avoid stress. Learn how to relax and spend more time doing things you enjoy.
5. If you have Raynaud's disease, then it is important that you try to keep your hands and feet as warm as possible. Going out of the house without gloves or warm socks on in the cold weather, can bring on an attack. You should also wear gloves when handling cold food or ice from the freezer. Warmth usually relieves all of the symptoms of Raynaud's disease, but don't just warm-up the affected parts; warming-up the entire body is important.

Diagnosis

If you suspect that you have Raynaud's disease then you must go and see your doctor for a proper diagnosis. There is a similar condition called Raynaud's phenomenon which may involve more serious long-term consequences. Raynaud's phenomenon can occur as a complication of other diseases and is a disorder of the circulatory system affecting the fingers and toes. Although the symptoms are the same, Raynaud's phenomenon is different from Raynaud's disease. The symptoms of Raynaud's phenomenon comes on suddenly whereas the symptoms of Raynaud's disease develop gradually over a period of years. Also, Raynaud's disease is a primary disease whereas, Raynaud's phenomenon can occur as a complication of other diseases such as connective-tissue disorders (e.g. scleroderma).

You must see your doctor if you have symptoms of Raynaud's

disease. If you have Raynaud's and your symptoms get worse in spite of treatment, then you must see your doctor straight away. Also, if you have ulcers on your fingers or toes as a result of Raynaud's, and you notice that they are not healing properly, then you should make an urgent medical appointment.

If you have Raynaud's, your doctor may prescribe drugs to help improve your circulation and to help dilate the small arteries. These drugs are known as 'vasodilator drugs'.

In severe cases, an operation may be performed to cut the nerves that control the diameter of the arteries.

Restless legs syndrome
(a.k.a. Ekbom's syndrome)

Restless legs syndrome (otherwise known as Ekbom's syndrome – named after the doctor who first recognised the condition) can deprive those affected of sleep, and bring misery to thousands of sufferers. It is characterised by uncomfortable feelings in the legs which worsen during periods of rest (i.e. sitting or lying down). Sufferers have reported relief from their symptoms once activity has been resumed.

Very little is known about what causes this neurological disorder, but there are many conditions that are associated with it. For example: rheumatoid arthritis, diabetes and kidney failure. A deficiency in iron, vitamin B12 or folic acid can also bring on the condition, and so can certain drugs such as beta-blockers, anti-epileptic medicines, lithium and even some anti-depressants. (Although certain deficiencies can cause restless legs syndrome don't attempt to treat yourself without having seen your doctor first.) In a third of cases, there is a family history of the disease.

Restless legs syndrome (RLS) is a common disorder and can affect anyone at any age but it does tend to be more common in the elderly. This condition varies in severity; some sufferers may experience only mild symptoms whereas other sufferers may find their symptoms incapacitating.

Symptoms may include:

1. Prickling, itching, aching, burning, tingling or crawling sensations which are felt deep inside the legs. These uncomfortable sensations are more predominant in the calves although they can affect the thighs or even the feet. Some sufferers have reported symptoms in their arms and more rarely, in their genital area.
2. Abnormal sensations may be felt in one or both legs or move from one area of the body to another.
3. Involuntary movements of the legs during rest and while at sleep. Involuntary movements can be violent enough to disturb sleep.
4. An overwhelming desire to stretch the limbs to ease symptoms. Sufferers have a tendency to fidget with their legs to try and ease their discomfort and in severe cases, they may find themselves pacing up and down the floor all night long just to gain some kind of relief. Symptoms are more noticeable at night.
5. Insomnia. Sufferers can have trouble getting to sleep because their symptoms can be so troublesome.

Treatment

Depending on the severity of your problem and of the cause, your doctor may suggest medication to help control your symptoms. However, treatment does not come without side-effects. Therefore, you must decide whether the side-effects are less problematic to you than the disease is. If RLS is secondary and the cause is treated then your symptoms should ease dramatically, or disappear altogether.

Self-help

Although restless legs syndrome is a chronic, progressive disease, the severity of the symptoms does fluctuate from time to time, and they have even been known to disappear completely for a short while. Meanwhile, these tips should help:

1. Massage the affected areas with oil or cream that is unlikely to irritate your skin.
2. Cold compresses can bring relief to the affected areas.
3. Try to abstain from cigarettes, alcohol, coffee and other stimulants because these have all been known to exacerbate the condition.

4. Lack of exercise can make your symptoms worse. (You should consult your doctor before taking up any form of exercise).
5. Try to keep your life as stress-free as possible because stress can aggravate the condition.
6. Some sufferers complain that their symptoms are noticeably worse when their feet are hot. If this applies to you, then you could try putting your feet in a bowl of cool water (ankle-depth will do) for half an hour before going to bed. Also, to help keep the feet cool, refrain from wearing socks, tights or slippers for at least a couple of hours before going to bed.

Retinal detachment

Retinal detachment is a separation of the retina (the light-sensitive layer of tissue that lines the interior of the eye) from the tissue beneath it. Retinal detachment can affect all ages and both sexes, but it tends to be more common in men. It is commoner among people with myopia (extreme short-sightedness) and among patients who have had cataract surgery.

Symptoms of retinal detachment may include:
1. Blurred vision.
2. Gradual loss of vision which may be so gradual that it is not noticed for some time.
3. Flashes of light.
4. Floaters (caused by spots of blood being released into the eye).

These symptoms can affect one or both eyes. Sometimes none of these symptoms may be present. The sufferer will eventually know that he or she has a detached retina when what appears to be a 'black curtain' covers his or her field of vision in the affected eye.

Causes of retinal detachment may include:
1. Injury to the eye.
2. Eye surgery – can sometimes cause the retina to detach itself, especially if there were complications.

Risk of retinal detachment may increase with:

1. Age.
2. Vascular disease.
3. Diabetes mellitus.
4. A family history of retinal detachment.
5. A previous retinal detachment.

How to prevent retinal detachment

Have any underlying disease (such as vascular disease or diabetes mellitus) kept under control. Wear a protective eye shield when playing sports which may cause eye injuries. (Eye injuries seem to be particularly common among squash players – possibly because the ball is just the right size to fit into the eye.) See your doctor straight away if you experience any visual disturbances. Treatment for retinal detachment usually involves surgery.

Sinuses (blocked)

Your sinuses are responsible for purifying and moistening the air you breathe before it reaches your lungs. Bacteria that enter, get caught and filtered out by mucus and cilia (which are tiny nasal hairs). If something stops the cilia from doing their job properly, then your sinuses may become blocked. Another cause of sinus blockage is a cold clogging up the opening to the sinuses. Blocked sinuses be painful as well as uncomfortable. The pain is normally felt behind the eyes, nose and around the temples. The flesh around the nose, and the upper part of the cheeks just underneath the eyes, may feel tender to touch.

Self-help

1. Humidify your room

Invest in a humidifier. This will help keep the air moist – something which is good for your sinuses. It will have a more beneficial effect on your sinuses if you put the humidifier in the room you sleep in at night and close the door. If you cannot afford a humidifier, then keeping a bowl of water in each room will help.

2. Turn down the heat

If you can bear it, turn your central-heating down. Central heating is renowned for causing blocked sinuses because it dries out the air.

3. Get some fresh air

Go for a walk in the fresh air to help clear your sinuses – this usually works.

4. The wonders of menthol

To help keep your sinuses in top condition put a small piece of menthol crystal (which can be purchased from your local pharmacy) in a bowl full of hot water. Put your head over the bowl and breathe in the vapour. Blow your nose gently afterwards. Do not use the menthol treatment more than twice a day because this can have a rebound effect and may actually make your sinus problems worse. However, you can breathe in the steam from a bowl of plain hot water as often as you like. The warmth of the water should also help with sinus pain. Do be careful not to burn yourself. Alternatively, take a bath or a shower, close the door and breathe in the steam through your nose

5. Beware of the rebound effect

Refrain from using nasal sprays, drops or other medicaments on sale at the pharmacy as these can also have a rebound effect – creating more problems.

6. Mind how you blow

When blowing your nose, blow one nostril at a time. This helps prevent bacteria from being sent back further into the sinus passages.

7. Drink more water

Drink more fluids. Fluids (particularly water) helps thin the mucus which means that the sinuses are less likely to become blocked.

When to see your doctor

If you have tried all of the above tips and still there is no relief (or your symptoms have lasted more than five days or are exceedingly troublesome) then you should see your doctor. You may have an infection of the sinuses which may need clearing up with antibiotics. You should, of course, seek medical advice straight away if you feel it necessary.

Slipped disc (see also backache)

One of the commonest problems to affect the back occurs when the nucleus pulposus – the soft, squashy part in the middle of the disc – bulges out through the tough, fibrous outer part of the disc and presses on whatever nerve or part of the spinal cord happens to be nearby.

The pain this can cause is often excruciating. If you've ever knocked your elbow – where the nerve runs across the surface of the bone and is easily trapped – you'll know just how painful a nerve injury can be.

A disc prolapse – often but inaccurately called a 'slipped' disc – usually develops gradually as the disc degenerates with age (though the problem can be accelerated by a fall or a sudden, unexpected movement and prolapsed discs can occur in younger people who take part in very strenuous activities – dancing and sport are common causes as is sex).

After the age of 30 the discs start to dehydrate and become slightly less pliable – that is when they are vulnerable. But after another ten years or so the fibrous capsule around the outside of the disc becomes stiffer and stronger and the nucleus loses much of its moisture and shrinks considerably, making a prolapse less likely. You may find your back getting slightly stiffer and less pliable as you get older and your inbuilt shock absorbers may be clearly slightly worn out but there is a silver lining – you are less liable to a prolapsed disc.

Disc problems are also slightly more common in men than in women – and they are particularly likely to affect individuals whose lifestyle is largely sedentary. They often develop after an unusually sharp movement. So, for example, many people who suffer from disc protrusions will admit that they had noticed a pain after moving some furniture, digging in the garden, turning to pick something up out of the back of the car or playing with a child or pet. There will have been a sharp twinge of pain, some stiffness and then – after a delay of a few hours or a day or so – a terrible pain and an inability to move.

In order to protect your spine – and reduce your chances of having a prolapsed disc – you need to exercise regularly to build up the flexibility of your spine and the strength of the muscles which hold the various parts of your spine in place.

Although disc prolapses can occur anywhere in the spine they most commonly occur at the bottom – in the lumbar region. The two discs that are most affected are the one between the fourth and fifth lumbar vertebrae and the one between the fifth lumbar vertebra and the top of the sacrum. These are probably more vulnerable than discs elsewhere because it is here that the spine moves most – and is under most potential strain when you are lifting, pushing or pulling. The prolapse is usually backwards and sideways and the pain usually develops over a period of a day or so as the inflammation builds up and spreads. The resulting low back pain is then frequently accompanied by pain in the legs as the nerves which supply the leg muscles are affected.

In the condition known as 'sciatica', for example, the sciatic nerve – which supplies the hamstrings and other leg muscles – is affected. It is usual for the pain to be restricted to one side of the body – according to the direction of the protrusion. If a disc between the fourth and fifth lumbar vertebrae has been squeezed out to the right, for example, then the right leg will be affected. In addition to pain a nerve that is being 'pinched' may also produce a wide variety of other sensations – with numbness and 'pins and needles' being among the commonest.

In those relatively rare conditions where the disc protrusion occurs higher up the spine the area affected by pain will again depend upon the position of the protrusion. If a disc has prolapsed in the neck then the shoulder and arm and head will be affected. If a disc has prolapsed in the middle of the back (and this is the most uncommon place of all because the middle of the back is relatively immobile) then the trunk may be the only part of the body affected.

Because the discs themselves have virtually no nerve supply it is only when a disc prolapses and presses onto a nerve or some other vulnerable part of your spine that you will notice any symptoms. The pain of a prolapsed disc tends to be deep, dull and persistent and it may radiate into all sorts of unexpected places. For example, a prolapsed disc in the lower back may produce pain in the buttocks, hip or groin. Some people find that these pains are worse if they bend in one particular way. Others find that their pains become unbearable if they stand up straight. And it isn't uncommon for people to complain that their pain is worse when they sneeze, cough or laugh.

If you have a slipped disc the first thing your doctors will want to do will be to make sure that your problem is caused by a disc that is misbehaving – and if it is a disc that is causing the trouble they will want to know which one.

To investigate your back problem an orthopaedic surgeon (who specialise in bone problems) and/or a neurosurgeon (who specialise in nerve troubles) will probably want to perform a number of investigations and tests: X-rays, CT Scans, myelography (in which a radio-opaque substance is injected around the spinal cord) and discography (in which a radio-opaque substance is injected directly into the disc itself so that it can be seen clearly on an X-ray) are all done by some surgeons.

In addition, tests of electrical activity in the muscles may be done to see which muscles are being affected.

Disc problems respond well to bed rest (though you may have to experiment to find the best and most comfortable position in bed) and although a protruding disc may return to its normal position spontaneously in a few days you may need to stay in bed for several weeks. (This should, of course, only be done under medical supervision and special care should be taken to avoid problems such as deep vein thrombosis.) The length of time you'll need to rest will depend partly on the position of the protrusion and the size of it and partly on how your body has responded to the pain. If your muscles have become very tense as a result of the pain you may find it difficult to move at all even though the disc has returned to its original position. You must have a firm mattress and it is important that you stay where you are for as long as the disc is out of position – getting up and moving about will usually make things worse because when you are standing the weight of the upper part of your body will press down on the disc, making it impossible for the protruded piece of disc to get back into its proper position and increasing the pressure on any nerve that is being squashed.

Roughly half of all sufferers will get better within a month – with quite a number of those making a full recovery within two weeks – and nine out of ten sufferers from 'slipped' discs will have made a fairly full recovery within six weeks whatever treatment they have. A small number of sufferers are left with a tiny patch of numbness or some muscle weakness. But most are so relieved that the main pains have gone that they do not mind too much about these.

Apart from bed rest there are lots of things that you can do to help yourself and your doctor will undoubtedly help by telling you which treatments you should try. Mobilizing exercises will probably be vital as you begin to recover and you may find the manipulation from an osteopath or chiropractor may help reduce the pain and improve your ability to get around. Acupuncture, which helps to relieve pain and to relax muscles, can be extremely effective. Doctors can, of course, prescribe painkillers to help deaden the pain though it is vitally important that you take pills properly. When you start to get up out of bed you may be advised to wear a special corset to support your spine – many people find that a corset doesn't just relieve the pain but also increases their confidence.

If, after a decent period of rest and treatment (six weeks or so is the usually accepted interval) the pain is still there then your doctors will – probably with some reluctance – start to think about surgery. But back surgery is never easy and wise surgeons don't rush patients into the operating theatre unnecessarily because there is always a risk that things may be made worse. If surgery is contemplated then your doctors will want to do whatever tests have not yet been done in order to find out exactly where the problem lies and how severe it is.

When a prolapsed disc stays out

If a disc prolapse does not go back – but stays out of position – it can cause chronic, long-term pain. The nature and extent of the pain will, of course, depend on the position of the prolapse and the nerve that is being compressed. The biggest danger is that if a nerve remains pinched for a long period of time then it may be permanently damaged – with the result that the muscles which are normally controlled by that nerve will become weak and ineffective.

If a disc in the lumbar spine stays prolapsed then you will probably feel a constant aching and stiffness in your back – particularly if you have been sitting down or stuck in any one position for a long period of time. The back pain will probably be on one side of your body and may be accompanied by pains or by 'pins and needles' in your leg.

You will also probably find that any heavy lifting that puts a strain on your back will lead to a worsening of the pain.

If the basic problem is in your neck then the general symptoms will be similar. In addition to generalised aching you may also notice occasional nerve pains, and sudden twisting or turning will probably make things worse – and may bring on a particularly painful episode. You may also notice some fairly unpleasant sounding grinding noises in your neck because of the strain on the ligaments and joints. People with neck problems invariably find that stress and tension and anxiety and pressure will all make things considerably worse – and, indeed, the severest problems may coincide with moments of the greatest tension at work or at home.

Wherever in your spine the problem lies you will find that to build up your resistance to pain you will need to exercise regularly. This will help to build up the strength of the muscles around your spine and to reduce the stress on the bones, ligaments and joints of your spine. You may also benefit from manipulation and acupuncture and you will almost certainly benefit if you learn to relax yourself thoroughly as often as possible.

The good news is that as you get older your spine will gradually stiffen and your ligaments will become thicker and tougher. As this happens so the pain should reduce.

Tests your doctor may do

1. X-rays

Discs – which are soft tissues – do not show up on X-rays but it is often possible to spot disc damage by looking at the size of the spaces between the vertebrae. A narrowed disc will show up on X-ray as bony vertebrae being closer together than normal. Most of the time, however, X-rays merely exclude more serious damage and do not show up anything useful. In at least 90 per cent of patients X-rays do not provide any positive diagnostic information.

2. Myelography

In order to perform a myelogram doctors will inject a radio-opaque dye into your spinal canal and then take X-ray pictures of the dye. Using a local anaesthetic the doctors will make a small hole directly into your spine so that they can inject the dye into the tiny space around the spinal cord and the nerves which come from it. The operation will be done on a table which tilts so that the doctors can move you up and down to make the dye run up and down your spine and around various different nerve junctions. The whole procedure lasts around half an hour. This is an unpleasant, tricky and potentially hazardous procedure and you will usually need to spend a day in hospital if you are having this test. The side effects – which seem to affect quite a number of patients having this test – include headache, nausea and vomiting. In the past some patients are believed to have suffered long-term problems as a result of damage – arachnoiditis – done by an oil based dye and so today most doctors use a water soluble contrast material. Because of the dangers associated with this procedure it is usually only performed when a surgeon intends to operate and wants to have an accurate idea of the sort of damage that may exist within the spine.

3. Discography

In this procedure a contrast medium which will be visible on X-rays will be injected directly into one of your intervertebral discs. You will be given a local anaesthetic and then, with a long thin needle a doctor will inject the contrast medium directly into your disc. X-ray pictures will then be taken. There may be some soreness at the site of the injection. The X-rays which are obtained will not only show a rough outline of the disc but if the outer part of the disc has ruptured then the contrast medium will leak out and be visible outside the disc.

4. CT Scan

Computerised tomography is painless and fairly fast. It uses a very sophisticated computer operated X-ray machine which takes a series of pictures throughout the spine and produces a three dimensional view of any damage that exists. Unlike an ordinary X-ray a scanner does not just show bones but also shows soft tissues such as muscles. A scan will probably help your doctor look at your vertebrae and discs more accurately than anything else.

5. Electromyography

By inserting fine needles into your muscles, and measuring the electrical impulses, electromyography enables doctors to measure the activity of various muscles – and it therefore helps them to decide which nerves have been damaged. (When a nerve has been damaged the muscles normally associated with that nerve will be less active). Electromyography takes about half an hour and is fairly painless.

Surgery – a decompression operation

If you have symptoms of a prolapsed disc which persist and which include chronic, intractable and untreatable pain then a surgeon may be asked to consider whether a decompression operation might help. Before doing an operation a surgeon will almost certainly want to perform at least one (and probably more) of the investigations described above.

Snoring

When we're awake, our throat muscles make sure that as we breathe air passes in and out smoothly and fairly silently. But when we're asleep these muscles relax, letting the throat sag inwards. This causes turbulence which is worst when we breathe in. The sound of snoring occurs when the turbulence makes the roof of the mouth and the base of the tongue start to vibrate.

Below is a list of just some of the things a sufferer can do to help prevent or lessen snoring:

1. Lose weight

Losing excess weight has been known to lessen snoring and in some cases, cure it. If you lose weight you'll lose fat, and with less fat in the tissues at the back of your throat and neck there is less chance that the flow of air will be obstructed. (For advice on losing weight see Vernon Coleman's book *Food for Thought*.)

2. Cut down on your alcohol intake – especially in the evening

One of the main contributory factors to snoring is heavy drinking. Drinking in the hours before you go to bed is most likely to cause trouble. There are two reasons for this: a high level of alcohol in the bloodstream suppresses the breathing centre in your brain and at the same time, reduces the amount you move around when you are asleep. Heavy drinkers often spend the entire night lying flat on their backs, and that is the position which is most likely to cause snoring.

3. Don't go to bed on a full stomach

Eating a large meal just before you retire at night can lead to laboured breathing because if there is too much food in it your stomach is likely to press up on your diaphragm.

4. Throw out a pillow

If you are one of those people who can only get to sleep by lying on your back, then don't sleep on too many pillows. If you're a two pillow sleeper try getting rid of one – this will ensure that your neck is kept straighter, and it will therefore reduce the amount of obstruction in your throat.

5. Try the marble trick

Sew a few marbles or a tennis ball into a sock and tie the sock to the back of your pyjama jacket or nightie. This uncomfortable lump should deter you from sleeping on your back – a position which makes snoring more likely.

6. Watch out for over-the-counter medicines

Look out for medications which contain muscle relaxants. For example, some over-the-counter cold and flu remedies contain muscle relaxants which have a tendency to affect your breathing. If you are a user of medicines which you buy over the pharmacy counter, check with the pharmacist.

7. Give up cigarettes

Smoking increases mucus production and causes the membranes in your nose and throat to swell. The result is that there is less space for the air to get through – and louder snoring.

8. Clear your nasal passages

Blocked nasal passages can cause snoring because they force you to inhale and exhale through your mouth. Those who suffer with hayfever or who have a cold, have a tendency to snore. To help clear your nasal passages, try inhaling the steam from a pan of hot water before you go to bed at night. (But be careful not to get too close and burn yourself.)

9. Beware of sleeping tablets

Although they may help you sleep better sleeping tablets may, by relaxing your head and neck muscles, make your snoring worse.

10. See your doctor

If these suggestions do not stop your snoring then you should see your doctor. If you snore very loudly the chances are high that not enough air is getting through when you breathe. Until your body's automatic defence system starts you breathing again you may stop breathing completely for ten seconds or so – or even longer. This syndrome is called 'sleep apnoea', and is more common in men than women, especially in the overweight.

Stomach ulcers

The term peptic ulcer, gastric ulcer and duodenal ulcer are often used as though they are completely interchangeable. In fact, however, there are differences. A peptic ulcer is simply any ulcer in the upper part of the intestinal tract. The word 'peptic' is used as a synonym for digestion. A gastric ulcer, however, is one that is found in the stomach, while a duodenal ulcer is one that is found in the duodenum. The phrase peptic ulceration can be used to describe both a stomach ulcer or a duodenal ulcer.

The most important symptom of a duodenal ulcer is usually pain, and indeed this is often the only symptom that occurs. The pain is usually localized in the epigastrium, a central point about half way between the chin and the umbilicus, and, unlike gastric ulcers, eating usually helps relieve the pain. People who have duodenal ulcers will often wake up at night and sneak downstairs to get a biscuit.

The other characteristic factor of the pain that people get with duodenal ulceration is that it tends to disappear for weeks or even months at a time for no apparent reason. Suddenly, just when you thought it had gone away for ever back it comes with a bang!

A gastric ulcer involves damage to the stomach lining or mucosa, which can be damaged by a number of different factors – tobacco, alcohol and fats, for example. This explains why individuals who have gastric ulcers will usually get better quicker if they cut out cigarettes and alcohol and if they steer away from fatty foods as much as possible.

Gastric ulcer pain is usually localized to the epigastrium, and eating usually makes it worse. Unlike duodenal ulcer pain, gastric ulcer pain doesn't usually go away once it has started.

Ulcers of all kinds result from an imbalance between the power of the secretions produced by the stomach and the resistance of the lining of the part of the intestine concerned.

For many years the standard medical treatment for peptic ulceration was either a milk and fish diet or surgery – the latter becoming the treatment of choice if the former didn't work.

All that is now in the past. Today, the surgeons who used to earn a fortune chopping out bits of stomach and duodenum have pretty much had to find some other way to earn a living. New drugs which actually help to heal peptic ulceration have turned this type of surgery (and its accompanying risks) into something of a historical oddity.

But powerful and expensive drugs aren't always essential and aren't always the best answer.

Drugs can treat the symptoms of peptic ulceration very effectively but they won't usually stop it happening again.

The most effective way to deal with peptic ulceration – and to prevent the same thing happening again – is to avoid the factors which caused the problem in the first place. This may sound absurdly simple but it is a philosophy which is ignored by the vast majority of doctors.

The basic rules for a healthy stomach are remarkably simple (though, admittedly, much easier to read than to follow):

1. Drink plenty of water

Cut down on fizzy drinks and drinks containing caffeine. Instead try to drink six to eight glasses of water a day. Drink bottled natural mineral water. You can add a little fruit juice to the water to give it flavour.

2. Minimise your consumption of alcohol

Ulcers are common among heavy drinkers.

3. Avoid tobacco smoke

Few things irritate the stomach lining more than tobacco. If you are a non-smoker you should make an effort to avoid smoke-filled rooms.

4. Avoid unnecessary stresses

Take a good hard look at your life. Which stresses are avoidable? Change your life so that you minimise your exposure to unnecessary stress.

5. Learn to deal with the essential stress in your life

Some stress is necessary. So learn how to deal with the stressful parts of your life most effectively. And learn how to relax and switch off so that you are better able to cope.

6. Take regular, gentle exercise

Check with your doctor before starting any exercise programme. Avoid any exercise which causes pain.

7. Don't eat too much – and lose weight if you are overweight

Overweight is a major cause of digestive problems.

8. Eat slowly

Eating too fast puts your stomach under strain.

9. Reduce your consumption of fat

Most of us still eat far too much fat.

10. Eat small meals often rather than eating big meals occasionally

Help your digestion by feeding your body small meals rather than huge ones.

11. Find out which foods upset you – and avoid them

If something upsets you cut it out of your diet.

12. Rest after eating

Don't rush around as soon as you've finished eating. Sit down and avoid mental and physical stress for 20 to 30 minutes.

Stroke

Strokes are the third biggest killer in developed countries and are also one of the most common causes of disability. Each year, thousands of people's lives are made miserable because of strokes; some sufferers end up wheelchair-bound. However, with the right care and attention, the misery of a stroke can almost certainly be avoided.

What is a stroke?

A stroke (also known as a cerebro-vascular accident) is a result of damage to the brain, either from a sufficient supply of blood not being able to reach the brain or from a ruptured blood vessel – or blood vessels – in or around the brain.

There are two main types of stroke: an ischaemic stroke and a haemorrhagic stroke. Although uncommon, a stroke can also be caused by a brain tumour.

An ischaemic stroke is the most common of all, and can be caused, either by a cerebral thrombosis (a blockage caused by a blood clot that has built up in an artery in the brain) or by a cerebral embolism (a blockage caused by a clot – medically referred to as an 'embolus' – which has formed elsewhere in the body and has been carried via the bloodstream into an artery in the brain). The lack of blood reaching the brain can cause damage to an area of brain tissue, and this tissue damage is medically known as an 'infarct'.

A cerebral haemorrhage on the other hand, is caused by bleeding around or into the brain, and is nearly always the most serious type of stroke. It is also the most common cause of sudden death.

There are two types of haemorrhage which can result in a stroke: an intra-cerebral haemorrhage where bleeding occurs inside the brain; and a subarachnoid haemorrhage where the burst blood vessel bleeds into the subarachnoid space that surrounds the brain. A subarachnoid haemorrhage is often caused by a weakness in the artery wall called an aneurysm, and mainly affects younger people.

Transient ischaemic attack (TIA)

A TIA can be an advanced warning of an impending stroke. A TIA occurs when blood cannot reach the brain in a sufficient supply for a brief period of time. Because the blood supply to the brain is quickly restored before brain tissue starts to die, the sufferer of a TIA usually makes a full recovery within 24 hours.

A TIA can also be an advance warning of a heart attack. Many people who have had a TIA suffer a heart attack rather than go on to develop a stroke.

Occasionally, a TIA can be caused by a lack of oxygen in the blood supply reaching the brain. This can occur if someone has a blood disorder such as severe anaemia, polycythemia or leukaemia.

A TIA should always be taken seriously because a person who has suffered such an 'attack', has a 50 per cent chance of having a stroke within the next five years. The cause of the TIA needs to be investigated, identified and treated.

Warning signs of a stroke

Depending on which part of the brain has been damaged (each part of the brain is responsible for a particular function), the effects of a stroke vary. Some strokes can cause mild symptoms which only last for a few hours while others can cause severe and lasting damage or even sudden death.

Many people who have a stroke experience some warning signs beforehand; these may include: brief episodes of confusion; noises in the ears; dizziness; weakness; falling suddenly to the ground for no apparent reason (this is known as a 'drop attack'); loss of sensation; pins and needles in an arm or leg; visual disturbances (blurred vision or loss of vision lasting for a few minutes); clumsiness and headaches on waking.

Some people experience brief warning signs during a couple of months before a stroke, while others experience symptoms only hours before. So it is important to report any unexplained signs as soon as possible. Symptoms of a stroke may take as quickly as a few minutes to progress or as slowly as a few hours. A cerebral haemorrhage usually comes on suddenly. The sufferer may experience a severe headache, quickly followed by paralysis down one side of the body, loss of vision to one side and maybe a serious epileptic-type fit.

Symptoms of a stroke may include:

1. Loss of consciousness which may result in a coma.
2. Numbness or weakness in a limb or limbs on one side of the body.
3. Confusion.
4. A drooping mouth.
5. Slurred speech.
6. Dizziness.
7. Headache.
8. The sufferer may become incontinent.

Depending on the severity of the stroke, the sufferer may experience only one or two, or all of the above symptoms. If a stroke is suspected, then an ambulance must be called immediately.

The brain is divided into two halves: the right hemisphere and the left hemisphere. The right hemisphere of the brain controls the left hand side of the body and the left hemisphere controls the right hand side of the body. Comprehension, speech, reading and writing are situated in the left half of the brain, except in a small number of left-handed people where they are situated on the right. If disability is experienced in the right side of the body, damage has usually been done to the left side of the brain. Depending on the severity of the stroke, this means that comprehension, speech, reading and writing will probably also be affected.

After-effects of a stroke may include:

1. Paralysis of one side of the body (hemiplegia)

This is the most common consequence of a stroke. The paralysis can be so mild that it may only affect part of the face, or it may be so severe that it can affect all the way down one side of the body.

2. Spasticity

This often accompanies paralysis.

3. Problems with speech and comprehension (aphasia)

Damage to the left hand side of the brain can cause 'aphasia' because this is where the centres for communication are nearly always situated.

Have you ever been at the dentist's, sat in the chair, with your mouth full of metal (probe, tongue retractor, mirror, pneumatic drill, zimmer frame and so on) when the dentist has asked you a question or said something deeply contentious? Have you ever wanted to say something but been unable to do anything but mumble something incomprehensible? That's how a patient who has had a stroke feels when listening to a visitor who won't stop talking. To say that this is frustrating is an understatement. And whereas the dentist will, in due course, remove the instruments from your mouth the stroke victim may remain frustrated for days, weeks or months.

Instead of subjecting a stroke patient to a series of lengthy monologues make a real effort to bring him into every conversation. This will almost certainly be possible even if he cannot talk to you in the normal way. As long as he has some control over a muscle or two somewhere on his body you will be able to work out a system of communication through which he can answer 'yes' or 'no' to simple questions.

If he can squeeze the fingers on one hand then you may, for example, decide that one squeeze means 'yes' while two squeezes mean 'no'.

Alternatively, if he can't control his hand muscles but can close one eyelid then make one blink mean 'yes' and two blinks mean 'no'.

The key, of course, is that you must remember to keep bringing the patient into the conversation at regular intervals. You must create and ask questions which can be answered with a simple 'yes' or a 'no'.

4. A shortened attention span

5. Depression

This can be caused by damage to the brain.

6. Memory loss

7. Post-stroke pain

Some sufferers describe the pain as a burning, stabbing or shooting sensation. Post-stroke pain can sometimes develop a couple of months after a stroke.

8. Confusion

9. Tiredness

10. Difficulty in swallowing

There is a risk of choking when eating or drinking. In a vast majority of sufferers who experience swallowing difficulties, the problem only lasts for a short while.

11. Incontinence

12. Visual problems

Some sufferers lose half their field of vision: the right or the left side of their vision is absent. This condition is known as: 'hemianopia'.

13. Personality changes

14. Epileptic fits

This only affects a small number of people, and usually for a few weeks or months after a stroke.

15. Disorientation

16. Problems with reading and writing

17. Difficulty in recognising familiar objects

18. Mood swings

Patients may be tearful one minute and happy the next for no explicable reason.

19. Sensory loss

Depending on which part of the brain has been affected, the sufferer loses awareness of one half of their body (medically referred to as 'hemi-neglect'). This form of sensory loss often accompanies hemiplegia (paralysis down one side of the body). The sufferer may have to keep being reminded that the affected limbs exist. There is, of course, a danger of accidentally hurting the affected limbs (or limb) because the sufferer just simply isn't aware of their existence.

20. Apraxia (an inability to coordinate movements properly)

Apraxia may affect dressing, and the sufferer might try to put his clothes on back to front.

Risk factors for stroke may include:

1. Heart disease.
2. Obesity.
3. A high fat diet.
4. Smoking.
5. Atherosclerosis (narrowing of the arteries caused by fatty deposits known as 'plaques'). Atherosclerosis is the main underlying cause of stroke.
6. High blood pressure.
7. Diabetes mellitus.
8. Atrial fibrillation (an irregular heartbeat).
9. Alcohol consumed in excess.
10. A previous stroke or a TIA.
11. Age – strokes become more common with age.
12. Hormone replacement therapy.
13. Polycythemia (an increased level of red blood cells).
14. A family history of strokes.

Complications

If a stroke results in immobility, then the sufferer may be at risk of developing a deep vein thrombosis which can break off and travel to the lungs where it may cause a blockage. This is called a pulmonary embolus. To reduce the risk of developing a venous thrombosis, it is important that the patient doesn't stay immobilised for long periods, drinks plenty of fluids to avoid dehydration and wears anti-thrombosis stockings. The risk of developing a venous thrombosis in an immobilised leg after a stroke is quite high, but it can be prevented if the above measures are carried out.

Pressure sores, another complication of immobility, can be prevented with good nursing care by making sure that the patient does not rest on the same part of his/her body for too long. Frequently turning the patient over should prevent pressure sores.

A heart attack is the most common cause of death in the few weeks following a stroke, but medical treatment to prevent further strokes may also help to reduce that risk.

Diagnosis

Sometimes, a diagnosis is made on the basis of the patient's medical history and by a physical examination carried out by a doctor or a specialist. An ultrasound examination of the heart (an echocardiogram) or of the carotid arteries in the neck (carotid doppler) may be required to find out the cause of the stroke.

If the cause of the stroke cannot be found, or the stroke victim needs special treatment, then it may be necessary for the patient to have an X-ray which produces pictures of the inside of the brain. A specialised brain scan called, a computed tomogram (CT for short) or an MRI scan (magnetic resonance imaging) might be used.

Other tests to find out the cause of the stroke may include: an arteriogram (an X-ray to view the insides of the arteries); a trans-oesophageal echocardiogram (a probe that is inserted half way down the oesophagus taking detailed images of the heart) and, very rarely, a lumbar puncture.

Treatment

Most people who have had a stroke may need to be admitted into hospital for care, investigation and assessment.

The first few days after having had a stroke are crucial as the patient's stroke might still be evolving from, what initially appeared to be a mild stroke to a much more serious one.

If paralysis is experienced then it is important that physiotherapy is carried out as soon as possible in order to get the affected limbs mobile again. Immediately after a stroke, the affected limbs become loose and floppy but within a matter of hours the limbs become 'spastic'. This means that the affected muscles contract and stiffen and if physiotherapy is neglected, then irreversible deformity will occur.

If the speech is severely affected, then speech therapy may also be required.

Daily exercising of the legs and support stockings are usually recommended to help prevent a venous thrombosis, which can be a complication of a stroke.

Treatment will also include dealing with the cause of the stroke as well as trying to prevent another stroke from developing. Treatment may include taking drugs such as anti-coagulants. This might simply consist of taking a daily aspirin.

How to prevent a stroke

Follow these tips to avoid a stroke:

1. It is important to have your blood pressure checked regularly.
2. If you're overweight then you should lose weight.
3. Giving-up smoking significantly reduces the risk of having a stroke.
4. You should eat a healthy diet which is low in fat and low in salt.
5. Take regular exercise, but do consult your doctor first before starting an exercise programme.
6. Mono-unsaturated fats (found in olive oil) are reputed to be beneficial in the prevention of atherosclerosis.

Outlook

Recovery varies from person to person but depends on the severity of the stroke and the health of the individual affected. Some stroke victims may take days to recover, some may take months and others may take up to a year or two; everyone's different. There are some sufferers who are left with a disability for life.

Like most illnesses, recovery also depends on the mental attitude of the individual concerned. Someone who is determined to get better stands a far better chance of a speedy recovery than a patient who approaches their illness with a negative attitude.

For those left permanently disabled as a result of a stroke, there are many ways to get around a disability and to lead a normal and rewarding life.

Temporomandibular joint syndrome (TMJS)

The temporomandibular joints are situated on each side of the face, just before the ears, where the temporal bone of the skull connects to the lower jaw. They are the most complex joints of the human body.

The temporomandibular joints, which are supported by tendons, ligaments and muscles, are responsible for jaw movements. These joints move each time we talk, eat and even swallow. As you can imagine, when we chew, these joints sustain an awful amount of pressure. The temporomandibular joints open and close like hinges and they also slide forwards, backwards and from side to side. No man-made joint could possibly withstand that variety of movement or pressure.

The commonest cause of TMJS is a combination of anatomical problems within the joints and muscle tension. TMJS is a very painful condition which brings misery to thousands of sufferers.

Symptoms of TMJS may include:

1. Facial pain which may spread to the neck and shoulders. The pain may also spread to the head, especially the back of the head and the temples causing severe headaches.
2. A popping or clicking sound (which may be so loud that it can be heard by others) on opening or closing of the mouth.
3. Facial pain when opening or closing the mouth.
4. The jaw locking open or even closed.
5. Earache which is not associated with an infection.
6. Dizziness.

7. Fatigue of the jaw.
8. Deviation of the jaw on opening wide. Deviation may occur to the left or to the right.
9. Difficulty swallowing.
10. Limited opening of the mouth.
11. Tinnitus (If you take painkillers to help with the pain of your TMJS then you should be aware that aspirin, and drugs which contain aspirin, may cause tinnitus).
12. Twitching of the eye muscles.
13. Pain in or behind the eye causing sensitivity to light.
14. Blurred vision.
15. Toothache for no known reason.
16. Depression can sometimes occur as a result of the pain the sufferer has to contend with.

You do not have to experience all of the above symptoms to be suffering with TMJS. Some sufferers may only experience the classic symptoms of TMJS such as facial pain and popping or clicking of the jaw, whereas, other sufferers may experience most of the symptoms on the above list.

If you have any of the above symptoms, then it is important that you make an appointment to see your doctor as soon as possible as some of the symptoms listed, may be associated with more serious diseases.

Factors which may cause and aggravate TMJS:

1. Stress is commonly responsible for aggravating the temporo-mandibular joints. Stress can cause people to clench or grind their teeth. This can result in severe muscle pain and tightness that can be felt on both sides of the face. Symptoms of TMJS may appear after a particularly stressful day or when waking up in the morning. If the latter is the case, then this may be due to you grinding your teeth in your sleep. Grinding of the teeth is known as bruxism.
2. Trauma to the jaw.
3. Diseases including systematic lupus erythematosus, psoriatic arthritis and rheumatoid arthritis may all cause inflammation of the temporomandibular joints resulting in much pain.
4. A whiplash injury.

5. Malocclusion (otherwise known as a 'bad bite') may be produced by: removal of teeth without any replacement, heavy dental work, an ill-fitting denture, poor jaw development or a displacement of the temporomandibular joint/s. TMJS has also been reported in patients undergoing orthodontic treatment. The reason for this is because malocclusion is temporarily produced by the gradual shifting of the teeth using an orthodontic appliance.
6. Very rarely, osteoarthritis can cause TMJS.

Diagnosis

A diagnosis of TMJS is usually made by your doctor or by your dentist after carrying out a medical examination and eliminating any other diseases which could be responsible for your pain. You may even be referred to your local hospital for X-rays to be taken of your temporomandibular joints.

Treatment

In a majority of cases, muscle relaxants and painkillers are normally prescribed for a short period only. (Remember, that benzodiazepines, which are often prescribed as muscle relaxants, can be addictive.)

If muscle tension caused by stress is the cause of your TMJS pain, then counselling may be offered to you. Your dentist may recommend that you wear a nightguard prosthesis to help stop you from grinding your teeth in your sleep.

If malocclusion is responsible for your TMJS, then your bite may need to be adjusted by the use of an orthodontic appliance.

Only in very severe cases is surgery needed.

Self-help

You don't have to rely on drugs to help control your symptoms of TMJS. There is plenty you can do to help yourself.

1. Applying heat to the side/s of the face can help to relax the muscle tension in your jaw. Try using a hot water bottle with a towel wrapped around it so as not to burn your skin.
2. Use your fingers to gently massage the muscles in the sides of your face to help try and relax them. You may find this painful

at first but the pain should subside after you've massaged the muscles for a while.

3. Try not to open your mouth too wide when you yawn as this can exacerbate the pain of TMJS. When yawning, put one hand directly underneath your chin, this should prevent you from opening your mouth too wide.

4. Cut your food up into smaller pieces to avoid opening your mouth too wide.

5. If you like to chew gum, then we suggest that you stop for a while. Chewing gum may result in overuse of the muscles surrounding the temporomandibular joints, causing pain.

6. If the TMJS pain has spread to your temples, gentle massage can help to reduce discomfort.

7. In some cases, TMJS pain can spread to the neck and shoulders. If this applies to you, then you can try getting a close friend or relative to give you a gentle neck and shoulder massage. Visiting an osteopath can sometimes provide relief from pain.

8. Throughout the day, try to be aware as to whether or not you clench your teeth. If you do clench your teeth, try not to do it.

9. If your TMJS pain is aggravated by stress, then try to relax more.

10. A facial steam has been known to ease the pain of TMJS as the heat from the water helps to relax the affected muscles. But do be careful not to use water which is hot enough to cause any burning. And don't get too close to the water.

11. Try not to eat food that is too hard. Chewing on a tough piece of bread or on a tough piece of meat can make TMJS pain worse.

12. Cold weather can make TMJS pain worse because we usually clench our teeth when confronted with cold air. So wrap up warm when going outside. Try wrapping a scarf around your neck and the lower part of your face as this will help keep your jaw warm.

Urinary incontinence

Urinary incontinence (involuntary loss of bladder control) can be embarrassing as well as debilitating to the sufferer. Urinary incontinence is not a disease but a symptom – although it is a cruel one and bad enough to force most sufferers to plan their lives around it. It is not uncommon for sufferers to become housebound because they are worried about having an 'accident' in public. However, this needn't be so because there are plenty of things you can do to help yourself.

1. Cut down your alcohol consumption

Cut down on your alcohol consumption, or even better give up alcohol completely. Alcohol has a diuretic effect which makes you want to pass urine more frequently. Alcohol isn't the only culprit as grapefruit juice and caffeine can also have the same effect. Caffeine is commonly found in coffee, tea and cola drinks.

2. Drink cranberry juice

Try and substitute your usual cup of coffee or tea with a glass of cranberry juice. Cranberry juice is reputed to be very beneficial to the bladder.

3. Eat more fibre

Avoid constipation as this can worsen incontinence.

4. Give up smoking

Avoid tobacco as the nicotine in cigarettes can irritate the bladder.

5. Lose any excess weight

If you're overweight, then start slimming. Losing excess weight has been known to ease urinary incontinence.

6. Keep a diary

Note down, every day for a week, what you've had to eat and drink and how often you have had to visit the toilet. This might help you find out what makes your incontinence worse.

7. Don't hold it in

It is important that you go to the toilet as soon as you feel the need to do so. Holding your urine in stretches the bladder and may lead to a bladder infection.

8. Go to bed with an empty bladder

Try to empty your bladder before you go out and before you go to bed each night to avoid any embarrassing accidents.

9. Gain bladder control

There are special exercises that you can do which can help with bladder control.

a) Try stopping your urine in mid-flow, count to five and then carry on and empty your bladder.

b) Women can tighten up the front part of their pelvic muscles by imagining that they are trying to squeeze a tampon as tightly as they can.

c) Men and women can strengthen up relevant muscles by pretending that they are trying to hold back a bowel movement. This helps to tighten up the sphincter muscles around the anus which will help with the muscles at the back part of the pelvis.

You should aim to do these exercises for a couple of minutes three times a day.

The above exercises are extremely helpful for those who tend to leak a little urine whilst coughing or sneezing.

10. Use absorbency pads

There are special pads made for those who suffer with urinary incontinence. These pads neutralise unpleasant odour, and hold 50 to 500 times their weight in water. Do ask your doctor for more information about these.

11. Take your time

Try to empty your bladder properly. Spend a minute or two extra on the toilet doing this.

When to see your doctor

You should see your doctor as soon as you become incontinent. Your doctor will probably give you a check-up to rule out any infection and to find out the cause of your urinary incontinence.

Men who have to pass urine frequently, who have to get up at night to pass urine and/or whose stream is slight and rather slow should visit their doctor. Prostate problems are commonest among men over the age of 50. Other symptoms include a stop-go urine stream and an inability to start easily.

Varicose veins

Varicose veins, which appear as bluish lumps on the legs just below the skin's surface, are extremely common. About one in seven adults have them. Women are more likely to have varicose veins than men. The disorder runs in families and tends to affect people who spend a good deal of their time standing still (for example hairdressers, shop assistants, factory workers and dentists).

The veins that become varicose are not the deep veins, but the ones that lie outside the muscles. Basically, varicose veins are caused by a breakdown of the valves at the junction between these veins. Blood tends to flow back into the vein outside the muscles if one of these valves becomes weak. In order to cope with the extra blood, the vein will swell, lose its elasticity and become lumpy. Although it happens very slowly over the years, once one vein has become damaged the one below it tends to become damaged too.

If you suffer with varicose veins, or would like to prevent yourself from getting them, read the following tips:

1. Get your circulation going

If your job requires you to sit or stand for long periods, then try to shuffle your feet or stand on tiptoe to get the circulation going. Try clenching your calf muscles.

2. Put your feet up

Varicose veins can cause discomfort in the legs such as, itching, aching and restlessness. You can help ease the aching and restlessness in your legs by putting your feet up (above hip level) on a chair. Putting your feet up will also help the veins to empty and reduce the swelling in your ankles which so often accompanies varicose veins. If you suffer from itching, try not to scratch because this can damage the skin and leave it open to infection. Try a simple, plain moisturising cream.

3. Watch what you wear

Do not wear tight 'hold-up' stockings or garters which may have a tendency to restrict the blood-flow around your legs. And watch out for girdles and other garments which may be restrictive.

4. Walk as much as you can

Exercise improves the circulation, and walking is just about the best form of exercise there is so do take regular walks. Always consult your doctor before taking up any physical exercise.

5. Stretch your legs

If you have to travel on long journeys, get up and stretch your legs from time to time. If you're on a bus, do take advantage of the stops and get out and walk around for a while.

6. Don't impede your blood-flow

Try not to sit with your legs bent or crossed.

7. Take the pressure off your legs

Lose weight. Obesity can make varicose veins worse because it puts extra pressure on the legs.

8. Mind how you go

If you have varicose veins, try and avoid any knocks and bumps to your legs if you can because any damage to the skin will take longer to heal. Poor circulation can deprive the skin of oxygen and slow down the healing process.

9. Support yourself

Invest in a pair of support-tights (or stockings) which can be bought from most pharmacies and some department stores. Support-tights help to push the blood into the deeper, larger veins instead of the blood vessels nearest to the skin, which then makes it easier for the blood to be pumped back up to the heart.

10. Eat more fruit and vegetables to avoid constipation

Try to avoid constipation as this can make varicose veins worse.

When to see your doctor

Blood clots and ruptures are two of the major problems caused by varicose veins. When a blood clot occurs, the area can become very painful and tender to touch and the leg can sometimes swell. If this should happen to you, then you must go and see your doctor straight away. This is a very serious condition which can result in death if left untreated. Varicose veins around the ankles have a tendency to rupture and bleed, this, too, is extremely dangerous because you can lose blood very quickly. If this should happen, put pressure on the bleeding to try and slow it down and call for an ambulance. You should ask your doctor for help if your legs are sore, painful or inflamed, if they are red or seem infected.

If the appearance of your varicose veins bothers you, do see your doctor about them. Depending on how severe they are, your doctor might suggest surgery or injections.

Wind (flatulence and burping)

Wind is one of the commonest of all health problems – affecting well over half of the population. Doctors don't understand much about it and can't do much to deal with it.

The normal gastrointestinal tract is said to contain between 100 and 200 millilitres of gas under normal circumstances. During an ordinary sort of day a normal individual will often produce one to two litres of gas. It is, therefore, quite obvious that there must be a tendency for wind to pass out of the gastrointestinal tract at one end or the other. (Wind consists of 250 different gases. The study of flatulence is called flatology. The most astonishing fact about wind is that it is normal to 'break wind' at around 100 mph.)

Not only can wind, otherwise known as flatulence, be embarrassing but it can also be fairly debilitating, causing nausea, pain and bloatedness. Gases are produced by bacteria reacting with food in the intestines. The gas is then eliminated from the body at one end of the intestinal tract or the other; either through belching or through passing wind.

Wind is produced within the gastrointestinal tract as food is digested, and some foods are more likely than others to result in the production of large quantities of wind. Certain carbohydrates in foods (i.e. beans, etc.) can make wind worse because they are not easily broken down and produce gas whilst they are being fermented in the gut. Brussels sprouts and cabbage are fairly widely recognised as offending vegetables and beans have a tremendous reputation in this respect.

It is, however, important to understand that not all of the wind in the gastrointestinal tract is a result of the normal digestive process. Some of the wind that causes such embarrassing noises gets into the intestinal tract in the same way that food gets in: it is swallowed. We swallow air when we eat and drink and even when we swallow our saliva.

People who chew gum, smoke cigarettes or eat too quickly will often swallow air as will those individuals who gulp in air as a nervous habit. Indeed, two thirds of the gas in your body is probably swallowed air. You're likely to swallow too much air if you gulp hot drinks or sip drinks through a straw. Habits like sucking mints can also cause wind to accumulate. Fizzy drinks are an obvious cause of wind. Chewing with an open mouth or talking with your mouth full increase the likelihood of wind too. Foods and drinks that are likely to cause wind include: beans, broccoli, cabbage, raisins, bananas, popcorn, peanuts, onions, chocolate, coffee, milk and carbonated drinks.

Apart from being inconvenient and embarrassing, wind can also be extremely painful – through stretching the sensitive walls of the bowel.

Coping with wind (flatulence and burping)

1. Eating simple sugars may make wind worse. Foods to avoid in particular include sugar, sweets, biscuits, cakes, crisps, white bread and processed breakfast cereals. Remember that around 80 per cent of the sugar we eat annually comes from packaged foods.
2. Tolerance to the amount of gas in the intestine varies enormously. Some people are particularly sensitive to it.
3. Eating too quickly can result in air being swallowed. Chewing gum and smoking cigarettes can both result in more air being swallowed. Every time you swallow saliva, you also swallow air.
4. Drinking water can help reduce bloating. You need two to three litres a day. Coffee, tea and cola drinks don't count because they tend to make things worse. Try drinking fennel tea – it can be very effective. Peppermint tea may also help.
5. Bacterial metabolism of food in the intestine may cause gas. Some foods – e.g. beans and cabbage – are worse than others. Wind sufferers should avoid the following foods: milk and dairy produce, fresh fruits, some vegetables. Avoid beans, onions, cabbage, broccoli and Brussels sprouts. These foods are renowned for causing wind. There are many other foods that can cause wind,

or make it worse, but everyone reacts differently so keep a diary. Note down in your diary what you've had to eat that day and how bad your wind is. After a couple of weeks, you should have a clearer picture of the foods you can eat and the foods you have to avoid.

6. Some people benefit by eating more fibre. Others benefit by eating less.

7. If the gas coming out smells unpleasant then you are probably eating too much animal protein (or failing to digest it properly). Animal proteins contain large amounts of sulphur – which smells a lot.

8. Too much fat encourages inflammation in the intestinal tract. And this can cause bloating.

9. The foods we are most likely to be sensitive to (and which are most likely to cause problems) are the foods to which we are addicted. So, if you can't stop eating chocolate you are probably sensitive to it. If cheese is your favourite food then you may well be sensitive to dairy produce.

10. Lactose intolerance affects around one in seven individuals of Northern or Middle European descent – and up to 95 per cent of those of African, American, Asian origin. Lactose intolerance can cause problems with wind. Lactose is found in a number of dairy foods.

11. Watch out for hot drinks and fizzy drinks. Do not gulp down hot drinks as this can introduce gas into the stomach. Consuming fizzy drinks also has the same effect.

12. Don't overeat. Your stomach normally contains some air and when we overeat, in order to relieve the distension and discomfort, the stomach expels the air upwards. This leads to bringing up wind.

13. Try not to eat your food too quickly as this can cause you to swallow more air. So can not chewing your food properly.

14. Learn to relax. Tension and nervousness can make wind worse because of the tendency to swallow more air.

15. It is better for your health not to hold your wind in. Obviously, out of social politeness, it is better to do it discreetly by going to the toilet or going out of the room.

16. Constipation can make wind worse because the food stays in the

bowel for longer, giving it more time to ferment.

17. Charcoal biscuits or capsules which can be bought from your local chemist or health store, can help with wind. Fennel tea is also good for dispelling wind. Chamomile is good for easing gut spasms which can often accompany wind.

18. You should see your doctor if none of the above suggestions help or if you are suffering from great discomfort. Your doctor should also be informed if your bowel habits suddenly change, if you start suffering from indigestion or if you notice any other unusual symptoms.

Appendix:
Aids and accessories to make life easier

For a whole variety of reasons (including, for example, stiffness in their joints) the over 50s sometimes have difficulty in walking, bending or reaching. To help overcome irreversible physical problems there are many products available. In addition there are many aids and gadgets which make life easier, which reduce the need for bending, reaching and lifting and which help to protect the joints and prevent the development of problems.

Some people are reluctant to use aids at all. They fear that to rely on any sort of assistance is to admit to a weakness; they even fear that it will speed up the disabling process. Nothing could be further from the truth. The best aids will help you to make the most of all your remaining skills and will minimise the effect that your disabilities have on your life.

The other fear, that gadgets and aids must inevitably cost a lot of money, is also ill-founded. There are, it is true, some pieces of equipment (particularly the electrical ones) which cost a lot of money. But there are also gadgets which cost next to nothing and which can be made at home.

This appendix does not attempt to offer a comprehensive list of aids but is designed to show the range of aids available. You should be able to obtain a full list of available aids from your family doctor or hospital consultant but if you have any difficulty contact one of the many charitable or commercial organisations offering aids. Big cities often have shops which specialise in offering equipment designed to make life easier.

Aids for sitting

Posture stool

The seat slopes forwards and you sit with your weight resting on your knees and your feet tucked in underneath you. The posture stool is designed to encourage you to sit in a healthier position so that you can get up at the end of a day's work without having a stiff and aching back.

Backrests, 'wedges' and lumbar supports

Most chairs do not provide enough support for the lumbar part of the spine. You can buy many different supports – including inflatable cushions which are suitable for travellers – which will help turn your uncomfortable chair into one which is much friendlier to your back and other joints.

Adjustable chairs

Properly adjustable chairs which allow you to sit in a comfortable position are available. But they do tend to be expensive. The seat height should be adjustable as should the angle of the seat and the backrest. You'll find it easier to get into and out of chairs which have arm rests which you can rest your weight on when sitting down or push against when standing up. If your feet aren't resting on the floor when you are sitting down then you need a footrest (dangling feet add to the stress on your spine).

Ejector chairs

It is possible to buy chairs which, at the touch of a lever, help to push you up into the standing position.

Aids for work

Writing slopes

If you work on a computer, word processor or typewriter you may need to have a flat desk. But writing slopes enable you to work at an angle which is better suited to your body.

Aids for picking things up

Pick-up sticks

Simple 'pick-up sticks' (such as are often used by park attendants employed to pick up bits and pieces of waste paper) help make life much easier if you find it difficult to bend or to reach for small objects. Pick-up sticks are probably the most versatile and useful of all gadgets. They are basically nothing more than a pair of tongs with a long handle which enable you to pick up something without bending or stretching. They are also useful for drawing curtains, switching on lights, pulling on socks and doing 1,001 other potentially painful little chores. With a little experience you will find that a pick-up stick extends your reach by three feet and enables you to pick up all sorts of things (clothes, books, magazines, newspapers, rubbish etc.) off the floor without bending down. It is possible to buy sticks which fold up (so that you can carry them around with you) and some sticks have magnets on the end to help pick up metal objects.

Aids in the kitchen

If you have lost strength or movement in your hands or wrists then you will almost certainly find that one of the most useful aids available is a small device which will help you to open a jar. There are also aids available to help you lift a heavy kettle or open a can (wall mounted can openers are sometimes helpful). Some useful aids can easily be made by anyone with a few basic carpentry skills.

Dealing with or preparing food can be tricky but the patient with only one useful hand will find that a spiked board will enable him or her to keep vegetables still while they are being peeled and chopped. To open packets it may help to stand them upright in a kitchen drawer, close the drawer as far as it will go and then cut the top of the packet open with a knife. Kitchen tools are easier to get hold of if they are hung neatly on hooks rather than placed inaccessibly in drawers. Cutlery should have large handles and you can adapt cutlery to make it easier to use by using tape or even bicycle handlebar rubbers.

One of the simplest and most useful gadgets you can buy is a 'grip mat' – a small, non-stick rubber mat that can be invaluable for opening jars, bottles or even doors that are stuck tight.

If you are planning a new kitchen think carefully about the height at which you have cupboards and electrical sockets placed (it is possible to buy electric plugs fitted with handles – these are much easier to pull out and push in than ordinary household plugs). Try to make sure that everything you need is within easy reach.

Remember that taps are easier to turn on and off if they are of the lever type.

Aids in the bathroom

If you have stiff or painful hands then you will probably find it difficult to operate ordinary taps, so long-handled, lever type taps (the sort used by surgeons in operating theatres) can be a tremendous help. A liquid soap dispenser which can be operated either by a foot pedal or by a lever will make washing much easier. If holding a nail brush is difficult one can be fixed to the side of the wash basin by screwing suction cups onto the back of the brush and sticking the suckers onto the basin.

As far as the bath is concerned one of the most important aids is probably the bathrail or handrail. A rubber mat at the bottom of the bath will prove useful for anyone who is slightly unsteady. People who find it difficult to lie down may be better off with a seat or board placed firmly across the bath. A lift suspended over the bath may be helpful (all sorts of hoists are available) and there are even special baths available in which the bather sits rather than lies.

There are many other useful gadgets for the bathroom: sponges with long handles, tap turners, long-handled brushes, toothbrushes with built up handles and so on. Often it is not necessary to buy an aid for a home-made improvisation will prove equally effective. For example, it is possible to make a tap turner with a piece of wood that has a hook fastened onto it. And it is possible to build up the handle of a toothbrush to a more manageable size either by wrapping pieces of sticking plaster around it or by fitting a bicycle handlebar rubber onto the handle.

As with everything else it is best to isolate the problems first and then look for the solutions. The solutions will then often appear quite simple. For example, if someone finds it difficult to operate a bathroom pull switch they may find it easier if a ball is tied onto the end. One of the 'air' balls that golfers use for practise will be easy to tie on.

There are things that can also be done to make the other vital piece of bathroom equipment – the lavatory – more accessible. The toilet seat can be raised so that the stiff person does not have so much bending to do. And soft absorbent loose leaf tissue is easier to handle than a continuous roll.

Finally, it is always wise to have several grab handles near to the lavatory. These should be very well secured.

Walking aids

Many people are reluctant to use a walking stick. They think of it as a badge of infirmity. It should be thought of as an aid to walking – just as good shoes are an efficient walking aid. There are many different types of stick available – ranging from the ordinary wooden stick (which should have a rubber tipped end to ensure that it does not slip) to the tripod type of stick (which has three feet attached to a single handle and which will stand up by itself – it gives a bit more security than an ordinary stick but is almost as portable).

The walking frame is held in front – usually with both hands. When moving the right side of the frame and the left side are shuffled forwards alternately. The frames are usually made of light but strong material and one major advantage is that a basket can be attached to the front so that small items (books, shopping etc.) can be carried around. Some frames can be converted into seats.

When choosing a stick or frame do make sure that it is the right size. Frames usually have adjustable handles. Sticks should be tried out for size. Some collapsible sticks and frames can be obtained.

A stick or frame can give you extra support, take some of the strain and enable you to rest when you need to. If you use a stick change hands regularly so that you don't get into the habit of putting too much strain on one side of your body.

Wheelchairs

There are many different types of wheelchair so when selecting a wheelchair you need to know exactly what you are going to use it for. Wheelchairs can be divided into three main groups: those most suitable for outdoor use, those suitable for use indoors and those which can be used either indoors or outdoors. Decide whether your chair will be pushed or propelled from inside. Look for a chair that is manoeuvrable and, ideally, collapsible so that you can take it with you when you travel by car, train or bus. Some chairs have detachable armrests and hinged footrests which make them easier to use because you can get in and out without too much trouble. Propelling wheels (the bigger wheels that the occupant moves to get a chair moving) are usually at the rear but if you have limited shoulder movement you may get on better with a chair which has the propelling wheels at the front. Pneumatic tyres are more comfortable – particularly over rough ground – but solid tyres make a chair easier to move and they do not puncture. If you are going to use your wheelchair over long distances you may get on better with a powered model. There are all sorts of different powered wheelchairs available: some suitable only for indoor use, some suitable for use on quite rough ground. It really is a good idea to shop around – but first, make sure that you know what you want.

Aids for getting dressed

If you have difficulty in bending or raising your arms you will find that some clothes are far more difficult to get into and out of than others. Avoid tight jeans or trousers. Wear slip-on shoes rather than lace-ups. Make sure that zips and buttons are easily accessible and replace difficult to reach and difficult to use fasteners with easy to reach and easy to use fasteners. Velcro fastenings are easy to close and undo. (Stiff or arthritic fingers will find buttons, hooks and eyes and other small fasteners difficult or impossible). Buttons, when you do use them, should be as large as possible. The long-handled shoe horn, the shoe which has an elasticated front and the long-handled pick-up stick can all help. For women a wrap around skirt is easier to put on than one that has to be pulled up, while a front fastening brassière can be a great help.

Disposable underwear, towels and handkerchiefs may be expensive but do cut down on washing and ironing.

If you have difficulty in dressing:

1. Lean against a wall when you need to raise a foot or leg (e.g. to put on a sock or tie a shoelace)
2. Roll up clothes (e.g. jumpers) so that you can put your arms through the arm holes as easily as possible
3. If you have difficulty in balancing and pulling on trousers or tights try dressing while lying on top of your bed. To get your

trousers over your feet pull your knees up to your chest. Then straighten your legs to pull your trousers up to your bottom.

Housing: general advice

Many of the minor hazards which the perfectly fit take in their stride can become major problems when joints stiffen and limbs don't work as well as they did.

For example, a flight of stairs which a fit and healthy individual can run up and down without any thought may provide considerable problems. Even a single high step or a couple of steps at the front door can suddenly become a restrictive barrier. High rise blocks of flats where lifts may be out of order for months on end can turn into high rise prisons for the disabled. And the lack of a ground floor lavatory can mean a disabled person becoming marooned on the first floor.

Just as important as the type of home is where the accommodation is situated. A bungalow may seem a wonderful idea. But if it is at the top of a steep hill, hidden away in the country miles from a bus stop or railway station, or can only be reached by clambering up a steep path or a long flight of stone steps, it may be completely unsuitable for someone who finds walking painful.

When planning a new home, or redesigning an existing one, it is important to be aware of the potential hazards and to think of future problems too. Uneven floors, steps between rooms and difficult passageways are all potential troublespots.

Aids for hobbies and leisure

Just because you are on the wrong side of the first flush of youth you don't have to give up all your favourite sports and hobbies. There are many gadgets that you can use. If you like playing cards you can make a 'card holder' by sawing a suitably sized slit in a piece of wood. If you like reading but find it difficult to hold a book then put a tray with a small stand on your lap. For the slightly creaky gardener there are plenty of useful tools: long-handled gadgets for hoeing and weeding and picking up the rubbish, lawn mowers that can be operated from a wheelchair, spades and forks that can be used without bending and tools that can be used with just one hand for cutting long grass and pruning small bushes and trees. There are long-handled trowels, kneeler stools for gardeners with dodgy knees and all sorts of gadgets for use in the greenhouse. Finally, gardeners who have a lot of difficulty in bending can try building up their gardens to waist height. Flower and vegetable beds can be separated by firm, even concrete paths. Raised gardens are suitable for gardeners who have to attend to their plants (and weeds) from a wheelchair.

For a catalogue of Vernon Coleman's books
please write to:

Publishing House
Trinity Place
Barnstaple
Devon EX32 9HJ
England

Telephone   01271 328892
Fax   01271 328768

Outside the UK:
Telephone   +44 1271 328892
Fax   +44 1271 328768

Or visit our website:

www.vernoncoleman.com

Also by Vernon Coleman

How To Live Longer

Good health is the foundation upon which everything else rests.
Without good health none of us can enjoy life to the full.

We know more about staying healthy – and fighting disease –
than at any other time in history. But finding the truth about medical
matters is just as difficult as it has ever been. Who do you trust? How
can you tell whether or not a doctor is being paid to do or say
something by a drug company with a product to sell? How can you
be sure that the doctor advocating a particular treatment technique
is not just trying to win another patient? And how do you compare
different medical and surgical techniques?

Doctors who practise as surgeons invariably claim that surgery
has all the answers, whereas doctors who practise as physicians will
often argue that surgery is barbaric, clumsy and dangerous and should
only be used as a last resort. Who is right?

Dr Coleman has always argued that every individual should have
the right to take control of his or her own health. Obviously, if you
follow this philosophy then you will need information and advice.

Dr Coleman's book is packed with information and advice and
the aim of the book is simply to enable you to make better decisions
about your own health and health care – and about how to live longer
and how to stay healthier and as 'young' as possible.

The advice Dr Coleman presents in this book is the advice he
would take himself – or the advice he would give to his own family or
friends. In a nutshell, Dr Coleman genuinely practises what he
preaches in this book.

Paperback £12.95
Published by European Medical Journal
Order from Publishing House • Trinity Place • Barnstaple • Devon
EX32 9HJ • England
Telephone 01271 328892 • Fax 01271 328768
www.vernoncoleman.com

Also by Vernon Coleman

Bodypower
The secret of self-healing

A new edition of the sensational book which hit the *Sunday Times* bestseller list and *The Bookseller* Top Ten Chart.

This international bestseller shows you how you can harness your body's amazing powers to help you cure nine out of ten illnesses without seeing a doctor.

The book also covers:

- How to use bodypower to stay healthy
- How your personality affects your health
- How to stay slim for life
- How to break bad habits
- How to relax your body and mind
- How to improve your figure
- And much much more!

'Don't miss it. Dr Coleman's theories could change your life.'
(Sunday Mirror)

'A marvellously succinct and simple account of how the body can heal itself.'
(The Spectator)

'Could make stress a thing of the past.'
(Woman's World)

'There are plenty of good books on health care in the shops and for starters I'd recommend Bodypower by Dr Vernon Coleman which shows you how to listen to your body and understand its signals.'
(Woman's Own)

'... one of the most sensible treatises on personal survival ever published ... It sets out an enormous amount of knowledge in the easiest possible way.'
(Yorkshire Evening Post)

Paperback £9.95
Published by European Medical Journal
Order from Publishing House • Trinity Place • Barnstaple • Devon
EX32 9HJ • England
Telephone 01271 328892 • Fax 01271 328768
www.vernoncoleman.com

Mindpower

How to use your mind to heal your body

A new edition of this best-selling book which includes:

- A new approach to health care
- How your mind influences your body
- How to control destructive emotions
- How to deal with guilt
- How to harness positive emotions
- How daydreaming can relax your mind
- How to use your personal strengths
- How to conquer your weaknesses
- How to teach yourself mental self-defence
- Specific advice to help you enjoy good health
- And much, much more!

What they said about the first edition:

'*Dr Coleman explains the importance of mental attitude in controlling and treating illness, and suggests some easy-to-learn techniques.*'
(Woman's World)

'*An insight into the most powerful healing agent in the world – the power of the mind.*'
(Birmingham Post)

'*Dr Coleman's Mindpower philosophy is ... an inspiring message of hope.*'
(Western Morning News)

'*It will be another bestseller.*'
(Nursing Times)

'*A guide to harnessing the hidden force of healing.*'
(Journal of Alternative Medicine)

Paperback £12.95
Published by European Medical Journal
Order from Publishing House • Trinity Place • Barnstaple • Devon
EX32 9HJ • England
Telephone 01271 328892 • Fax 01271 328768
www.vernoncoleman.com

Also by Vernon Coleman

Food For Thought

Between a third and a half of all cancers may be caused by eating the wrong foods. In this best-selling book Dr Coleman explains which foods to avoid and which to eat to reduce your risk of developing cancer. He also lists foods known to be associated with a wide range of other diseases including asthma, gall bladder disease, headaches, heart trouble, high blood pressure, indigestion and many more.

Years of research have gone into the writing of this book which explains the facts about mad cow disease, vegetarian eating, microwaves, drinking water, food poisoning, food irradiation and additives. It contains all the information you need about vitamins, carbohydrates, fats and proteins plus a list of 20 superfoods which Dr Coleman believes can improve your health and protect you from a wide range of health problems. The book also includes a "slim-for-life" programme with 48 quick slimming tips to help you lose weight safely and permanently.

' ... *a guide to healthy eating which reads like a thriller.*'
(The Good Book Guide)

'*I consider it to be one of the most brilliant books of its kind that I have ever read. Not only are the contents a mine of information and advice but the style is such that it makes the whole book so thoroughly enjoyable to read; indeed it is a book difficult to put down.*'
(G.P., Streatham)

'*His no-nonsense approach to all foods makes finding your way through the nutritional maze that much easier.*'
(Evening Times)

Paperback £12.95
Published by European Medical Journal
Order from Publishing House • Trinity Place • Barnstaple • Devon
EX32 9HJ • England
Telephone 01271 328892 • Fax 01271 328768
www.vernoncoleman.com

Also by Vernon Coleman

Spiritpower

Discover your spiritual strength

- Find out who you are (and what you want)
- Three words that can change your life
- How to get what you want out of life
- Use your imagination and your subconscious mind
- Why you have more power than you think you have
- How you can control your own health
- Why you shouldn't be afraid to be a rebel
- How to stand up for yourself
- Know your fears and learn how to conquer them

What the papers say about *Spiritpower*:

'The final tome in his trilogy which has produced the bestsellers "Bodypower" and "Mindpower", this is Dr Coleman's assessment of our current spiritual environment, and his prescriptions for change. He advises both awareness and rebellion, recommending ways to regain personal autonomy and fulfilment.'
(The Good Book Guide)

'"Spiritpower" will show you how to find freedom and give meaning to your life.'
(Scunthorpe Evening Telegraph)

'This is a handbook for tomorrow's revolutionaries. Dr Coleman offers an understanding of the society we live in, in order to show where our freedom was lost.'
(Greenock Telegraph)

Paperback £12.95
Published by European Medical Journal
Order from Publishing House • Trinity Place • Barnstaple • Devon
EX32 9HJ • England
Telephone 01271 328892 • Fax 01271 328768
www.vernoncoleman.com

Also by Vernon Coleman

Superbody

A healthy immune system won't simply protect you against infection – it will also prove to be an essential factor in your body's ability to fight off all other diseases – including cancer.

The first two parts of this book explain why and how our bodies are under siege – and why the incidence of cancer and infectious diseases is rising rapidly (and likely to continue rising).

Infectious diseases started to become resistant to antibiotics a quarter of a century ago. Since then the situation has steadily worsened, and it is now probably too late for the medical profession to reverse the situation. Infectious diseases are coming back in a big way and the incidence of cancer is also going to continue to rise.

And so the third part of *Superbody* explains how you can protect yourself against these, and other threats, by improving the strength, efficiency and effectiveness of your immune system.

- How to boost your immune system
- How to increase your resistance to infection and disease
- How to protect yourself against cancer
- The best 101 foods in the world
- Improve your mental health
- How to spot early warning signs of disease
- How to de-stress your mind and body
- How to avoid environmental risks
- And much, much more

'A helpful and informative read for those who have been swept up by the lifestyle and excesses of the 20th/21st century.'
(Evening Chronicle)

Paperback £9.95
Published by European Medical Journal
Order from Publishing House • Trinity Place • Barnstaple • Devon
EX32 9HJ • England
Telephone 01271 328892 • Fax 01271 328768
www.vernoncoleman.com